TALES FROM INDIAN COUNTRY

Authentic Stories and Legends from the Great Uintah Basin

TALES FROM INDIAN COUNTRY

Authentic Stories and Legends
from the
Great Uintah Basin

GEORGE EMERY STEWART, JR.

MaryEllen Gardner
PO Box 900983
Sandy, UT 84090

ISBN: 1-57636-044-X
Library of Congress Catalog Card Number: 97-69111
Typeset/Designed by: *SunRise Publishing, Orem, Utah*

TABLE OF CONTENTS

OUTLAW STORIES

THE OPENING

JOURNEY THROUGH A LOST COUNTRY

ACKNOWLEDGMENTS

To Penny and Stewart Gardner, grandchildren, whose many hours and efforts have made this book possible.

To daughters Renee Millett and MaryEllen Gardner for their compilation and editing work.

INTRODUCTION

George Emery Stewart, Jr., now deceased, was one of those colorful 'old timers' whose life spanned the 'old days' and the 'modern days.' He was born in Vernal, Utah in 1906. As a small boy, he lived with his family in the Ouray, Utah area. His father was a mining prospector.

These circumstances brought him into close and intimate contact with the Ute Indian Tribe and their chief Red Moon. Because his playmates were Indian boys, he soon spoke Ute fluently. Until the day he died, he always spoke and visited with the Utes in their own language. Through this association and friendship, he developed a keen understanding of their ways and beliefs. He respected and defended them throughout his life.

He met Chipeta several times when he was a young boy. She gave him the name of 'Frightened Boy' which he did not like. George was not frightened of Chipeta, but only stood in reverent awe. Seeing this, she changed his name to 'Uviev' which he liked very much. He showed his approval with a smile. It means 'Turkey.' Chipeta said that George walked like one. From then on, he was known by his Indian friends as 'Uviev.'

Later, his family moved to Myton, where his mother ran a hotel. It was at this time that he met Elza Lay, a former member of the Butch Cassidy gang. When he was not in school, young George spent much of his time sitting with Lay on the bench in front of the saloon. He listened for hours and asked so many questions that Lay became worried that George was being badly influenced. But already being an avid reader and well supplied by his father with many of the 'Classics,' his values were well founded. George just had a natural interest for history, the facts, and how they happened. His brilliant mind never forgot a detail.

George was sent to Westminster Boarding School. Later, he graduated from the University of Utah. He received a law degree from George Washington University. As an attorney, he received several offers to practice law in the East. But his roots were in the Uintah Basin and there he stayed. For many years, he was 'The Voice Over the Mike,' the M.C. of all the celebrations and main events.

George married Elva Gagon (August 10, 1929), who was also raised in the Uintah Basin. They are the parents of three daughters; MaryEllen Gardner (Garth), Renee Millett (Therrol), and Nancy Harrison.

George was the founding attorney for Moon Lake Electric Association and was their attorney until his retirement. His legal forms were adopted by the federal government in gaining right-of-ways for power lines constructed by the Rural Electrification Association nationally.

His law practice was interrupted during World War II, when he served in Europe under General Patton, 76th Division. He was among those who liberated the Jewish people at the Buchenwald concentration camp in Germany.

George Stewart was a member of the Utah Historical Society and also the Utah Western Historians until his death in March, 1990.

—MaryEllen Stewart Gardner

INDIAN STORIES AND LEGENDS

THE STORY OF THE HEADHUNTERS

It was many years ago, in a teepee on the banks of the Duchesne River, that I first heard the 'Legend of the Headhunters,' as told by the Indian people. The old man sat in the embers glow and we thought he was napping. Then, in a voice so low, at first, we could hardly hear him speaking, he started to tell his tale.

"Many moons ago in the time of my father's fathers, the head hunters raided this land and struck terror in the hearts of the people. They came always in time of falling leaves when the hunter's moon rode high in the sky. They caught us where we camped together, snuggled in for the coming winter. These headhunters traveled the hidden ways; sleeping by day and walking by night so they could strike us unawares, usually while we were celebrating the luck of the hunt. First here, then there, then some other place, they raided and we could never tell which village would be their target. So when the red leaves came, we were ever watchful and ever fearful, lest we should be the unfortunate ones whose heads would be carried over the hills and far away to perform their rites of worship.

"They came in pairs, one round and one square. Their stature was gigantic; in their moccasins they stood so tall they could almost reach the smoke hole of a teepee. Their visages were the picture of death when the flesh is falling and the bone is showing. They were horrible, horrible, horrible!

"The round one carried a shaft, like a spear except on the end was a knife shaped the same as a white man's sickle. The square one walked beside him with hands bare and empty. They hit the camp like a thunderclap, whooping and yelling and screeching. When the people, in alarm, either ran, stood stupid, or came fighting—snick snack; the bright blade flashed and there rolled a head. Snick snack and there rolled another. Each time, they took six heads; the round one cutting, the square one gathering. Then they vanished, like wraiths in the night, to be gone for another year."

For ten, twenty heartbeats there was a pause in the old man's story. Then someone asked, "Did you really see them?"

"Oh no," the old man said. "The headhunters came here long before my time. I tell the story to you like it was told to me, like it was told to my father and my grandfather's father. But old as it is, I believe it. Now it is said that sometime the headhunters will come again. Maybe, even yet, I shall loose my head, although I hope not. You see, the people found out the headhunters could hear much better than they could see. So when the leaves are falling like now and the moon is bright like now, the best way to keep them away from you is to be quiet, be very quiet. That way they will choose the noisy ones. I have been quiet all my life and I believe that is the way of winning."

It was quiet in the teepee, very quiet.

In later years as I looked back, I thought, how clever that old man was. He told an interesting yarn of terror and in the process quieted all the noise kids will make as they rant and play at bedtime.

Then one day, as I followed the trail of a hidden way as it twisted and turned through the desert, I came upon a petroglyph and I took a picture of it. I call it 'The Headhunter Panel.'

Later, I traveled a hidden trail and I saw a petroglyph—another headhunter petroglyph. This one is more remarkable than the first one. There are the two headhunters, one round and one square. See the scythe-like weapon the round one holds in his hands. Look at the terrible faces of these two. Would you like to meet them some moonlit night? Above all this, notice the lower left hand figure; it is a headless torso. Of course, there are the other interesting details about the carving but I haven't space to point them out to you or to tell you what they mean. Perhaps you can read it as well as I can. Both these carvings are on hidden ways. They are very old and they are fifty miles apart.

Is there, do you suppose, a basis of fact for the old man's tale?

The Woman Who Was a Man

Aug-gu-saw, (meaning half and half), an Indian woman, lived far up on Bitter creek. She lived alone. A passerby saw her, now and then. Once in a while, she went to ouray to trade. She was a pleasant person with a ready smile and a friendly manner. People thought she was somewhat queer, though, because she never spoke. She always used sign language; it seemed she could converse with her hands much more readily than she could with her tongue. In other ways too, she was not quite right. She was a little touched, they say, but she had her charm and everybody liked her.

Then, one day, when she was old and bent and gray, the death wind blew for Auggusaw. She was hurriedly taken to the agency hospital at Ft. Duchesne in an attempt to save her life. At the hospital, they took off her shawl, her dress, and her undergarments. They stood amazed, for they found that Auggusaw was a normal male who had lived as a woman for many, many moons.

Auggusaw's spirit walked away. His body was buried and the strange story of his life came out. It was the last chapter in the tale of the famous old Meeker Massacre.

Many years ago, an Indian boy dwelt close by the Whiteriver Agency near Meeker, Colorado. He was an orphan and lived with his grandmother, Mus-i-mutts, the desert flower. There was no man in the teepee, so as the boy grew, he had little chance to learn the ways of an Indian brave. The Desert Flower, grown old and quiet, taught him mostly the ways of peace. The lad was lively and gay, with a happy disposition, so he got along well with all those living around him—even the fierce war-chief, Captain Jack. He had the usual amount of boy's curiosity and he passed his days observing the activity near the agency. Especially, he was interested in the affairs at the agency headquarters.

One day, as he watched the White men at their work, he passed the house where Meeker, the agent, lived. He stopped short in the door yard. There, wafted to his nose, was the most delicious smell he had ever known. Josephine Meeker, the agent's daughter, saw the boy standing there testing the air like a questing hound. She smiled in response to his broad grin and beckoning, said, "Come here a minute."

The Indian came with alacrity. Jo gave him a handful of freshly baked sugar cookies. Thus, a friendship began between the young lady and the bright, young boy. As time went by, Jo and Mrs. Meeker always gave the youngster some tidbit when he came to visit; there was bread and honey, cake, pie, and sometimes stick candy. The two women and the boy became fast friends.

Suddenly, trouble was brewing on the reservation. Meeker had the river bottom plowed and planted where the Indian pony herd grazed. To add insult to injury, the agent ordered the land fenced where the racetrack of the Red men stretched across the meadows. This was too much for Johnson, a Ute sub-chief. He went to Meeker's house, forced him outdoors, and began to beat him. The agent's life was saved only by the timely intervention of the agency employees.

Meeker was angry and frightened as a result of Johnson's acts, but he palavered with the Utes. During the course of the conversation, the agent said, "If there is anymore violence offered to my person, or if you Indians threaten me or any White man here at the agency, I shall send for the soldiers and you will be sorry."

"If you send for the blue coats to come to Indian country, it is you who will be sorry, because, before they get here you will die," replied Douglass, another Ute sub-chief. Josephine's friend, the Indian boy, was worried. He had heard the talk of the more hotheaded tribesmen. He knew many of them wanted the war trail. Some painted their faced yellow and black and left the settlement, riding to join those planning to fight. Time after time, the Indian tried to tell Jo that she and all the Whites were in danger; but his English was poor and she understood no Indian. The Meekers went blissfully on, never dreaming of the terror to come.

Meeker, never understanding Red men, and in spite of the warning given to him by Douglas, sent a message to the Army asking for aid. In response to Meeker's summons, Major Thornburg, with one hundred and forty men and a wagon train was ordered out of Ft. Steele, Wyoming to the Whiteriver Agency in Colorado. They were to do whatever was necessary to quell the hostile Utes.

Twice, Captain Jack, the war chief, held a pow-wow with Thornburg. Each time, the chief warned the soldiers not to march into Indian Country. But the Major had his orders. He kept coming on. War drums throbbed in the mountain valleys. Finally, the Utes, at least three hundred strong, attacked the blue coats at the narrows of Milk Creek Canyon and hemmed them in. The engagement went on for days, lasting until reinforcements arrived from Ft. Steele.

At the agency, the morning of September 29, 1879 was calm and peaceful. The Whites didn't know a battle was raging over on Milk Creek. It is possible the Indians at the agency didn't know of the encounter either, thinking the soldiers would halt before they crossed the reservation line.

The sun climbed the sky. Noon came and went. And then, the storm broke. Perhaps a courier arrived from Captain Jack, telling Douglas and Johnson about the fight with Thornburg's command. The two sub-chiefs, true to their promise, sent twenty-five or thirty warriors in war paint to strike the agency. Caught unaware and outnumbered, the White men had little chance to defend themselves, or to escape. All the men present at the time, including Meeker, were killed.

The women and children of the employees, Mrs. Meeker and Josephine with the rest, hid in the milk house first, then in the

Meeker residence. Knowing that sooner or later, the dwelling would be raided, the frightened women watched for a chance to leave the house for a better hiding place. At last, they broke cover and ran for some sagebrush on the far side of a plowed field.

The Ute boy, friend of Mrs. Meeker and Josephine, watched his rampaging elders from close by. He sought an opportunity to help the two women. He saw the party run from the house and cross the plowed ground. Instantly, he ran to aid them, hoping he could lead them, unseen, to the teepee of Desert Flower. Unfortunately, his were not the only eyes to see the fleeing party; other warriors came pursuing and caught the women and children. The Ute boy stood there among the captives, weeping. He thought that now, they too must die.

He was only twelve or thirteen years old at the time of these stirring events at Meeker, but despite his young and tender years, the boy was put on trial before the Council for cowardice in battle. The verdict came and he was found guilty; only Captain Jack voted in his favor. The final judgment was spoken by the Awat-ta-pah-gi (Big Talker) Colorow, who said: "We cannot change the way you are made, but we can make a half man of you. From this time on, you shall dress like a woman, live like a woman, and you shall do a woman's work. Never, in this world, will you ride as a Ute warrior. Since you stood among the women and children crying, a thing no Ute boy may ever do, you are half woman already. So your name, from now until you die, will be "Auggusaw.""

Most warriors, given this sentence, would have slipped away, riding to a far country to live with white men or some renegade band. Perhaps this is what the lad was expected to do. But Auggusaw showed great courage. He bowed to the edict the Council had issued; he lived his whole life through as a woman of the Ute Nation.

You see, there was a religious overtone in all of this. Because such a judgment, when given—especially if the Healer, the Sky Reader, the Vision Dreamer, the Spirit Talker, in other words, the medicine men—concurred in it, it was a Decree of Heaven. It said in effect, "Live your sentence during the short time you are here on earth and be free of it when you die. If you fail, you shall live it throughout eternity in your after-life, for we shall know you in the Land of the Sky. You cannot avoid us or our judgment."

At first, his people poked fun at Auggusaw. But as the years went by, and he never failed or faltered in paying his debt; the Indians came to respect him. They ceased even to tell about him. After he was dead and buried, those who knew his story told it. But there were no derisive grins on their faces as they did it.

They say, somewhere great warriors ride wearing eagle feathers and mounted on fine war-horses. In that Land of Somewhere, Auggusaw rides, not as a woman, but among the warriors of his race. He displayed great steadfastness and courage unto death. He proved himself. The days of his retribution are over. Where he is, he is known as an Awat Towatch (Big Man or Chief); and they call him 'The Half Chief.' Auggusaw Awat Towatch.

THE FORGOTTEN CHIEFTAIN

RED MOON

He had the right to eagle feathers. Around his neck and down his breast, he wore the band of death. For he was a chief, you see. The last living war chief of the Whiteriver band of Indians, the fiercest band of the whole Ute Indian Nation. He was as wild and free and tempestuous as the desert wind in springtime. Where he walked, the enemy, especially the hated paleface, best beware.

The band of death is the tanned and cured skin of a rattlesnake. It must be caught and killed by the warrior using only his bare hands; he must use no weapon such as gun, knife, club or rock. In the old days, only a chief could wear it. In the photograph of Red Moon, you can see his snake skin. It is large. He must have searched for it many days to get one this big in the area where he lived. Note too, that on the left side of his hat he has one lone eagle feather.

* * *

No scribe has ever touched him. No legend, no story has ever been written about him. He disdained the white man's language. Although he understood it, he never spoke a word of English if he could possibly avoid it. If you talked to this Indian, you spoke to him in Ute or he ignored you. Perhaps this is why the White men passed him by.

It was in the days of Indian Summer, when the dreamy haze falls on the land. The woman lay in great travail. As the first yell of her warrior baby echoed in the nearby forest, she turned her head and saw through the teepee door the red moon climbing slowly above the mountain peaks to the east. Her great ordeal was ending. She spoke softly to her husband, "Our son will be known as Com-matt-too-its (Red Moon)." In reply, the young father quietly nodded his assent. And so it was, from that time onward, this boy was known as Red Moon.

The peacemakers among the Indians, like Ouray and Tabby, have been blown by historians into heroic proportions. But the fighters, who wanted to assert the rights of the Indians, even if it meant bloodshed, received hardly a mention and now are all but forgotten.

Red Moon, is almost forgotten now. Hardly a word has been written about him. He was the last War Chief of the Whiterivers and he was no peacemaker. It was he who led all or at least a portion of the Ute warriors facing Cook across the Uintah River.

In later years he said, "I remember when the walking soldiers first came to Ft. Duchesne. It was I who led the Indians who stood across the river from them. I also saw the riding soldiers when they came and we were not afraid of all of them. If we had wanted to attack, we would have attacked.

"There were not seven hundred of us. There were only two hundred warriors maybe, the rest were women and children.

"Do you think I don't know the white man? I knew then and I know now, they are like the flies in summer—you can kill them all the day, but tomorrow they will be back in even larger numbers than before.

"When we lined up on the Uintah River, we wanted to say: 'See, we are on the bank of our river. All the land you see from here, even to the tops of the mountains is ours. Do not cross the river. Stop where you are and come no farther, or we will fight you.'"

Now, Red Moon, brave warrior chief, rides free and wild in the Happy Hunting Grounds.

"I knew Red Moon, the last War Chief of the Whiterivers, many years ago, when I was a boy living near Ouray. I also knew

Wahpanah, an old, old Indian when he lived at Myton. Wahpanah dressed, when I last saw him, in the fashion of the Utes before the white man; leggings, breech coat, moccasins, feather, long hair, painted face, etc. He used to sit by the hour staring afar with his faded eyes. I used to wonder what his thoughts were. When I studied speech in college, I learned to give from memory the orations of great Indian orators. This poem is a composite of them as well as Red Moon. I hope I have caught enough of the feeling, to affect others as they have affected me.

RED MOON

I am Red Moon, War Chief of all the bands.
Once my people ruled, at my commands,
These hills, these valleys, all the lands
Where now the lodges of the white man stands.

The warrior bird once screamed and ruled the sky.
The singing water near my lodge flowed sweetly by.
I saw the buffalo, in hundreds, thunder nigh,
At night, I heard the coyote's wailing cry.

The Bighorn climbed the rocky steep,
The deer from out his hiding place, would leap.
The beaver swam the mighty rivers deep,
The bear, in his mountain cave, could sleep.

The wild horse roamed the grassy hills,
Lions stalked and made their feeding kills,
The fishes swam in all the mountain rills,
The woodland echoed to the bird song trills.

I loved an Indian maiden fair
With flashing eyes and long black hair.
When I am dreaming, unaware,
I seem to see her in the campfire's glare.

The morning sunlight brightly bathes
My feathered headdress, as it dips and waves.
I hear the war cry of the braves
I led to victories or their graves.

That was many, many moons ago.
Now I sit in firelight and afterglow.
I hear the paling death wind softly blow
For me and all the friends I used to know.

The Warrior's time has come and passed away;
His flowing blood could never stem nor stay
The relentless coming of this day,
When he and all the wild things stand at bay.

The white man's works close all the old domains;
The hills, the valleys and the grassy plains,
No place now in all the land remains
Where wild, free life can be sustained.

The autumn time is showing on my face.
Soon I shall join the spirits of my race.
The red leaves falling o'er my place
Will hide where I have been without a trace.

This is the sunset evening hour
For all the ancient Indian lore.
Gladly shall I walk beyond death's door
And to this place, I shall come no more.

In the Happy Hunting Ground beyond the hill,
I shall know again the things I love so well.
My grateful chant the morning breeze will swell
In that great land, forever, I shall dwell.

Note: Author used to have a photograph of Red Moon but it has disappeared, along with many others.

CHIPETA, "QUEEN OF THE UTES"

This picture of Chipeta was probably taken after the death of Chief Ouray, since she is pictured alone. During his life, she was always seen by his side.
—Used by permission, Uintah Regional Library, all rights reserved.

I suppose you have heard of Chipeta, who as a young girl, married Ouray. Ouray's mother was a Ute and his father was Apache. In spite of this, became the head of the whole Ute Nation. He was the chief of chiefs. Chipeta was all Ute, a member of the Uncompahgre band.

When the Meeker trouble flared with the Sun Blanket Indians, now the Whiterivers, Ouray was already ill with the sickness that would kill him. He sent word through Chipeta for the Indians to stop fighting. Or, was it as some people say, Chipeta, acting on her own initiative? Ouray respected his wife and like many a man before and after him said, "That wife of mine, she is usually right. When she speaks to me, I always listen."

It was Chipeta who got Mrs. Meeker, her daughter Josephine, and the other white women released from captivity. She cared for them until their friends arrived.

After Ouray died, Chipeta, to all intents and purposes took his place. She was the second woman known in Ute history who achieved the right to sit at the Council of Fires to decide all questions which might arise. She was the one who decided war or peace between the white man and the Indian. She always, always kept the peace.

When the Whiterivers wanted war because the army, violating agreements, was building Fort Thornburg at Ouray, Chipeta, wanting peace, was overruled by the Council. Next day, on her great white horse, she rode alone to see the commander of the bluecoats. So great was her influence that the Army listened to her and moved the fort off the reservation to the west end of Ashley Valley.

When I was a small boy, I met Chipeta in Matt Curry's old trading post at Ouray, Utah. I can remember the awe I felt as I stood, hat in hand, before this Indian woman, who even then had become known as the 'Queen of the Utes.' Her kind, smiling eyes took my fear away. She spoke to me, in Ute, saying something about a "nee-poots ap-ats yavo-gai" (a little boy afraid).

After that, I met Chipeta several times because I went out of my way to see her. She never forgot me. Though she knew English fairly well, she always spoke to me in Ute. I deemed this a special favor, whether I understood or not.

The years went by. Chipeta died. Ouray, the Indian village on the banks of the Green, never seemed the same again. Chipeta's fame spread in all directions. Today, many campfire stories tell of her. Though many know about her, there are few who can say, as I do, that they knew Chipeta when she was alive and rode the trails of her desert country.

SONG TO CHIPETA, QUEEN OF THE UTES

It is difficult to write of Chipeta for too much time has come and gone since she lived and died. The records of her deeds are few and far between in the books of white men. Since her people had no written language, what she did is remembered only in the minds of the Old Ones, who long since have ridden away across the Misty River to the land of Shades and Shadows.

But what we have is precious for it tells us of a beautiful woman, a leader of her people, whose finger always pointed down the trail to peace in the days of turbulence and anger between the white men and the Indian.

She was one of the two Ute Indian women, in the history of her tribe, who had the right to sit in the circle of the chieftains to decide what to do for the welfare of the whole Ute Indian Nation. Even before her husband, Ouray, the great Chief of Chiefs, died—her voice was heard around the council fire. It is probable that Ouray insisted on it. He loved this woman deeply and trusted her honesty and judgment beyond all his other aides.

From the night she swam the swollen Gunnison River to warn and save the white settlers on the other side; through the bloody days of the Milk Creek Battle and the Meeker Massacre in Colorado; to the days of 'the opening' of the great Ute Indian Reservation in eastern Utah; Chipeta was known as a woman of intelligence, reason, and peace.

Her medicine was powerful. Not only did the common people need her, but so did the mighty and the strong. She had access to the chiefs, the Indian agents, the commander of Ft. Duchesne. Even the men along the Potomac heard her when she spoke.

Through the turbulent years, she stepped, time after time, into the breach—to cool the hatred and prevent bloodshed. By many she was called "The Peacemaker." In the end, her fame had spread. It was of a sort that made her seem almost saintly. She was a person loved by all men, both red and white.

By the time Chipeta died, August 9, 1924, she had become a legend of the west. Because of her character, intelligence, and wonderful disposition—not because she ruled—she was given the accolade of 'The Queen of the Utes.'

She was old and bent and gray when I knew her. I first met her at Matt Curry's old trading post at Ouray, Utah. My uncle, Buckskin Shirt, introduced me to her white man fashion. That was many, many moons ago when I was just a boy. I knew a part of her story and I remember that I stood before her, head uncovered, abashed and a little frightened to be so closely noticed by this famous Indian woman. But, she smiled at me, touched my face with her hand and spoke to me in Ute. She said something about a little boy afraid. The kindness in her eyes and her smile made me comfortable standing quietly in her presence.

From time to time after that, I saw her. I went out of my way to meet and speak to her. She always answered me in Ute. I was flattered, for she spoke English; to talk to me in Ute indicated that I was special to her, I imagined.

One year, when the time of the Ripe Moon came, I went outside to boarding school. While I was gone, I heard that Chipeta had walked over the misty river in the twilight to join the spirits of her race. I felt badly because I knew I would never see again a friend I had cherished.

Years later, during the Moon of the Bear, an old Ute and I rode together across the desert which was in full bloom. That night we camped under the cottonwood trees of Chipeta Grove.

The evening chores were done. As the night was falling, we talked together in the flitting shadows of the embers' glow. Far away, the night birds called, a coyote howled, and on the wings of the breeze that comes at dusk was the delicate perfume of the blooming desert lilies. There was peace around us in this sylvan setting where the leaves whispered softly in the trees above our heads.

It was a fitting time to speak of Chipeta, whom we both had known. Where we sat was near the place where she had spent her final days.

I, thinking as a white man thinks, proposed a monument of stone to be erected in this grove to the memory of Chipeta. My Ute friend spoke quietly to me, telling me his philosophy of such things. "Do not disturb her that way," he said.

Then he told me of the trees, the birds, the animals, the flowers, the sky, the clouds—all natural things in this land of hers were paying tribute to Chipeta. It was strange but it was beautiful.

The main thing he said was, "We all remember Chipeta in our own way, the cactus roses, the lilies, the birds, the leaves on the trees, even the clouds, the earth and the sky and all animals tame and wild. You, with your pen, can sing about her on your talking paper. That will be better than a monument of stone. Write it for us and put it where everyone can see it."

While he chanted softly, slowly in the shadows, beating time with a stick on a stone, I penned our song to Chipeta.

I have kept my promise, though my friend, too, has walked away to the Happy Hunting Ground. Here and there in the chanting, I seemed to catch a word or two in Ute. I put them down as they were sung. The result is a poem in mixed languages. I am sorry, but I can't change them now because this would change the beat time of the chant. The English translation of the Indian words are given below. Sing it in your mind as you read it and you will pick up the song that will please Chipeta.

SONG TO CHIPETA

Ne-ka-ki[1], Ne-ats[2]
Chipeta[3] Ta-goo-eu[4],
Softly blows the petals
From the cactus roses blooming
Over the lonely land
Where you walked
Your final days.

And your Greening Grove
Is chanting
Soft and low
In Indian language.
As the soughing wind
Stirs the leaves
To whisper your name.

A-woo-its[5] sings at sundown
From yonder butte
In mourning,
Remembering the comely
Mamuts[6], the queen of
Uncompahgres[7], whose
Cabin stands deserted
By the Smoky River[8] Streams

Too-wits[9] serenades you
In the sunlight of the morning
From the tree
That shades your dwelling,
So that men will always know you
Where you ride
In golden glory,
In the land of Too-woop-paw-eu[10].

Though the paths you trod
Seemed humble
Still, your fame is ever-growing,
Among the wild things
Of the wasteland
In the legends of your people;
In the talking books
Of Whitemen.

Oh, Chipeta,
Who, mated with the Arrow[11],
Spread kindness and wise council
To the people, White and Indian.
Your name will be engraven
In Western Skies forever
As the greatest of Ute women;
A Spirit of sweet beauty,
Beloved by all Mortals
Who live on Mother Earth
Here below.
Ha-eyah e ooo[12]

Notes:
1. *Ne-ka-ki* means Listen
2. *Ne-wats* means Listen to me
3. *Chipeta* means spring of clear water
4. *Ta-goo-eu* means friend
5. *A-woo-its* means coyote
6. *Mamuts* means woman
7. *Uncompahgre* means Red Water People—one of the bands of Utes among whom Chipeta lived.
8. *White River*—Indians called it the Smoky river
9. *Too-wits* means small birds
10. *Too-woop-paw-eu* means Land across the misty river
11. *Ouray* means the Arrow in Ute
12. *Ha-eyah e ooo* means the song is ended

THE LEGEND OF SPIRIT ROCK

An early Ute Indian Brave.

In the mountains of Eastern Utah, along a stream of surpassing beauty, is the spirit land of the Ute Indians. In the summer, it is a land of cool air and greenness. In the autumn, it is a land of colored splendor. In the winter, it is a land of silent whiteness. Over its mountains, the clouds linger always; in its canyons and valleys, the mists gather, giving to it great enchantment and an air of mystery.

This land is beloved by the Ute Indian people. It is here they see and feel most keenly the hand and presence of the Great Spirit. Around this land are woven many legends of the Indians, legends which go back to the beginning of their race. These stories are kept alive now, as they have always been, by the elders telling them to their children, in the evening, at story telling time, as they sit around their fires.

It was on a night in June, at story telling time, that I first heard the legend of 'Spirit Rock.' I sat by a campfire with an Indian friend. It was the night of the young moon, when she cast her pale, soft light over all the land. High above us were the peaks of the mountains covered with caps of eternal snow; on these the moonlight shone, turning them to things of great ethereal beauty. The summer breeze whispered in the tree tops with a silver tongue as it flowed by. It was a bewitching hour, a time of perfect peace that comes only in the great outdoors.

For a long time, my friend and I sat silent, drinking in the magic. Neither of us wished to break the spell cast upon us by the time, place, sights, and sounds. As we sat, the fire burned to embers. In its soft red glow, I watched my partner's face. He was deep in reverie. An educated and learned Indian, he had reverted this night. He was remembering the lore of his people. Finally, he glanced up and found me staring at him. He began to speak quietly, telling me the Legend of Spirit Rock. This is what he told me:

"Many, many moons ago, before my father's father was born, my people came to this river. They made their camp at this spot where you and I are sitting. It was in the time of red leaves and the snows of winter would not be long in coming. Each year, when leaves are falling, my people came here to hunt, so they would have meat to last them through the long days of cold and white silences.

Among those who came to hunt that year, was Young Bear, who, one day, would be chief of all the bands. But at the time of which I'm speaking, he was only a young warrior just lately proven. Young Bear, though young, was a mighty hunter. Many times, while yet a boy, he had proven his skill by bringing in more game than any other hunter. On the night of which I'm telling, he prepared his horse and his weapons to go on the hunt the next morning. Then he went to sleep.

As the eastern sky first began to lighten into dawn, Desert Flower, Young Bear's wife, cooked breakfast. When it was ready, she awakened her warrior. After he had eaten, Desert Flower sent her husband forth, with her blessings, to hunt.

In the sunrise, Young Bear, mounted his horse and rode up that long, high ridge you see across the river. He knew that where the bareness of the ridge meets the timber is the place where the big bucks linger into daylight. So that is where he went. It was a year of dryness. The horse made many noises as it climbed up the trail toward the darkness of the pine trees. Thus it was that the deer, hearing the noises, fled before the hunter to the cover of the thickets in the forest. All this Young Bear read in the signs the deer had left on the ground.

Young Bear tied his horse to a tree on the eastward side of the ridge, so the morning breezes would not waft his scent to the hiding place of his quarry. Then he began to hunt more quietly on foot. He went into the forest, moving as silently as a ghost, looking for the big game he knew was hiding here.

Moving quietly on his hunt, Young Bear came, unheralded, upon a band of renegades, who had come to raid his people. They were camped in a clearing where a mountain spring was flowing. The warrior lay hidden long enough to count the outlaws. Then he tried to move away, without alarming the camp, so he could go warn his people.

In the camp of the renegades was a dog—a huge, black beast. This dog's nose was keen and his ears were sharp. He heard and smelled Young Bear, who was a stranger to him. The dog howled the alarm and charged Young Bear. The warrior, to save himself, stood in full view and sent an arrow flying down the throat of the vicious beast. Then he turned and ran.

The outlaws, on the instant, ran to their horses, mounted, and began the pursuit of the hunter. It was their intent to run Young Bear down and kill him before he could warn his people of their presence in these mountains. But the raiders did not know this warrior with whom they had to deal. This Indian was strong and fleet of foot. Besides, he was a master woodsman. He did not run down the trails or in the open; he chose to go where the trees and underbrush grew thickest. It was hard for men on horses to go where Young Bear led.

This hunter ran for his horse where he had left him tied. But the outlaws blocked his path in that direction. So he was forced to get away, if he could, on his own two feet.

As the chase grew long, the outlaws strung out, the fastest and more skillful leading the rest. The fleeing warrior seeing this when he glanced behind him, paused to pick off the leaders. He killed four before the renegades became wary and stayed together. In this way, for awhile, the hunter gained a little time and distance.

As he ran, Young Bear always ran in the general direction of his teepee, but finally he came to the edge of the timber. He had to make a choice. He could run in cover in the hopes of eluding his pursuers, which would lead him away from his people; or he could break cover and run down the bare ridge in full view of his enemies. Quickly he made his decision, he broke cover, but he ran parallel with the crest of the ridge, down along the steep hillside where the rocks were loose and rolling. Here, again, it was hard for mounted men to overtake him.

The outlaws were smart and wily men. When Young Bear ran

along the hillside, the renegades split into three parties. One party rode to the canyon's bottom and raced along the trail at the foot of the ridge. A second party rode down the crest of the ridge where the running was easy for their horses. A third party stayed behind, on Young Bear's trail. The parties above and below the hunter passed him. Then the renegades on the hilltop circled down; the band on the canyon floor circled up; the outlaws behind came on. Young Bear was in the circle; he could not get away. No man alive can outrun a horse on equal footing. Besides, the warrior was tiring fast now. His lungs were near to bursting. His feet and legs were growing numb. His eyes were blurring from his terrible exertion. He could hear the death wind blowing; he knew his time had come. He looked for a place to make his stand.

There, halfway up the ridge yonder, where the shadows are the deepest, is a small meadow. It is flat and strewed with boulders. It was to that place Young Bear ran to make his stand. He mounted to the top of a great boulder. He stood straight as an arrow, with the sunlight glistening on his wet, sweating body. He raised his face and arms to heaven and gave one last, long cry to the Great Spirit.

The renegades launched their arrows. But before they reached their mark, Young Bear toppled from the rock upon which he was standing. Down he fell and disappeared.

The outlaws, crying their yells of victory, raced for the rock, expecting to find the body of Young Bear lying there dead and bristling with arrows. Instead, they found nothing.

The raiders searched for the warrior. They beat through all the thickets. They walked up and down the hillside. They prodded in every crack and crevice. They followed the tracks of the running brave. They did not lead beyond the rock. They could not find their victim, he was gone.

In the deepening shadows of twilight, the outlaws grew afraid. This man they hunted could only be a phantom warrior. Their arrows had not killed him; when surrounded he had disappeared before their eyes. He was a spirit. They must leave before this spirit chieftain called his spirit warriors to take his revenge upon them. In the gathering darkness, the renegades fled from the scene.

When all had grown quiet, Young Bear, came from his hiding place. He came out of the rock upon which he had stood when he had made his last plea to the Great Spirit. The rock is hollow, like the hogan of a Navajo. It has one small entrance to the hollowed out shelter within. Over the entrance is a small, flat stone which is easy to move. It is blended and fitted, until it completely conceals the entrance to the space inside the rock. The Great Spirit had hidden Young Bear away from his enemies by placing him in the center of a rock.

Young Bear reached home that night, he told the chief about the outlaws. In the night, he led all the warriors of the band to the camp of the renegades. In the pale light of dawn, they surrounded and took the enemy, ending their lives forever.

In the years that followed, Young Bear's name was changed to Great Bear. In time, he became the chief of all the bands. During his mortal life, Great Bear guarded this land against all evil. It is said, by my people, that Great Bear and his warriors, even now, guard this country. And I believe it. On bright nights, you can hear the guards. They call to each other in the language of the night birds. Their horses gallop in the sky; they sound like distant thunder. But you need not be afraid of them. They will keep all evil from you while you are here. That is why it is so peaceful along this mountain stream.

The rock in which Young Bear hid is still there. We call it 'Spirit Rock,' because it belongs to Young Bear and the Great Spirit who made it for him. If you wish, I shall take you to the small meadow, where Spirit Rock stands. But, after that you will have to find the Rock yourself. I cannot show it to you, it is forbidden."

So my friend's story ended. The next day I was taken to the

meadow. I found Spirit Rock. It is as the legend describes it—hollow, with an entrance to the interior, small and concealed. It is, in truth, like a hogan of the Navajo.

But, strangely, the rock was not hollowed out by man. There is not a man-made mark upon it. There is no mark of tool or delving. The rock was made and hollowed out by the forces of nature, by the processes of erosion. Or ... some other way unknown?

WILD MAN OF THE WASTELAND

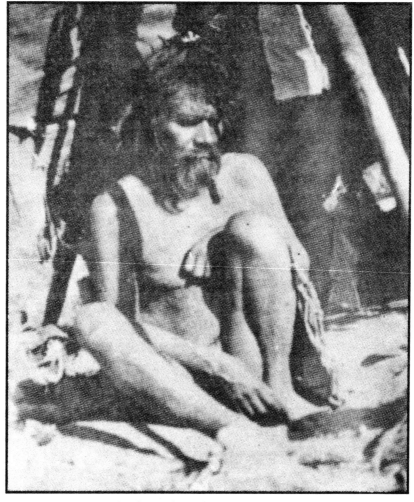

Nipcut ('The Crazy One') lived as a wild animal in the
vicinity around Whiterocks, Uintah Basin.

'The Crazy Indian,' the white men called him. 'Nipicut' (meaning The Crazy One in Ute) was the name given him by the Indians.

Regardless of his sobriquet, he was the strangest human being the Annals of the West has ever known. Around the turn of the century he lived and died near Whiterocks, in Utah's Uintah Basin.

Nipicut ran in the wilderness like a lobo wolf. Like a wolf, he hunted. He followed the trails of his prey like a questing hound, nosing out the spoor until he ran his quarry to earth and caught it. He had no weapons like gun, knife or spear. With his own hands, he bagged his game, drank the blood, and ate the meat, growling as he devoured raw what he had killed.

Though the sun blazed down in summer and the temperature dropped far below zero in the winter, he ran barefoot and naked in the wilds. His skin became rough and wrinkled like the hide of an elephant. The soles of his feet were so callused and tough, he could walk through the coals of a fire without wincing. He had no house, no home, no shelter. At times, he built himself a crude teepee out of rags to fend the biting wind. Or he dug a small, round pit in the ground, kindled a smoldering fire of cow dung and around it he curled, canine fashion, to keep himself warm.

He spoke no word to any man. When they talked to him, he did not answer, nor did he by sign or sound, indicate that he had heard them. The only sound he was ever known to utter was on nights when the moon was full and bright. At such times, he crouched on the crest of his favorite hill and howled. The children, hearing him, crept deeper under the covers and shivered. The adults slept uneasily, their hearts filled with a nameless dread.

Twice they carried him away, to make him live far from human habitation. But though the men who moved him were on horses leaving him afoot, he beat them back to his old familiar haunts. Finally, they allowed him to remain near the base of the hill where he chose to be. Time and time again, he was given tents, nice blankets, warm clothing and food. But he took nothing, preferring to use only what he got by his own devising.

As Nipicut's fame spread, the legends grew and have persisted to this day. Stories are still told around the fires of Uintah of the prowess of the Crazy Indian. They tell of how he could outrun a horse in the mountains; how he could chase a deer down in the aisles of the forest; how he could catch a jack rabbit on the open range land; how he led a lost child to home and safety.

As the stories grew, so did the superstitions. It was agreed by most that a person who could live like Nipicut, must have supernatural powers. To the Utes, he was a special creature of the Great Spirit, therefore, none would harm him. To some white men, he was a werewolf or some monster of the nether regions. But since he had never been known to harm a single child, or man, or woman, he was left unmolested.

For thirty five years, he lived like a wild thing. Then, on October 8, 1912, he died. They found him lying cold, still and dead. Nipicut's long, hard life was over. He was buried on the hill, from the crest of which he had bayed at the moon and near the base of which he had slept. That hill bears the name of 'Crazy Hill,' named after the 'Crazy Indian.'

The mystery of this remarkable man has lasted all these years. Few have known the facts about him. But he had a past; it has been kept hidden by the silence of his people. Now, it is time to tell his story:

Once, Nipicut was known as Neu-wafe (meaning winter snow). His home was near Spanish Fork, Utah. In those early days, he was a promising young brave of the Ute Indian Nation. He was proud, free and warlike. One day, the order came that his band must leave this land where Utes had camped for centuries. Neuwafe would rather have fought than go, but his young voice was not heard around the council fire. His band, the Paw-gwan-nuance (meaning Lake Shore People) must leave for Himpaw (the River of Pines) in Uintah Basin. Neuwafe was not pleased.

As the long calvacade of Indians rode into Heber Valley, they saw farms along the side of the road. Neuwafe, was fond of the light bread white women made, so he stopped at a farmhouse to get some. He walked into the dwelling without knocking as was the custom of the Indian. He frightened the lady of the house, who screamed to her husband. The farmer, a big burly man, came running. The white man, assuming the boy was molesting his wife, beat and kicked the Indian unmercifully, continuing the chastisement out in the yard in front of the boy's people.

The Utes continued their journey, but Neuwafe was angry, ashamed, and despondent. In order to get the boy out of his depression, his mother rode up beside him, teasing him gently as they rode. Neuwafe was playing with his rifle. He had it across the saddle in front of him, cocking and uncocking the hammer. Suddenly, the horse jumped. The boy's thumb slipped from the hammer and the gun went off. The bullet struck his mother. There, by the side of the road, the son watched his mother die.

The Indians had an unwritten code of crime and punishment. The capital offenses drew one of the four major sentences. First, the most severe judgment in Indian eyes, was the 'No Person Edict.' No one spoke to him, no one ate with him, no one slept with him and no one lived near him. He was disgraced and alone for the rest of his life. The second in severity of punishments was the 'Woman Judgment.' When a warrior convicted of cowardice in battle, received this sentence, he became a woman for the rest of his life. He dressed like a woman, did a woman's work and in all his associations, he was treated as a woman. Third in line was 'Banishment.' The man, receiving this sentence was stripped to the buff and sent barefoot, alone, naked, and without weapons from tribal territory. He must never return during his lifetime. Last of all and least feared was 'Death.' The convicted person suffered death in the manner prescribed by the chief or council, but he retained the position of a respected warrior. He was dressed in full regalia including war-paint. He died proudly, was buried respectfully, and his favorite horse was shot at his grave so he could ride in the 'Great Beyond.'

Women, except in some rare individual cases, were not subject to trial or punishment by chief or tribal council. If a woman committed an offense, her husband punished her as he saw fit. But the man was held responsible if he failed in his duty to see that his wife paid for her crime.

In rare cases, without the action of tribal council or chief, a person punished himself for a crime he deemed he had committed. He did this because he thought he must clear his name so he could ride proudly in the 'Happy Hunting Ground.'

If Neuwafe willfully killed his mother, then he had committed the cardinal crime in the Indian law; he would have been subject to the cardinal punishment. He would have been sentenced to become a 'No Person.'

The facts were that Neuwafe, after the death of his mother, became Nipicut, the No Person. But, there is no record now and no one alive today who can say, whether or not, he was sentenced by the tribal council or the chief; or whether he imposed the judgment on himself. Whatever the facts were, no human being since the dawn of time, lived such a primitive existence, so lacking in human comfort as did Nipicut. It was a miracle that he was able to survive so long under such bitter conditions.

It is true, that whatever the penitent Indian set out to do, he accomplished it. Wherever the sun shines brightest; wherever the game runs in teeming plenty; wherever warriors ride in the sky, it must be that there rides Neuwafe, The Winter Snow. Wherever he is, he is a respected warrior of the Great Ute Nation. For if any man who ever lived, earned his right to be in the Great Beyond of the Indian, it was this penitent warrior, the Wild Man of the Wasteland.

ARAPEEL

I noticed him sitting quietly against the south wall of the trading post, where the sun of springtime shone bright and warm. He was dressed in a costume from out of the past, fringed leggings, beaded moccasins, calico shirt, and a blanket of many colors. His hair had long since been turned to silver; he wore it parted in the middle, hanging down in braids on either side to his shoulders. His face was painted in red and yellow, in accordance with the old custom of his people. When he walked, there was the faint tinkling of the tiny, silver bells he wore fastened to his leggings. Once in a while, he took tobacco from a small buckskin pouch, and, fining it between his hands, rolled a slim cigarette, which he smoked in long, deliberate puffs. As he smoked, his faded, old eyes seemed to look far out over the horizon. In his fancy, I suppose, he was going over the sights and sounds of many days ago.

I saw him quite often after that. Never did he fail to rouse my interest. Yes, he was an old warrior. I knew he had seen many moons in the sky and had many true tales to tell, if he would talk and I would listen. But, at the time, I thought he spoke no English and I could speak no Ute. So I could only imagine what he had seen and what he had done in a long and active life. It was later, after he had died, that I learned he spoke English well and had already told his story.

This was Arapeel. When he died in 1927, he had lived long over a hundred snows. His life story reads like fiction, only it is true. It began a long time ago when white men, horses, and guns were new in Ute country.

Some Arapahos were camped one night in a secluded spot near a small stream. They were returning to their homes from a foray into the country of their hereditary foe, the Utes. Five horses, they had stolen. Now, where the great buffalo plains began, they deemed themselves safe from any reprisal from their victims. They slept quietly, relaxed and unguarded. They were sure they could not be tracked down before they were well within the Arapaho lands, among their tribesmen and safe.

But the Arapahos, had not calculated on Tomahawk, the tracker. Tomahawk could see, hear, and smell better than any man alive. He could follow a trail as swiftly as the wolves of the prairie. He moved faster in pursuit than his quarry could flee. And he was coming to find the raiders of the horse herd. Long ago, he had detected the slight scent of smoke on the evening breeze and now he knew where the enemy of his people rested. He hurried to the chief, Greyhawk, and pointed out the campground of the horse thieves.

As the first streaks of dawn lightened the eastern sky, Greyhawk and his warriors struck. Vengeance came by surprise and swiftly to the Arapahos. They were dead, some without weapons in their hands.

After the looting and scalping was over, the Utes started back for the Shining Mountains. As they passed a clump of bushes, they heard the lusty cry of a man child. The baby boy was seated under a bush, where he had either crawled or his Arapaho mother had placed him.

Red Hand, the Terrible, leaned from his horse and snatched the boy up by his long, black hair. Death was but a whisper away, for Red Hand's knife was streaking swiftly to disembowel the child. But in the instant before the strike, a strong hand grasped Red Hand's wrist with a grip like iron.

"Give the boy to me. One day he will be a great Ute warrior," Greyhawk said. So saying, he took the baby in his arms to still the silent terror in the big, black eyes.

The baby was called Arapeel. Greyhawk and his wife, Meadow Lark, reared him to the day he became a warrior. He was an Arapaho by blood, but in heart, he was a Ute.

The years passed swiftly. When Arapeel had seen sixteen summers, he danced the dance of the sun and became a warrior. He had learned all the skills of an Indian brave. He was an expert bowman. There were times when he had won horses for himself and for others in his village by outshooting all the braves from other bands.

He had heard of guns, the white man's fire stick made of iron. But he had not seen one until some Mexicans stopped to trade one day. He and some other braves went hunting with the Mexicans and he saw the fire stick used. It had a voice of thunder and more smoke came from it than from a campfire made from punkwood. It killed the deer but he was sure such a weapon, used once or twice, would drive the game far away. He did not want one. Greyhawk, though, traded many beaver furs for a gun and Arapeel learned to use it. At first, he thought it would never equal the bow and arrow. But after awhile, he found the gun was an excellent weapon. He wanted one badly. His father's fire stick was a good one, but many the other Indians acquired, were worthless. He said, "When you buy a gun, try it before you pay for it. That way you will always get a good one. All my guns are good ones."

The year Arapeel became a warrior, in the time of red leaves, the band was camped beside the great trail along which the Spaniards came to trade. The braves were hunting and the women and children were gathering berries from the mountain berry bushes. It was the time when food must be gathered and stored for the cold, snowy days of winter. Along the trail, came a party of white hunters and trappers. These men did not speak Spanish as did the Mexicans, nor did they speak French like the men from St. Louis. They talked in a tongue few of the band had ever heard before. These men were Americans; they spoke English. The white men camped a little way upstream from the Indians. When the campfires burned brightly in the evening's first dark, the white men came to visit with Greyhawk. The leader was of medium height and had dark brown hair and blue eyes.

With the visitors was a Shoshone Indian. The Shoshone could speak both Ute and English; it was he who acted as interpreter. The American leader said, "I am Kit Carson. I am searching for other white men in these mountains. Do you know where I can find them?"

Greyhawk answered, "I know where the men you mention are. They are on Awatpaw (Big Water, Green River). They are trapping and trading there."

"Is there a brave among you who can lead me to the camp of my comrades?" Carson asked.

Arapeel spoke up quickly, not waiting for Greyhawk to answer. "Yes, I will take you there, but you must give me one of your rifles."

Carson looked the youth over carefully by the light of the fire. Then he said, "Well, I guess it would be worth a rifle to have someone to guide me. But son, I had in mind an older brave. You ain't much more than dry behind the ears."

Greyhawk looked at his son. On his face, he read the strong desire of youth written plainly. Then he spoke, "This is my son. He is a warrior and will one day be a chieftain. This is a truth all Utes know. White man, your party is small and many will want your horses. Maybe you are strong enough to keep them, you can wait and see. But with my son to go with you, you will make your passage safely, for no Indian of my tribe will dare attack you. You had better take Arapeel with you."

Kit Carson smiled when he heard what Greyhawk had to say. "Chief," he replied, "I will take your boy. I know that years do not tell the story. We thank you."

Turning to Arapeel, Carson spoke, "All right, you are hired. I will give you your gun in the morning."

"No," the young Indian said. "I want my gun tonight. At first light in the morning, I must test it."

Carson complied; no further word said.

BEAR TALK

The five fingers of light had not even begun to show over the tops of the Shining Mountains to the east, heralding the rising of Tana (the sun), when old Many Tails, the great medicine man, began his 'by yi' and chant accompanied by his eldest son, his first understudy, on the largest tom-tom he had.

In his teepee, Mountain Sheep, the chief of chiefs of the Whiterocks Band of Ute Indian Nation, sat straight up in his bed. "What goes on here," he said to himself. "Are we being raided this time of night by an enemy or what?"

He reached for his rifle and prepared to order all his warriors to repel an attack. But being fully awake now, it dawned on him that Many Tails was at it again. He'd had a dream, he supposed, an important dream; or the Sachems of Manitou had visited him again and he had a great prophecy to foretell. Everyone must hear; must hear it as quickly as possible for there was no time to waste; it must be told while his mind was still sharp so that no detail would be missed.

Mountain Sheep's wife turned over in her bed and to her husband said, "Get up and go out and make that old man be quiet. This is our busy time. The meat must be smoked and dried. The Yampas must be dug. The ripened berries must be picked and dried. Everyone needs their sleep and how can they sleep with all that commotion? Go! Go!" she said.

"Oh, no. I won't," the chief said. "The last time I did that, old Many Tails stopped all right, but before he did, his chant changed. He pointed four fingers at me, two on each hand; it was a curse. Much sick came to me; my eyes turned red, many, many tears ran. My head ached like it had a tom-tom inside it; my nose ran like two rivers were running out of it; my throat was red and it was so sore I couldn't eat. You ought to know woman because it was you who took care of me. You were frightened, remember that?"

"Yes, I remember," she said. "Even Old Crone's doctoring did no good. I was frightened and so were you. In four days, as the day was fading, he came to you with his eagle's wing and with his magic powder. He went over you good, front and back and down each side. All the while, he sang a weird song. When he was through, you were all well. It was just like that," she said, snapping her thumb and fingers together. "Let him go, I don't care. I'll sleep anyway," she said.

Mountain Sheep wrapped his bear robe around him and went outside. "If Teele, my little granddaughter, has left my tender, as she always does, I'll make me a little smoking fire, light my pipe and maybe Bent Legs will come and we can talk all this over." He reached down and moved the square of brick laid to keep the dew away.

Teele had not forgotten, she never did. There was the fired up cedar bark, a bundle of small sticks and his flint and steel. In a minute, he had a small fire burning, his pipe filled and lit. Now he would sit and watch.

Now the five fingers of light were stretching up into the eastern sky. In the dim, light he could see Bent Legs coming from his teepee across the parade ground to talk with him.

Teele came from her bed and sat in his lap. "Grandpa, I think the stars are going out over that way," she said pointing to the sky in the east.

"Yes," he said. "That's the butterfly's work. Every morning, they have to go up and blow the stars out with their wings. Then at night they have to go up and light them again. It's a lot of work, don't you think."

"Yes! Grandpa, what do butterflies eat?"

"Well," he said, "at the bottom of every flower, there is a little cup. The flowers fill the cup with water, like sugar water. The butterflies have long tongues and with their tongues they drink the water from the cup of the flowers. The butterflies like it and so do the flowers."

"Grandpa, here comes Bent Legs."

"Yes," he said. "But you mustn't call him Bent Legs to his face. His real name is Running Antelope. You see, many moons ago, he and I went hunting. In those days, his legs were as straight or maybe straighter than mine. But on that day, when we went hunting together, we came down a ridge of the mountain. His horse slipped and fell. It rolled over him two times. It broke both of his legs so bad the bones poked through his skin. His horse wasn't hurt much, just skinned here and there. So I built a travois and brought him home. Old Crone fixed him up as best she could but it left his legs bent as you see them now. So call him Running Antelope because that is who he is."

"I'll remember," she said. "I think I'll go now." She jumped up and ran to her friends so they could watch Many Tails.

Around his waist Many Tails had a belt with a turquoise buckle. Fastened to it were six wolf tails, each dyed in a different color. The tails swirled and swirled, first one way then the other. He was doing a fancy dance like no one had ever seen before, all in double step time, perfectly in time with the beat of the giant tom-tom. His costume and his painted body and face were the most beautiful and elaborate any of the villagers had ever seen.

Now, the five fingers of light rose into the eastern sky; it was the twilight of the morning. How the distant Shining Mountains, with their snow caps, seemed ethereal and transparent in the eastern sky.

At all the teepee doors, people were up and watching as the great medicine man, dreamer of dreams, seer and revelator, carried on his ceremony. Not one among them knew that soon he would make a great prophecy for the benefit of the chief of chiefs and the people.

Round and round the fire burning in the center of the big parade grounds, Many Tails danced. Then just as the sun's first beam of light shone on the Shining Mountains, turning them red with its light, Many Tails lay down. The tom-tom was still beating, but muted—so much the people could barely hear it.

Now, after he had regained a little of his breath, Many Tails spoke his prophecy. "I have been visited by the Sachems of Manitou. The one dressed in red said that in the next two sleeps, there will be born to the tribe, four great chieftains. One will be Bear, one Lion, one Eagle, and one Light Eyes. Light eyes will be chief of chiefs and the others will be chiefs of different kinds. They will win four great battles. Prepare and beware," he said. Then he fell into a deep slumber, almost the same as the sleep of death.

"Humph!" Old Crone said. "Why didn't he tell me something I didn't know already. Desert Blossom's papoose is due but she is so small in body and her baby is so large, I doubt that she can have it and live." Holding a certain leaf in her hand, she continued, " Send Bear Talker to me. If anyone knows where more of this is, he will."

Bear Talker, the smiling warrior, arose from where he was seated and walked over to Old Crone. He said to her, "I know the leaf you hold in your hand. But the last time you harvested it, you took it all. Mother Earth knows you were greedy and now she won't grow anymore at that place. I know where there is more but it is a long, long way from here. It will take me four sleeps to go, there and back, to get it."

"Too late, much too late," Old Crone said. "You would have to kill at least two of your best horses to get it here in time."

"Wait," Bear Talker said. "I'll find Big Bear and ask him; maybe he knows where some grows closer."

"You make me much angry, pretending you can talk to a great bear. You go near him, he will kill you."

Bear Talker reached and took the leaf from Old Crone's fingers.

"Be still healing woman. Your tongue is too loose. You talk too much."

Bear Talker spoke to a pony herder. "Bring me my mountain horse, not any of the mules, and hurry."

"Here he is. I've already brought him to you. Something told me you would need him. Look, he is ready to go."

Bear Talker mounted and left, saying to his big black horse, "Save your strength. You've got much climbing to do. We must find Big Bear with white spot on legs. You must smell him out for me."

As he left, Bear Talker heard Little Crone run to her grandmother and say, "Grandma, come. Come quickly. Desert Blossom is beginning already."

Black climbed fast and ever faster, stopping now and then in good places to catch his breath, then he climbed on. Finally, they came to a little gushing stream that flowed into falls and rippled down the mountainside. There stood Big Bear. He stood on his hind legs in fighting stance. But when he saw who it was, he came down on all fours and lumbered over to meet his friends. Bear Talker took the leaf out of his medicine bag, showed it to Big Bear, and let him smell it. Then he asked, "Do you know where some of this grows? Desert Blossom will die if she doesn't get some quickly."

Big Bear grunted and groaned in bear language, then took off on a lumbering run which was much faster than it looked. He came to a place where a ridge flattened a little. There, thickly growing, was a whole acre or more of the burning plant.

Bear Talker pulled the plants up by the roots and stuffed them in his buckskin bag. In no time at all, the bag was brimming full. He mounted his big horse, bid good-bye, thanked Big Bear and was on his way home.

When Tabby had reached the noon mark on the time stick, Bear Talker was home again. Both he and his horse were tired and weary but when he heard Desert Blossom moaning and yelling in travail, he washed his plant roots and using a pot, put them on the outside fire to simmer and stew for one full mark on the Tabby stick.

Old Crone hurried out, "Are you back? Did you get the plants I sent you for? What are you doing using roots and all. Pick the leaves off and use only the leaves."

Bear Talker said, "In many things you are right, but Big Bear said the roots are four times stronger than the leaves. Get me the honey, the pine gum, and the bugs. I'll do the rest. Hurry back to Desert Blossom."

"Hurry! Hurry!" Old Crone replied. "Already I can feel the head. It is the biggest papoose ever born to a little woman. If the woman lives, medicine man must call the Shaman to ask them for help."

Bear Talker picked the clay jar up and one bug at a time he gently squeezed one clear drop of liquid from each bug, then gently turned it loose. "Go play," he said, "and I thank you." He had killed not a single one.

He measured and poured in the wild honey, the pitch pine gum, and the finest of moss from the north side of the pine tree. The medicine grew thicker and thicker. He touched a spoonful to his elbow; it was done but must be cooled.

He saw Pink Butterfly standing near. "Butterfly, take this to the spring of many cold waters and cool it until you can put your finger in it. Then bring it back to me. Don't spill a single drop. Hurry! Hurry!"

Butterfly was back. The liquid had turned to a thick paste; it was just right. "It will burn like fire but leave no scar," he said to himself.

"The baby is born. He is big, the biggest baby boy I have ever seen. Desert Blossom is sleeping from the sleeping medicine I gave her, but is bleeding so fast I doubt I can save her. I hope your bear medicine can save her. If not, she will die," said Old Crone.

"Bear says it will do it like a red hot iron but it will leave no scar. Here is a new, slim paddle I have made for you. Hurry! Hurry! Use it!"

Old Crone used it and now the bleeding slowed until there was none. Now Old Crone thought to herself, "I must keep her sleeping. This stuff is as hot fire. It will weaken, though, as time goes by. And when I let Desert Blossom waken, she won't feel it. But she must rest; she must have a long, long rest."

Into the teepee came Little Crone. She was weeping; the tears were pouring out of her eyes copiously. "Oh! Grandma," she said, "I am so afraid and I feel so bad I don't know what to do. Pansy's baby has a cat's mouth. They say that such a one is either a demon or an imp."

Old Crone grabbed her to her and said, "Be still. Be still and wipe your tears away. I know they say and believe such things. But I don't and neither did my mother, the oldest Crone of all. Find me the smallest needle in our basket and also the smallest cat gut thread. I'll hurry over there with my sleeping potion. Maybe I can fix it before anyone else can see it, especially old Goat Horns, the medicine man."

Then off she went in a flurry. She went into Pansy's teepee and said, "Let me see your baby."

"No, no, no," Pansy said. "This is my baby. You just leave him. You will kill him. Someday he'll grow up to be a big chief, if you leave him be."

Old Crone petted her face. "I haven't come to kill your baby; such a thing is foolish. I don't believe these old tales and neither must you. I have come only to help you. Let me see him. Maybe I can fix him. He won't be the first like this you know."

Pansy handed him over. She knew she could trust Old Crone.

"It is bad, very bad, all I can do is try. If I don't win, then there is another way to fight for his life."

Old Crone with her smallest needle and small, tough cat gut thread, sewed up the lips of the deformed baby after she had put him to sleep with her herbal brew. And we can only guess that the baby grew to fulfill his destiny.

BELIEFS AND WAYS OF THE INDIAN

SKY READER

All my people can read the sky a little bit, but there is always one who can read it well. By a Sky Reader, I mean a man who, upon arising in the morning as the sun rises, can look at the sky and tell you what will happen that day. For example, the sky reader arose in the morning and he said, "Before the sun goes down, we shall take the war trail." That was the day the Japanese Bombed Pearl Harbor. Another time the sky reader said, "Today the great chief dies." That was the day they assassinated John F. Kennedy. These are the men we call the Sky Readers. There are not many, usually only one, and he foretells only for a single day.

VISION DREAMER

Among my people is the man we call the Vision Dreamer. He sleeps and dreams. In his dreams, the future is foretold, for months, maybe years, in advance. So we know that it is well to listen to the vision dreamer. It is believed by our people that if they use peyote, each man will have his dreams and in so dreaming can foretell his own future and perhaps the future of his tribe.

PRAYER MAKER

The prayer maker is he who chants to heaven. He asks the great spirit for the help that his people need. We find that ordinarily there is one man who has more influence with the great spirit than another, and it is he upon whom we call to aid us. Sometimes he will not always help. He tests the wind with dust. He views the sky. He sleeps. And if he sees fit, then he will make his prayer. Thus it is, we call him the prayer maker.

HEALER

In the making of Indian magic, there is always the healer. Sometimes this might be a woman. They are the ones who take care of the wounded and the sick. They know the creatures of the fields. They know the plants. They know all things that should be used to cure. In the use of herbs and other medicines much has been forgotten. We have turned to the white man's medicine. Once in awhile, we find that only the Indian medicine will work, and to get this, we must inquire of the healer.

CHARMER

The charmer is he who makes believe. He can also make you believe. He can make you happy; he can make you sad. He can make the wind blow; he can make the rain come. He can make the trees sway and the dogs bark. He can make plants grow. Sometimes, he can even move mountains. Because he can do this, everybody is afraid of the charmer and they treat him well. Many times the charmer has white eyes, whiter even than the white man. When he looks at you, it gives you an uncanny feeling. One day, I shall introduce you to a charmer, and you know what I mean.

The Sky Reader, the Vision Dreamer, the Prayer Maker, the Healer, and the Charmer are those known by the white man as Medicine Men. But few white men know that each of the Medicine Men have their specialty. These I have told you are the specialties belonging to the medicine men and only they know how to work it.

INDIAN RELIGION

You white men say there are three Gods: The Father, the Son, and the Holy Ghost. We Indians do not believe this. We worship the great spirit as you do. His symbol is the sun. He is too holy for us to approach him directly, too holy for us to mention his name. So we use the sun as his symbol, but he is the father. Then there is the mother. The mother is the earth. She produces all that there is of life, plants, all other things by the action of the great spirit through the sun upon her. And so the Indian religion is the father and the mother and we are the children.

We do not mean that only the humans are the children, so too are the beasts, so too are the plants, because they are born of the earth. Everything has its rights. The lion, the coyote, the bear, the horse, the dog, all things have their rights on earth and we cannot take these rights from them. We may kill, but we cannot kill just for killing sake. We can only kill if we need the creatures. When the creatures die, us included, the things they are made up of now return to the mother earth and become a part of her again. Only our spirits travel on.

The white man's heaven is not like ours. The same requirements to get to your heaven are different from the requirements to get to ours. We call ours the Happy Hunting Ground. Each person, and everything, when he dies will go there. We have no hell. Every living creature goes to the Happy Hunting Ground. If he does wrong in his life here on earth, he is punished here and is punished enough; when he dies he goes to the Happy Hunting Ground with all the rest.

There are times when one man, through his actions, may punish the whole tribe. The whole tribe must suffer for him. There are times when the whole tribe does wrong, in which case the whole tribe must suffer. This is the reason there are periods of famine, drought, floods. This is why the coldness of the winters. This is why we must go through all of our sufferings which may arise here on earth, because we must suffer for what we have done wrong. But when we die, the Happy Hunting Ground will be ours.

TWINS
There can only be one spirit born at each birth. There can never be two. If there are two spirits born at one birth, the one child is a

witch's child... a thing of evil. It is difficult sometimes to tell which one is which. So the time must run on until you are able to determine which one is your child and which one is the witch's child. When you find out, then the witch's child must die because if you keep it and raise it, there will be evil and you and your tribe will suffer. For this reason, you will not find living twins of any great age among the Indians.

ANGEL BEINGS

There are people who are not Gods and yet they are spirits. They usually control a section of land. These we call angel beings. If they are in control then you have nothing to fear and everything will be good for you in the land where the angel beings are.

Then there are the Devil Beings. They control sections of land, too—sometimes the same sections as the angel beings. And control of the land swings back and forth between the angel beings and the devil beings. It is not well to go into strange country when the devil beings are in control, for then accidents will happen to you, sometimes even death will occur. When you go into strange country, look at the land about you. If it is frowning stay away because it will be rough upon you. But if the land is smiling, then you may go for the angel beings are in control and they will see that you are happy.

TRICKSTER

Almost anywhere you might find this fellow. There are lots of them. There is no danger in him because he is a joker. He will make you forget things that you should do. He will pull little tricks upon you. When you are thinking that you have done things right, you will find you have done them wrong. He will keep you awake at night with funny noises. He will make funny winds come and blow away. He will cause the showers to fall when you least expect it. He does this all for fun. The only way you can get along with the trickster is to laugh at him. Then he will never do anything very serious to you because he loves laughter and fun.

WITCH'S CHILD

Sometimes, if you aren't careful upon the birth of your children, the witch will trade children with you. If she does, you have a thing of evil. Then you must allow it to starve and slowly die, and if you keep it you will bring disaster upon yourself and maybe upon your tribe. Therefore, destroy the witch's child. Most of the time only the mother can tell if she has her own child or if it is the witch's child. You must listen to her.

WATER PEOPLE

I saw one of the water people. It sat on the bank and watched us swimming. Of course, if we drew close it dove into the water and we saw it again no more. Once for a long time, day after day, we watched one of these creatures. It looked like a human but it was much smaller. It loved to watch humans play and swim in the water. When I told my mother of it, she would not let me go swimming again for many days, because she was afraid. But I have never known of one of them to harm anybody.

SAWATCH

In the high mountains, when the snow is deep, there is a giant man. We do not know where he comes from. We do not know where he goes, but he is a giant. He need not wear clothes for his skin is covered with fur like a bear; but he is not a bear. He is like a man and he walks on his hind legs. Sometimes, when you have seen one you can go where he was and see his steps in the snow. You will know that he is gigantic. There are those who have met him face to face and have suffered no evil. But we do not trust him because he is too big and too savage. He can kill a horse, or any other animal we know of, with one blow of his hand. I have never seen a Sawatch, I have only been told about him. I have looked many times, but then those who say they have seen him I believe, for they have no reason to lie about it. Maybe before I die I shall see one. No white man that I know has ever seen one, but I read in the papers that there are those who say that white man has seen them in far away Tibet. But among my people there has been none for many generations.

GOVERNMENT OF THE UTE INDIANS:

It is difficult for whites to comprehend the loose organization of early Indian government, if it could really be called that, but it went as follows:

A chief was a leader of his people. He was selected not by vote but by prowess as a warrior; as a general and sometimes as a medicine man. Many times he ruled by force.

Chiefs were ranked as sub-chiefs, chiefs, and chiefs of chiefs. Whether he was one or the other depended upon the number of warriors willing to follow him. This, you see, could change from time to time and sometimes did.

The name Sanpete came from a band of Utes called San-Piche or San-Pits. The name of Utes usually came from the characteristics of the land in which they lived.

The Bureau of Indian Affairs made a census of Indians in 1875. The San-Piche were listed as numbering 336.

The Utes of Spanish Fork and Utah Valley were divided into several bands controlled by several sub-chiefs and chiefs. Their name as a whole was Paw-gwau-nuance (Lake Shore People) or Paw-gooz-caw (Fish Eaters).

Looking back, I find there were several chiefs at the time of the migration eastward to Uintah: 1. Santaquin (Sagebrush); 2. Tabby (Sun); 3. Sowiette (Slim Belly).

It is possible that one of the above chiefs could have made up his mind and led his following eastward without concurrence of the others. However, in affairs like this, they held a grand council. There would be the chiefs, big and little, and the old men of the tribe rich in age and wisdom. The council would decide the movement.

Tabby was a Shoshone. He was a chief of chiefs. He spoke the Ute and Shoshone languages with equal facility. He led his people east to Uintah. His band were both Utes and Shoshone.

Sowiette was a chief of chiefs, a Ute. He led his people east to Uintah. When he died his wife, Ta-Tach (The Preacher) took his seat at the council. This was unusual because, so far as I know, she was the first Ute woman allowed to do this. Chipeta (Spring of Clear Water) was the second.

Santaquin was a chief of chiefs. He led his people east to Uintah. Hand died a short time later on the west shoulder of Tabby Mountain.

Who was superior between the above three? I don't know. From all accounts, Tabby was.

Who controlled the San-Piche or San-pits? It was either Sowiette or Santaquin, I don't know which.

In the very near future, at Bottle Hollow near Ft. Duchesne, in connection with the museum, there will be an archive set up containing all the written documents about the Ute people. Research should disclose the Awat-towatch (Big Man) among the above three chiefs of chiefs.

SOME INDIAN RULES:

When the sweat dries quickly from a man's body, it is a time for much water to drink, but it is a time when there is little sickness. This is a good time for babies to be born.

The white man says, "Where there is a circle around the moon there will be a storm." This might be true but the day will be hot and the sweat will not dry quickly.

You will not get sick from drinking water made from melted snow or ice.

In the winter, camp where the rising sun will shine on your teepee, but not where the shadows strike before the sun goes down.

When it is hot, camp where the breeze blows off the water to you and it will be cooler.

When the red star is in the sky, watch your temper.

When the great blue star is brightest, it will be colder.

When the smaller blue star overhead is brightest, it will be hotter in the daytime.

When the heat bothers you most, sit in the sun while you slowly throw 15 stones to the distance. Then go rest in the shade against a tree trunk. This will cool you.

When you want to save water in the heat on the desert, drink plenty, even if it is all the water you have and then move slowly. If you drink your water little by little, you will always be thirsty and you will drink more.

When you have only a little water, sit quietly in the shade till evening comes. Drink plenty of water before you start for the next water hole. Do this even though the one drink takes all your water.

When you are hungry and thirsty never eat anything but something green.

Rest in the shade during the hottest part of the day, travel only in the morning and evening.

Two meals are best for a long journey: a big breakfast and a big supper. Do not eat in the heat of the day.

JOHNNY HARPER NICK

Johnny Harper Nick, a Ute Indian, died here today.

With his passing comes the end of a living legend for he was an American hero. He was near the top of the roll of honor in that long list of men who fought in World War I.

In his younger years, he attended Riverside, Haskell, and Carlisle. He was offered a scholarship to Harvard or Dartmouth, but he turned them both down. He was tired of book learning, he said. He wanted to come home to live with the people of his tribe.

Johnny played shortstop on the Myton Baseball Team. When the United States entered the World War I against Germany, all the single men on the ball team enlisted to a man. Among these was Johnny Harper Nick.

He was with the first contingents of doughboys to land in France. They marched down the streets of Paris while the band played Yankee Doodle.

General Pershing was determinded to have an independent Armerican army so he refused to throw his men into battle sandwiched in with the English and the French. The speed of the American arrivals, division after division, caused Hindenberg, Leudendorf, and the Crown Prince to decide on a great offensive. They tried to capture Paris and win the war before the full strength of America could be felt.

The Germans started a drive at Chateau Thierry. This was originally planned as a front but it worked so well, it turned into the real thing. And the French Sixth Army came reeling back almost in a rout.

The 'Old Contemptibles' of the British Army stood pat, fighting with quiet ferocity on the left and on the right. The veterans of the Battle of the Marne stood their ground. In the center, however, the

Sixth Army couldn't withstand the onslaught of the Kaiser's Shock Troops on the way to Paris.

Foch and Petain planned to bring in veteran outfits to fill the gap, but they needed time. Time was extremely critical. They prevailed upon Pershing to let them have Americans to stop the Huns until they could set their trap.

Johnny Harper Nick, with his outfit, a machine gun battalion, went forward with all haste. As they watched the Americans going by, a British colonel said to Petain, "Those untrained men don't have a chance against those Prussian shock troops, General. This is murder."

Petain replied, "I know it but it's all I can do. Send them in and pray that they will give us time."

The Americans went to the crossroads this side of the Marne, where the road ran west to Paris. Here they formed a perimeter in the form of a horseshoe. It just so happened that Johnny Harper Nick occupied the position right on the point of the horseshoe. It was here he dug in and waited.

He didn't wait long. The Germans, after re-grouping, sent over a big artillery barrage followed by their infantry. These advanced swiftly, thinking all they had at this point, was a mop-up operation. What they struck was a hornet's nest.

Of course, the Krauts tried to drive in the point of the horseshoe first. They couldn't leave machine gun nests behind them. Nick kept firing, knocking men down in windrows like wheat before the scythe. They tried snipers next. But who in the world could dream that a man could aim a machine gun like a rifle and knock out those snipers? Well, Johnny Harper Nick did.

Then the enemy tried to creep up and use grenades. But they came against a baseball player who outmatched his opponents with counter grenade throwing. His accuracy was uncanny.

They abandoned the assault on the point of the horseshoe. The tactics were unorthodox anyway. They tried to the left and then to the right but this didn't work either because the farther they came, the more guns they faced. The crossfire was terrific.

Then, here came the 'Fokkers' led by the Red Baron Manfred Von Richthofen. They tried to strafe the machine guns out, but after a few passes the Flying Circus was met by the Lafayette Escadrille, led by Eddie Rickenbacker. The air was soon filled with dogfights.

In the end, the Germans were rocked back into the cold and gray twilight. They never came on again.

When everything was over, Johnny Harper Nick and Clyde Wing won citations for bravery above and beyond the call of duty. It was debated whether they should receive the Congressional Medal of Honor or the Croix de Guerre. They could have one but not both. Chief Nick and his helper were under French Command at the time of their exploits. French President Walstem decreed that these two men, in accordance with the French request, be allowed to receive the Croix de Guerre, the highest medal for valor of the French Army.

Petain decorated the men in Paris, kissing them on one cheek, then the other. Here was the citation:

"In the course of violent action disputed foot by foot on the northern outskirts of Chateau Thierry, these men covered themselves in incomparable glory. Their valor and skill caused the enemy sanguinary losses. They barred the Boche [German soldiers] on the road to Paris."

So, now, at Johnny Harper Nick's passing let us pause while the bugle blows the strains of Taps. Let us give a last salute to a valiant soldier while we stand and whisper a last farewell to a great American hero. May his name be engraved forever on the highest honor roll of American fighting men.

Johnny Harper Nick, the scion of a long line of Ute chiefs, died here today. With his passing, we lost one of the last great heroes of World War I.

THE PIT OF HADES

Muse Harris, the Indian chief, known to the Indians as Chief Red Moose, told me of a spot in the desert country of Uintah Basin so incredible, a man can hardly believe it even when he sees it with his own eyes.

As spring was breaking, Red Moose guided me to this place. "We climb to the top of that low ridge yonder," the old man told me. We climbed and, at the crest of the ridge, without warning, 'The Pit of Hades,' fell away beneath our feet.

The view was utterly fantastic. Down in the pit, carved in stone, are unbelievable creatures: imps, demons, gargoyles, goblins, witches, monsters, devils and all kinds of creepy, squirmy, crawly, slimy things. They stand there forever frozen in the midst of the desert. There is no pen on earth that can describe the place, for it is like the nightmare of an opium eater. I took some pictures and from them you can see what I mean, although the pictures too are inadequate.

Aside from the nightmare figures, and sometimes as a part of them, are flutes, pipes, spirals and carvings—a wondrous filigree as delicate as the lace on Molly's hem. Such erosion is strange and far beyond belief.

There is an Indian Legend about this place in the desert. One day, the story goes, the evil creatures of the nether regions, tired of living in the dark and dank, decided to dig up to the surface and take over everything above and below the earth. They dug and the ground trembled and rumbled in their work.

Two coyotes heard the rumble. Curious, as all coyotes are, they couldn't resist the urge to investigate. The pair discovered the plot of the creatures from down under and in a trice howled the alarm to all their fellow mortals round-about.

A great council was held to decide what to do. It would take more than mortal power to stop the invasion of these supernatural beings, this they understood. Finally, they determined to send for the greatest medicine man they knew.

Two eagles flew with the summons, and on the very first day, they found the great one in his mountain fastness.

The wild horses set up a relay of the fleetest stallions on earth; they bore the mighty one with the speed of the wind over mountains, rivers, valleys and plains. And it was none too soon, for as he came up Whiteriver the Sachem could see the red light in the sky where the under-world denizens had broken through.

Without sleep or rest or food, the Medicine Chief went to work. First, he called on the Wind of the West and a great hurricane blew, carrying dust, dirt, rocks, and trees to fill in the awful hole. But all this went for naught. It fell through to be burned in fires down below.

Then, the Rain God was asked for help. He sent water in clouds and torrents, but it vanished away in steam and mist, while the Devil Chief laughed loud and long and his minions screamed with glee.

The Sachem called to the God of the North, "Help us, help us," he chanted and drummed, "Oh, Great Lord of Ice and Snow."

Help came as swift as an arrow—intense, deep, bitter cold. The North God caught the denizens of the deep as they gathered to spread over the world. In a wink of an eye, he turned them all to ice. The Devil Chief, the Great Mother Witch, the magician, and all the rest, stand there just as they stood at the instant the cold struck long ago.

When the warmth came back, again the West Wind blew and as the ice melted, the dust took its place. Now the monsters stand in the pit they dug, all of them turned to stone. It is a warning to the evil ones down in hell to leave the good green earth alone.

THE FIRES OF SPRING

On my little pony, I rode toward home. It was a very cold winter's day. I was freezing, in spite of the warm clothes I wore. My horse's breath, as it blew back from his nostrils, was turning his chest white with frost.

As I rode farther on, I came upon an Indian's camp pitched in a sheltered cove. Out in front, seated cross-legged on a Navajo blanket, was a gray-haired old Indian woman with a fire burning briskly in front of her. She had a big pot boiling on the fire, full of clothes which she was preparing to wash, I guess.

I rode up to the old woman and asked, "May I come to your fire and warm me and my horse before I go on home?"

"Oh, yes. It is a very cold day and you are welcome to come close and warm yourself by my fire," she said.

Without further ado, she poured me a scalding hot cup of coffee. She handed it to me said, "Drink this. It will help to get you warm."

As I sat on a log by her fire, sipping slowly on that wonderful cup of coffee, she began to tell me a story. To my mind, as the years have gone by, it has become a legend. This is how she told it:

"Many moons ago when I was a small girl, as you are still a boy, my people lived in tall teepees both winter and summer. In the summer, we raised the edges so the breeze would blow through and keep us cool. In the winter, we put the edges down and banked them with dirt or snow so we could keep warm. We always had a small fire in the center of our teepee to keep it warm and to cook on. The smoke rose straight up and out the smoke hole in the top.

In the daytime, the men hunted to find us meat. The women sat in the teepee by the fire making clothes, mending and cooking.

In the evening, when the men were home, we all sat in a circle around our fire. And this was storytelling time. It was fun and from the stories the old ones told us, we young ones learned many things.

Before my father went to bed at night, he notched the stick to keep track of the days, the weeks, the moons. This is the way he kept time.

White men have a saying we Indians knew also as, 'When the days begin to lengthen, the cold begins to strengthen,' and 'It is always darkest just before the dawn.'

We lived on in the winter, but in spite of the stories we heard and the games we played, the days of winter became tiresome and tedious after awhile. We became restive and sometimes quarrelsome and sometimes mean. We were waiting for the time when winter would lose his grip on the land—and on us.

Then one day, my father would count the notches on his stick and say, 'These are the coldest days of the winter. Soon it will be spring. We must light our spring fires now. It is coldest just before the warming days of springtime.'

We all began to search for the oriole's trees. It must be the oriole trees because no other trees will do. You see, the oriole trees are those which have deserted nests hanging down from the limbs like baskets. When we found oriole trees, we shouted. These were cut down and dragged home. We built a big fire up wind from our camp and burnt the trees we had found.

We children would be so happy and so gay. We would look far away over the country. And we could see the smoke from other fires where other bands were burning oriole trees. Then we would dance round and round and sing and sing, 'Oh! Look, Oh! See, the fires of spring are burning; soon we will be playing in the warm sunshine.'

When I was a little girl, the fires of spring would be burning today because spring is not too far away.

My young friend, you must be riding for home now before darkness closes in on you and the cold gets colder. But remember as you ride, my fire is a little oriole fire. And spring is not too far away."

INDIAN ANECDOTE

I live on the Uintah-Ouray Indian Reservation in eastern Utah. I have a Ute Indian friend whom I have known for many moons. Time was, when in accordance with Indian custom, my friend, wore his hair long and painted his face. This was the mark of a brave; Indian women did not do these things.

After several years, during which time we had not met, I saw my Indian friend again. His hair was cut and he had no paint on his face. I jokingly asked him, "How come you've cut your hair and have no paint on your face?"

Jesting back, he replied, "Last week I went to Salt Lake City to visit my granddaughter. All the girls out there, including my granddaughter, wore pants, wore long hair, and painted their faces. I'm afraid to go around anymore like a man should, because if I do, everyone will think I'm a squaw."

UTAH BIG GAME HUNT: CIRCA 700 A.D.

Utah Big Game Hunt
"One member of an Indian hunting party more than a thousand years ago
took the time to preserve his peoples' hunt in carvings in rock." This is not
the photo of the one in the article but from same area, Nine Mile Canyon.
—Used by permission, Utah State Historical Society, all rights reserved.

In Nine Mile Canyon, south of Myton, hidden away on a ledge is scratched the picture story of a hunt that took place over a thousand years ago. One member of the party, elated over its good fortune, carved on a panel of rocky wall an account of the kill in picture form, capturing a moment in time from a day long, long past.

Who these hunters were, where they came from, and where they went is a mystery. Scholars say they were Moquis or Anasazis who vanished from this region centuries ago.

But, back to the petroglyph. Studying its design, one can see the hunting party, their hair, the fashion of their dress, their weapons and even the strategy of the hunt. Crude bows used by the hunters, as shown in the petroglyph, were not very long, consequently effective range was short. In hunting big game, their strategy was simple—get close to the quarry, either by ambush, or by stalking the unwary animal, or by running it into a cul-de-sac. Then, having trapped the prey, slay it!

The primitive artist used the natural features of his stone canvas to depict the character of the terrain. He is saying quite plainly that wild goats have been driven into a dead-end, the edge of a high ledge. The rest is obvious. While the goats stirred in confusion, backs to the sheer drop, the hunters brought them down.

When I first saw the panel, I sat studying it for an hour or more. As I slowly unraveled its meaning, I wondered if I could find the spot where the kill occurred. Surprisingly, the scene wasn't hard to find, as the drawings almost were made on location. To the east was a saddle in the hills marked by a deep, worn trail which must have been started by wild animals ages ago. On one side of the pass, a ridge runs westward for a quarter of a mile or more and ends in a high, ledgy point. Following the ridge about three quarters of its length, you become trapped; there is no way down except back the way you came. At the base of this ridge are the drawings. Over the hills beyond the saddle is good grazing ground. Even today, mule deer frequent the area.

More hunters than those depicted may have been in the party. Nevertheless, the hunt must have been well-planned. After the goat herd was spotted, hunters evidently were hiding at strategic points along the trail route. One or two men must have circled east beyond the grazing ground, then acting as beaters, came noisily back. The wild goats, frightened by the approach of humans followed the trail through the notch. Herders hazed the goats down the ridge and soon the herd reached the point of no return. The pursuers closed in and the action began.

In the upper left of the panel, a goat lies sprawled out dead. Behind the bowman, another beast has fallen, struck in the base of the neck. In front of the archer, a goat has been hit by an arrow; the shaft protrudes from its side and blood flows. It will soon fall. Far right on the panel, another animal lies dead.

Now, the artist catches the most dramatic moment of the hunt. A prize trophy is alive; the magnificent ram at the top of the panel has turned at bay on the edge of the precipice. You can almost hear him blow and snort with anger, his front hooves stamp the ground. He will fight; in another instant, he will charge. It is a moment of danger. Can a bowman stop the giant?

There are four hunters shown. To the left is a bowman, wearing a single feather in his hair. The feather curls forward over his brow. He has put an arrow to his bow while intently watching the big ram. His position is not favorable for a shot so he waits for a better chance. One of the figures is a brave who appears to be walking from left to right. His right hand is empty, but in his left, he holds a sling—like the sling David used against Goliath. This brave wears a headdress with one feather, curling toward the back of his head. Perhaps the headdress and the curl of the feather indicate rank. If so, this man is the leader of the hunt; his headdress and the curl of the feather set him apart from the other men.

One of the hunters is a woman. Her sex is indicated by the absence of a feather, her female shape, and her dress. She is waving the pelt of a small animal in her right hand. It is probably a tanned fur which she may be using to haze the ram toward the other hunters.

All the figures are clothed. The men are bare from the waist up but wear a short skirt or breech cloth, reaching about midway down the thigh. The woman wears a Mother-Hubbard-type dress, reaching just below the knees and belted with a narrow belt. All have footgear of the ankle, moccasin type.

There they stand, caught and held, unmoving for hundreds of years. Did they kill the giant ram? Unfortunately, the man spun his yarn but left it dangling for all time. Perhaps they did not get the ram, so the author allowed it to live forever, poised for its breakaway charge.

This is the age old story upon which fishermen and hunters dwell. This is the yarn of the big one they almost had; but somehow it got away.

DID YETI ONCE ROAM
THE VALLEYS OF UTAH?

Last spring, after the coils of winter's civilization had grown irksome on us, some friends of mine and I decided to escape into the real wilderness. We planned a backpack trip into a region rough and remote, to see places seldom scanned close up by the eyes of man. We drove up the winding, dusty road to the Land of the Sun in eastern Utah. (Tavaputs, means Land of the Sun, in Ute).

Here, by chance I met Ouray McCook, an Indian, who knows Tavaputs country foot by foot. When I told Ouray where we intended to go, he walked with me to the edge of the great chasm and we gazed down from the heights. We looked on the backs of eagles, soaring below us on the tides of the shifting wind.

My Indian friend stretched out his arm, spread his fingers wide and motioned from left to right. He smilingly said, "Down there is the home of See-atch. If you walk those trails ta-goo-an (friend), take strong medicine with you, so I won't have to bring you out across my saddle, and so your wife won't have to cut her hair and sing her song of mourning."

"See-atch, what is that?" I asked.

Ouray explained, "The See-atch are giants. They are half man, half creatures. They run as fast as deer and are as strong as que-au-gut (bear); they wear no clothes but grow fur to take the place of garments.

"They talk, but their tongue is strange; you cannot understand them. When you first come to where they live and hunt, they will try to scare you away. They will stand where you can see them, raise their arms above their heads, beat upon their chests, and bellow like bulls. If they know you are frightened and will not stay in their country, they will let you go. But, if you camp and they think you have come to stay awhile, they will try to kill you. They roll big rocks down on you from the hillsides. They drop rocks on you from the ledges, so keep a sharp lookout above you always.

"If you camp in their country, keep your campfire burning. They are like lions; silently they creep close and watch you from the darkness. If they catch you unaware, they will raid your camp and pull you limb from limb; or they will take you to some high ledge and toss you over. They know you have guns and can kill them, but they won't give you a chance to do it. You must be watchful, do not let them steal up on you. Do not take children into See-atch country with you; they will try to steal them from you. You will have to fight to keep them."

Ouray McCook is the nephew of Chipeta, famed Queen of the Utes. He is an educated Indian, a wonderful conversationalist, a skilled story teller, and a gifted painter of the western scene.

I do not always know when he is in earnest, or when he repeats an interesting tale from the hundreds of Indian legends handed down to him from his fathers. But then, this was not the first time I had heard of the See-atch from the Indians. I had heard about them first years ago, when I was living at Ouray, Utah.

That was long before the mountain climbers told about the Yeti or Abominable Snowmen of the Himalayas, so one story was not borrowed from another. Nevertheless, I have always classed the See-atch as an Indian myth on a par with our own stories of unicorns and dragons. The story Ouray told me hadn't changed my opinion about the giant, beast-like beings of the Bookcliff Mountains. They still remained mythical to me.

With packs on our backs, we hiked down the zigzag mountain trail. We were searching for the deserted houses of 'Cliff Dwellers,' who inhabited these canyons centuries ago.

In the distant past, I am told, when a large group of people moved from one place to another on long journeys, they did not travel blindly, they sent scouts out ahead. These scouts left messages carved on the rocks, directing the main body coming behind them. Usually, you can't miss the messages; they are still there and will be at prominent places close beside the main trail. There will be directions, information, and warnings as to what lies ahead.

As our party came to a ledge on the border of what McCook had said was See-atch country, we came upon a message carved in the rock by an Anasazi a thousand years ago. It was startling. I took a photo of it, and here is my interpretation of it.

Look at the figure of the man on the left, his head-dress is the upward thrusting, back curling horns of a wild mountain sheep. Ten to one, his name was Ram or Mountain sheep. Farther to the right in the photo, is the second man, his head and head-dress resembles a flying bird; his name was probably Flying Eagle. The last man to the right in the panel, has the short inward curving horns of a buffalo; his name likely was Big Buffalo. To get the names as I have read them, look only at the head and head-dress above the shoulders.

Now, look at the giant, central figure with his powerful arms upraised. He appears to be half human, half beast. He wears no clothes and his body is furred. Is he a See-atch?

This is how I read the message: "We are the Scouts—Mountain Sheep, Flying Eagle, and Big Buffalo. Beware! You are in See-atch country. We saw one. He stood there beating his breast and bellowing like an angry buffalo. Move quickly, have your weapons handy, keep your campfires burning, and guard the children."

If the Anasazi knew the tale of See-atch, then the myth, if myth it is, pre-dates the Utes. If both peoples knew about the giant creature, the question naturally arises: Did beings like this actually exist? Do some of them still live in this remote region? If the answer to both questions is no, then how come an Anasazi drew this picture on the rock?

HIDDEN PETROGLYPHS

Taken May 14, 1966
Down Canyon past the old gelsonite mine. The left half of 'picture rock'

Hidden away near the mouth of a waterless canyon in the Uintah Basin is my favorite panel of petroglyphs. I like it because it is unique in a dozen different ways. It contains mysteries unsolveable now, but someday the why, the what and the wherefore may appear as new pages of an old history, like the discovery of the "Scrolls." Mainly, it says there are stories of mankind on the North American Continent, ancient, guessed at, but completely unknown.

The horse figure shows that the Petroglyphs over which it is imposed are very old. You can tell this by the brown-off of each drawing as compared to each other. This is one rare instance, I suppose, where a vandal deserves our thanks; he has helped to date our pictures.

Before we leave that horse though, let's study it a bit. It was drawn sometime after the Spaniard re-introduced the horse to the continent and the Indian had a chance to acquire them, it is, therefore, dated within a few decades or so. To most casual observers the figure is poorly executed, but to those who have dug deeper, it tells a story. The man was probably a scout for a following main party. He is in hostile country because he is leading his people from the Duchesne River valley up a hidden way; a dry, deep draw or canyon where they cannot be seen from very far away. He seeks to conceal their passage. The figures are out of proportion. The mount is much too long. This is purposely done by the artist to make his message clear. This says prepare for a long trip to the next camp where there is grass, wood and water. Below the front feet of the animal is the name of the scout. His name could be "Tailfeathers" or maybe "Turkey." Notice the feathers are spread like the tail of a bird. Those two limbs coming down, bending to right and left, with forks on the end, are the legs and feet of the bird. We are looking at him from the rear with his tail feathers spread.

Now let's look at the rock where the figures are drawn. It has the natural shape of an Anasazi lodge. One of the corners has outlined a door made of skins, I guess. In the upper right hand corner are fastenings, maybe these indicate that this was sort of a curtain which slid back much the same way your drapes do in this modern day.

The Ute, the Sioux, all the hunter tribes lived in teepees and in many cases they are decorated by painted drawings on the outside walls. But this panel indicates that in Anasazi life, the mud or rock walls were to rough to decorate so they decorated only the skin door of their lodges.

But that isn't what makes this panel remarkable; this is a message rock, much used over a long number of years. You find message rocks like this at the mouths of all canyons that were used for travel. I have often wished I could understand all the messages left on these rocks by the ancients, but I can't. Still over a period of fifty years, I have learned to interpret some of them.

It takes no special training or study to see what is obvious here. To the right is a headdress, there is no head of face under it. There is the crown; the ear, the bead bangles hanging down. It is almost an exact duplicate of a female head dress from Burma. There is a line reaching from the head dress out in a square and there falling down to the wavy lines. This is a name and has something to do with water because the wavy lines in Indian sign writing means water.

THE DEMON OF HORSESHOE BEND

As elsewhere in the "Old West," the history of the Uintah Basin is replete with colorful tales. They tell of outlaws, close calls with gun play, battles won and lost. Interlaced among the rest are humorous stories characteristic of the "American Frontier." Among all the funny incidents I have heard the old-timers relate, the one I think takes the cake is the story I call "The Demon of Horseshoe Bend."

It begins with Newt Stewart, a young cowboy, who was camped on the banks of the Green. In the night, Newt's horse herd got spooked and took off for parts unknown. But Stewart had old Dan, his favorite mount, tied fast to a cottonwood tree. When he checked him out and found Dan was safe and sound, he decided to wait until daylight to round up the rest of the horses. As the sun peaked over the eastern hills, Newt got on the trail of his runaways. He followed slowly because the country was full of horses and this was a difficult tracking job.

Down below on a river bend was the camp of a very good friend. Yamp, an Indian, and his band always stayed there until the heat and the mosquitoes drove them to the mountain peaks. As the sun declined toward evening, Stewart neared Yamp's camp. He decided to stop awhile, visit, have supper and maybe stay the night. "Who knows," he thought, "maybe Yamp will have my horses corralled and waiting for me."

Newt topped a ridge. Looking down the river, he could see the Indian village. The tents were there and everything looked natural except there wasn't a single live thing moving; not a man, not a child, not a woman, not a dog could be seen about the camp. Stewart rode on down, thinking there must be some explanation. But when he got there, the mystery deepened. The empty tents flapped idly in the breeze; the campfires were cold; on the bushes newly washed clothes were hung out to dry; a buffalo robe was draped over a pole, a meal was cooked and set out to eat, but the flies and dirt had ruined it. Everything was deserted, as if in an instant some catastrophe had struck and wiped everyone from the face of the earth leaving their belongings behind. By the time his inspection was over, it was growing dark. So Stewart camped in the place that night, although he wished he hadn't.

"I never got much sleep that night," he said. "The place was too damn spooky. It was eerie there in that deserted camp and there were a lot of whispery noises. Besides, I was worried about Yamp and his people. I wondered what had become of them. Surely they must be dead, or they would have come back by now from wherever they had been."

Next morning Stewart was on the trail again, but this time he followed the Indians. About noon, he came upon Yamp and his band camped in the bushes along the river. Yamp told his story. Moctoose, a boy about fourteen years old, had gone rabbit hunting. He shot a few rabbits and was on his way home, riding under the trees for shade, when he saw a strange creature perched on a limb in a tree. The thing had the body of a dog and the face of a Navajo, he said. Surely, no one had ever seen a creature like it. Moctoose had shot at the thing, but his horse was jumpy so he missed. The creature had chattered and screamed at him. The boy became frightened and rode home down the trail as fast as his horse could run. Yamp said that the Indian boy was as pale as a White man when he dismounted to tell his story. Of course, before he was through, the Indian boy drew a crowd. They all stood there around Moctoose, poking fun at him. And then all hell broke loose at the other end of the camp! A yelping, howling dog came like the wind from somewhere and sped right through the tents, leaping campfires, scaring horses, drawing other barking dogs. In an instant, there was bedlam, all noise and dust and dirt. But that wasn't all. Astride the running dog, riding him like a jockey, was a demon kind of a thing. And over all the other noise, they could hear his high pitched, maniacal laughter he vented as he rode. It was as Moctoose said—a beast with hands, with the face of a Navajo, and the body of a dog. It was a demon. We all know that it was an angry demon, too. Who could tell what he'd do? So we gathered what we could in an instant and took off to get beyond the demon's jurisdiction before the coming of night.

"Well, here we are and I guess if you slept in our camp last night the monster's anger must be cooled. We'll go get our stuff and head for the mountains without waiting any longer. By fall everything should be all right."

After hearing the yarn, Stewart was mighty puzzled because he knew Yamp didn't lie. So what could an animal be that fit what Yamp described except for a demon—the demon of horseshoe bend.

Note: Newt Stewart was the Uncle of George E. Stewart and told George this story. The 'demon' was a pet monkey. There is another story which George wrote about who this monkey belonged to and how it got away. However, the story somehow got away from us—misplaced.

HORSE THIEVES FROM BROWN'S HOLE

The following tale is true. It has been gleaned from the pages of an almost forgotten journal of the long ago. Some of the names used are fictitious. The tale has been elaborated as to detail. The author guesses as to what must have happened from the brief general accounts. The places mentioned are not imaginative but actually exist. The tale is laid where the events took place.

The main characters—Carson, Thompson, Meek, Craig and Clair (Sinclair)—are the men who actually took part in the incident. There were Indian chiefs mentioned, but the author was forced to invent names for them, since their names were not given in the journals. This is all the fiction the story contains.

In the United States, the westward trend was rapid. Always in the forefront were a few hardy souls who, by a few years, preceded their fellows into the distant, wild places of the old, old west. Into the Rocky Mountains, along the streams and rivers, came the legendary mountain men. They trapped and traded with the Indian for 'plew' the fur of the beaver.

They were adventurers and explorers of the first order. The events of their lives were stranger, and many times, more thrilling than anything the pen of fiction can write.

Grazing in the mountain meadow were most of the horses of the men of Ft. Davy Crockett. Brown's Hole was a secluded spot along the Green River in what is now the Uintah Basin of eastern Utah. Never had marauding bands of horse stealing Indians raided this valley. So the trappers were lax in their guard, feeling secure in their assumption that their horse herd would be unmolested.

That morning in the late summer of 1840, a small band of Sioux warriors had ridden quietly to the edge of the timber surrounding the meadow where the horses grazed. Well they knew the lethal power of these white men sleeping quietly inside the palisade of the trading post. Whatever move they made, must be quick. They must strike and be away before the men in the post had time to collect their thoughts. Otherwise, some Sioux would be lying prone on the grass spilling their lives upon the ground for nothing.

Quietly the warriors spread out. As the first rays of the dawn tainted the eastern sky, they charged, fan shaped, into the meadow. They were fast. In a minute or two, they had the trapper's horses on the run going up the trail leading east to the distant plains.

The mountain men heard their horses go. This was not a new game to them. Horse stealing was a custom of the Indian. Any horse herd of white men or of other Indian tribes was fair game. The trappers knew their horses were fast vanishing away over the mountain ridges. In this land, the horse meant life or death; it was by far the most valuable possession a man had. They must retrieve their mounts or get others in their stead.

Not all the horses were stolen. Those in the corral by the palisade were left. These, they knew, would be their salvation. Quickly the pursuit formed. Carson, Meek, Thompson, Sinclair, Vasguez, Charlosseau, and Reynard took the trail of the Sioux.

Along the trail, beside the Green on the way to the east, there is a narrow pass. The ledges here are vertical and high on either side. It is an ideal place for an ambush. Here men on the ledges above, behind cover, can stop a whole army of men. So it was that Red Tail, the leader of the horse thieves, smiled a knowing smile as the last of the horses entered the narrow defile. Here he would lay his trap for any pursuing white men and stop them.

"Big Bear, Shawnee, Yellow Feather, Big Nose, Barking Dog— you will keep the horses moving on the trail for home. You must drive them as fast as you can. I know these white men. They will come for us. The rest of you braves will stay with me. Half of you will get on the ledge on this side, the other half will come with me.

We will get on the ledges on that side. When the white men come, we will stop them when they get here."

But the pursuing trappers were wary. These men were experienced mountain men. Besides, they knew all the tricks of a wily Indian. As the small group came to the gorge, Kit Carson said, "Hold on thar, old coon. We cain't go in that cut. Someone will get killed, if we do. There are Sioux up in them ledges."

So it came about that the white men stopped their pursuit. It would be of little value to pursue and die.

Back at the post a council was held. At least half the horses were gone. Too few remained to carry on the business of trading. Either their own horses must be recovered or other horses must be obtained.

Now in those days, horse stealing was developed to a fine art. It was a game. It was wrong to steal horses from your friends. In fact, a clever horse thief had the admiration of all his fellows. The trappers had adopted the ways of the Indians with whom they lived. In this emergency, it was decided that Thompson and Sinclair with three other men would follow the trail of the Sioux. If they could, they were to recover the post horses. If they were unable to do so, they were to steal others and return to the trading post.

Day after day, the track of the raiding party was followed. But somewhere on the buffalo plains, the trail was lost. When this happened there was only one answer—find other horses, the closer the better.

As evening fell one day, the smoke from campfires could be seen rising in the sky. As the small party topped a ridge, they saw, lying below them, an encampment of Cheyenne. Up the stream, about a half mile from the Indian camp, the band's horse herd was grazing, guarded by half grown boys. These horses were to be the white men's target.

In a secluded spot behind the ridge, the trappers waited for darkness. They ate the cold food in their saddle bag pockets to prevent any warning of their presence in the vicinity. As the night wore on, they crept to the top of the ridge to observe the camp of their intended victims. That was a night of a bright moon. They could see the horses of the Indian band. They had been driven in close to the lodges and were contained in a rope corral. There were no visible guards.

Gradually the fires burned to embers, the camp quieted into the night. After midnight, the trappers made their move. Sinclair moved silently down to the rope corral and with his big knife, cut it. The other four men came on. Now they began to drive the horses away. It was easy, there was no discovery. Finally, the crest of the ridge was reached. But here luck changed. A night prowling jack rabbit broke cover in front of the horses. The frisky leader pretended fright and bolted. In a moment, all was chaos. Horses ran in several directions. It was impossible to keep them all bunched. It was useless to stop for a roundup; with all this noise, the Cheyenne would be upon them in a matter of minutes. They went whirling away with a bunch of fifteen horses. The rest were left behind. At least, it would take time for the Indians to gather and the pursuit would be delayed probably until daylight.

All through the night, the trappers rode. There was no pause, no rest, no hesitation. They must put as much distance between themselves and the Cheyenne as possible before dawn. When the light came, they could see to the west the high Uintah Mountains. Once within those mighty defiles, they were safe; for in there, the plains Indians rarely ventured. The warlike Ute Nation was death to the invader in the mountains.

But far on the back trail was a rapidly moving cloud of dust. It must be the Cheyenne. Well, if worst came to worst, they would abandon the driven horses and make a run for it.

They forged on and finally rode into a river bottom. They were safe, for there before their eyes was a large camp of friendly Shoshone. Here the Cheyenne dare not come.

In the camp of Big Bear, the mountain men rested for several days renewing their own strength as well as that of their horses. Fifteen horses was not enough; they must have at least thirty to equal the number they had lost. They would take these horses to Brown's Hole and then venture forth again.

When they were sure no lurking Cheyenne were still about, they prepared to bid farewell to their Shoshone friends. Early one morning, they were on their way.

As they rode up the river, they came to a small lush valley. Here was a band of forty or so Shoshone horses. It was only a part of the mounts belonging to their friends. There was no guard and none to see if they took them. No one could be sure who had driven them away, especially if the impending storm was heavy enough to wash out the tracks and dim the trail.

There was a short conference. These men knew well that to stay at the camp of a friendly chief, eat his food, and then steal his people's horses was a rank violation of the laws of the west. But Thompson and Sinclair, over the arguments of their lesser companions, decided to take the Shoshone string. Quietly, they drove them away.

Arriving back at Ft. Davy Crockett, they made a triumphal entry with at least fifty five head of horses. There was drinking and celebration far into the night, while the returnees told their tale of the successful raid. But they said nothing of stealing the Shoshone horses; supposedly they were all Cheyenne.

In the morning, Kit Carson and Meek went to view the stock herd. With seeing eyes, Carson picked out the Cheyenne from the Shoshone. He even saw a horse belonging to Big Bear, the Shoshone chief. It still had the paint markings on its hide.

"Thompson," Carson said, "you are a fool. You stole Shoshone horses from Chief Big Bear. Purty soon he will come here. We will have to return the horses and talk and talk to save your no good hide. You saddle up, you and Sinclair, take yer possibles and clear out of the country. Leave the horses. We will return them to Big Bear."

Sinclair wanted to go. But Thompson said, "Look Kit, when did you git to be the boss of this post? I ain't taking no horses back, but if you are ascairt, I'll drive these horses on. I'll go to the mouth of the Winty in Ute country. No Shoshone will come there to bother me and if they do the Utes will help me run them out."

Carson replied, "Dang your no good hide. I cain't make you leave the horses. But if Big Bear comes after you, don't ask me to help you because you're wrong and you know it."

Early next morning the renegades left with their ill-gotten gains. They headed straight for the mouth of the Winty. They traveled leisurely. In a day or two, they arrived at the old Robidoux place on the Green opposite the mouth of the Uintah (now the Duchesne.) The old post was deserted and in poor repair, having been flooded by high water in years past. But it made a good place to camp for awhile. So the renegades moved in.

The stolen horses were hidden on a large island in the river. If anyone came looking for them, it would be difficult to locate them.

Back at Ft. Davy Crockett, more men were sent to the east to look for horses. They were to steal only from the Sioux, Cheyenne, Arapahoe, or Comanche. The Utes and Shoshone were to be left entirely alone. These men were in charge of Craig. Carson and Meek remained at Davy Crockett.

As the raiders rode the trail toward Ft. Bridger, they came face to face with Big Bear and his braves. Big Bear was in an angry mood. The lives of the mountain men hung on a single thread. It was only when a Shoshone girl, the wife of one of the hunters, told the story of what had really happened that the white men were allowed to continue on their way.

One morning, when Meek went out to see to the horses, there facing him a short distance away, was the band of angry Shoshone in war paint. Quickly, he went back inside to tell Carson. Carson looked the situation over. With Desert Lily, a Shoshone woman at his side as interpreter, he walked unarmed to where Big Bear sat on his horse. Carson said, "I know why you have come and you are right. But those here now did not steal your horses. We were angry when we heard about it. The men who stole from you are not here. They have run away to Ute country. If there is any way I can help you, I shall do so."

Big Bear answered, "White man, it is known you speak with only one tongue. I believe you. But still, you must get our horses back from the Ute country or we will kill you and all that live here with you, even this woman. If one of my braves ate your food, then stole your horses, I would get them back for you and I would kill the brave who wronged you."

Carson replied, "There are only two men here, Meek and myself, the rest have gone hunting. If you will go with us, you and your braves, I will take you to your horses. We will get them. But I am not a chief like you; I cannot decree the death of those thieves. If they fight us, I will help you kill them."

"White man," Big Bear said, "I hear you. At sunup in the morning, we will leave for the Uintah. But, you had better know, this is a war trail that we follow."

As the sun rose the next morning, the cavalcade was on the way, Meek and Carson riding out in front and the Shoshone strung out behind.

It is true that this was Ute country, but the Utes and Shoshone were at peace. It was permissible for one tribe to visit the lands of another, if there was peace between them.

In late afternoon of the second day, the Shoshone band reached the area of the mouth of the Uintah (now the Duchesne). They pitched their camp on the river bottom near the White River.

Next morning Meek went scouting. He located the stolen horses on the island in the river. It was not the wish of Meek to get Ben Thompson and his cohorts killed. After all, a white man was a white man. Even though he was wrong, it went against the grain to allow his death at the hands of Indians. Consequently, Meek, with the help of some Utes, attempted to spirit the horses from the island to the Shoshone without bloodshed. But Thompson discovered him.

Thompson knew he and his men were outnumbered. They couldn't take the horses alone, so he went to Red Moon's village close by. He said if the Utes would help him, he would divide the horses with them.

Meek got wind of Thompson's offer to the Utes, so he rode there himself. He told Red Moon the whole story. He said, "If you help Thompson, it will mean war between you and your friends, the Shoshone. You will have to stand alone against the Shoshone, the Arapahoe, and the Comanche."

The Ute chief decided to stay neutral.

Under those circumstances Thompson had no alternative, he had to let the stolen horses go. Meek talked Big Bear out of making an attack against the old fort. The horses were back. So what was the point now of useless bloodshed, Meek argued. Big Bear agreed.

So it was that the traders of Ft. Davy Crockett went their separate ways. Thompson and Sinclair were not trusted anymore by Indian or white because of what they had done to Big Bear, so they moved on to New Mexico and California.

Craig and Meek stayed on for awhile and then left for parts unknown.

EARLIEST WHITE HISTORY OF

UINTAH BASIN

PASSAGE THROUGH THE LAND OF THE SUN

The Green River going through Red Canyon.
—Used by permission, Utah State Historical Society, all rights reserved.

I was a boy of eight when I first stood on the banks of the Green River and watched the water roll by. It was spring and the first heat of the year was melting the snows in the mountains and the river was rising fast. It was the biggest stream I had ever seen. Its great flowing majesty impressed me as one of the grandest sights I had ever seen. I knew then, as I know now, that there were other rivers in the world bigger than the Green, but like the hills of home, this was mine. The fascination that I felt then has never left me. I can still spend uncounted hours gazing at the stream, watching the passing show as it goes by on the crest of the flood.

My father was the general superintendent of the Uteland Mining Company, a corporation organized to exploit the large copper deposits which lay not far from the river. Uteland was a tent village—boarding house, bunk house, and tents for married men. All these were neatly boarded up and floored. They were located along company streets in small town fashion with plenty of space in between. The only permanent buildings were the assay office, the big double-decker, stone walled ice house, and the copper mill itself.

The copper mill had an engine house, with two horizontal steam boilers and the other machinery necessary to work the mill. The engine house was at the base of a hill. The mill stretched up the point to the top, housing big wooden leaching tanks, installed in stair like fashion. On the very top of the hill was the two story building which contained the crusher where the ore dropped into the tanks. My family never lived in the tent city. My father had built a log house on the flat of the ridge not far from the mine. It was to be our home. At the time I first saw the house, I wondered why it had to be out in the sun and not down in the shade of the trees. Before the summer was over I knew why. The thick roof was cool and the mosquitoes were fewer up here than down in the tent village.

We lived in... and that is where us kids went to school. But every spring when school was out we moved down on the river. The first year we were at the river, my father, Frank Davis, and Hank Stewart in addition to their regular work, operated a ferry boat, as partners. The ferry crossed the main channel to an island called Long Island. The car crossed the island and a cable, or swinging bridge reached from the island to the east bank. Later, when the Uteland Mining Company built a road, the ferry boat was moved up stream to a point about five miles below Ouray. Hank Stewart bought out Frank and Dad. From then on Hank operated the ferry until the bridge at Ouray was built.

There is little left now at the sites of the copper mill or Stewart's Ferry, to indicate they were ever there. There is the old concrete foundation and the rock walls of the ice house at the site of the mill. There is nothing at Stewart's Ferry.

My family lived at four different locations on the banks of the Green. We had homes near Ouray, at the copper mill, at the mouth of Willow Creek and far downstream at what we called Cow Bottoms, but which has since become known as Stewart's Flat.

During most of those old days there were no automobiles, no radios, no television, and no mechanical refrigeration. People, traveling by team or horseback over the long, hot miles, took time to stop, to eat, and to visit. There were no strangers, either white or Indian, riding the roads or trails—if there were they didn't remain a stranger long. Sometimes in the heat of the summer a cowman got so hungry for fresh meat, he killed a nice fat beef. Knowing he couldn't eat it all before it spoiled, he delivered meat to the neighbors up and down the road. A neighbor was anybody within a thirty mile radius.

Almost from the outset of my life on the Green, I began to gather in my head the lore of the river. I knew old-timers who knew old-timers. This was as far back in the white history of the place as you could go. I sat around many a campfire and heard the yarns spun by these master story tellers of the Old West. I heard of trappers, traders, outlaws, cowboys, and Indians without end. I heard about locations and places and things along the stream. I heard of ghosts and mysteries that once in a while I hear repeated even today.

I saw the great clusters of foam come floating on the flood. I knew that these were formed in the great white water passages of Flaming Gorge, the Canyon of Ladore and Split Mountain Gorge. I knew that down below me was Desolation Canyon, where the river cut its way through the 'Land of the Sun.' I knew that Desolation was filled with great cataracts, that only expert boatmen could run and live.

I knew high above was a town called Green River, Wyoming, and down below was Green River, Utah. Intertwined with the stories of the river were the stories of White River, Duchesne River, and of the Creeks—Willow Creek and Hill Creek.

Most of the old-timers have passed on to their reward. Today I have become an old-timer of the river myself. I pay attention to admonitions that people give me, "George, if you don't write it, it will die with you." This is true, for most of the histories are already dead, passed on with the early settlers. I know only a small fraction of it, and some of that is as tenuous as a small boy's memory.

As I grew, I often sat on the banks of the river to daydream. It was on such occasions that I built my castles in Spain. Someday, I thought, I shall go to the beginning of this stream and follow it to where it ends in Colorado. As time went by, I did this. But my most loved is my first love—the country with which I am best acquainted—from Ouray, Utah to Green River, Utah.

There has been much written about Flaming Gorge, Ladore Canyon and Split Mountain. One way or the other, they have received much deserved publicity. But Desolation Canyon, to my mind, has been neglected. Maybe because of its name.

Now in a small way I shall attempt to bring it out of its obscurity. I shall write about the river that flows from Ouray to Green River—the land of the sun. Put an arrow to the string of an Indian bow; draw it back quickly for a speedy shot and let it go. You will hear oooray. The ray is said sharply. Ouray in Utah gets its name from the famed chief, Ouray of the Uncompahgre (redwater land) band of the Ute Indian Tribe. Though part of the Uncompahgre band was allotted near the village, the chief never saw the place in Utah named after him. It is certain that he never lived near or in the town. The Indians never named the village. The white men did. Although it had an Indian name from times immemorial, that name has been lost now in the realms of unrecorded history.

Today you drive through Ouray and the uninformed sees only a little somnolent Indian town on the banks of the Green. The picturesque atmosphere of the Old West still lingers there, but few will know the remarkably historic spot they visit. Here, beside the turgid river is the home place of the Whiterivers, the wildest and fiercest warrior band of the whole Ute Indian Tribe. In their day the Utes were fully a match in combat for any Indian tribe alive—especially if they were attacked in their mountain fastnesses. No Sioux, no Comanche, no Apache, no Navajo band dared intrude into Ute country without permission—and these Movitaviats (Sun blanket Indians) were the fiercest band of all.

It was the Whiterivers who killed Meeker and his men. It was they who planned and accomplished the defeat of Thornburg. Even today, I have heard it said, "Don't push a Whiteriver too far, because if you do, he will fight you."

Of course, the Whiterivers didn't always live at Ouray. They wound up there after the Meeker Massacre when they were forced to move into a portion of the Uintah band's reservation. Movataviats is their real name—sun blanket Indians. The white man calls them Whiterivers because they lived along the White and Yampa rivers all the way back to the Rocky Mountains in Colorado, even as far as Denver. The Indians always called the river, Whiterivers, but they used the Indian name for it, "Sun Quitches." The old fur traders and trappers converted it into English.

How far back in history does Ouray go as a settlement? This is hard to say, but because of its location it probably reaches far back into antiquity. Ouray in ancient days and as late as fur traders was a great cross-roads of the west. Water, wood and grass were the primary requirements for travel in this arid land. From Ouray, the White River comes from the top of the high Colorado mountains to the east. The Duchesne stretches away to the west, almost to the Wasatch Mountains. It drains most of the Uintah Mountains to the north. Willow Creek, with its tributary Hill Creek, flows out of the Bookcliffs. All of these streams enter Green River almost within shouting distance of each other. Travelers invariably came to the spot where the village of today is situated. In certain times of the year, after the river has been high and gone down, mud along the banks of the stream makes fording difficult, except in selected locations. At Ouray there are gravel banks on both sides. In addition, there is a sandbar in the middle of the channel which provides a mid-stream rest. As far back as memory goes, the sandbar has always been there. There is hardly a doubt that even in the days of the Anasazi, Ouray was a stopping place for those moving across the arid land. I might say that the proof is upon the ledges in petro-glyphs, drawn there by the Moquis and by the Utes. This is an indication that from ancient days to the days of the white man, men traveled along these stretches.

Standing in Ouray and looking north you can see a high, prominent point or bluff. It was on this hill that Father Dominguez and Escalante stood to view the confluence of the Duchesne, the Green and the White, on September 17, 1776. Having viewed the meeting of the rivers from afar, the party, for some reason never mentioned ever having been there. The party turned westward and came to the Duchesne River farther along its path. This is the first time Ouray is mentioned in recorded history.

Across the river from the Indian town, stretching along the bank all the way to the White River, used to be a grove of giant cottonwood trees. As a boy, I rode along the old trail when the sun was blazing high and never saw the sun. The shade was solidly deep and dark all the way. To the east is the White River plain, reaching for miles upstream. It was always covered with green grass and made the finest horse pasture imaginable.

Entienne Provost came to this spot in the summer of 1824. He had traveled since late spring from the city of Santa Fe. He had followed the old Indian trails over the mountains from far away and at last had reached the great cross-roads of the west. At this place under the giant cottonwood trees on the left bank he established his headquarters.

From there he branched out with the object in view of collecting plew—the beaver skin—the life blood of the great fur trade. From his headquarters on the Green, Provost and nine of his men proceeded westward. They went across the Kamas Prairie then a mountain stream to Utah Valley. There he met a band of Shoshone (Snake) Indians. The Snakes laid a peculiar ambush on the banks of the river. It is difficult at this late date to determine whether the event occurred on the banks of the Jordan, or on the banks of the Provo River.

They went into council preparatory to trading with the Indians. They sat in a circle to smoke the peace pipe. The chief said his medicine wouldn't work if there was metal near, so he persuaded Provost and his men to lay aside their weapons. After the council started, the Indians attacked Provost and his men. Provost was an athlete and quite strong. He and one of his party were the only ones who escaped alive. They reached their horses and fled. They came back to the headquarters on the Green, across the river from the sleepy little town we know as Ouray. The river which he traveled to Utah Valley bears his name. Later, when a town was set up on the banks of that river, it also was called Provo.

After Dominguez and Escalante, this was the next white man to visit the cross-roads. It was in the spring of 1824, that William H. Ashley, the famous man of Mississippi, came down through the Uintah Mountains, passing Flaming Gorge and the rapids of Ladore. It was he who first saw Split Mountain because his passage was by way of Bull-boats. He reached the mouth of the Uintah River, crossed the Duchesne on May 23, 1825 and established his camp there.

It was this same summer that Antione Robidioux came to the area. All were in search of valuable beaver pelts that could be taken from the clear streams of the mountains. As you drive through Ouray, on the right bank of the river sitting on the bank is a small log cabin, which the older Indians say was built by Robidioux. Across the river bridge and on your right are two old log cabins. Indians say that there were originally three cabins here. By searching the records carefully, I have come to the conclusion that these cabins were built by Kit Carson in the year of 1835.

About a quarter of a mile south at the end of the river bridge, you walk westward into the trees. There next to a giant sand dune is what most of the old-timers will tell you is the old Fort Kit Carson. It was a sizable place, 95 feet by 70 feet wide. On the southwest and northeast corners were rounded towers like a castle. Succeeding years of overflowing water from the river have eroded the adobe, so that now there remains only the round mounds. Reading the journals of the early explorers, we find that this at one time was an adobe fort. Careful pursuit of the records indicate that this was the first trading post of Antione Robidioux. If this is so, and undoubtedly it is, then this was the first white settlement in the state of Utah.

Across the river from Ouray and against the hill are the remains of the first Ft. Thornburg. The military started to build it, but because the Indians objected so strenuously, they left it half finished.

They constructed the first Fort Thornburg at Ashley Valley.

The Whiterivers came to Ouray in 1882. In that year, the Ouray Indian agency was established at Ouray. Originally, there were two Indian agencies in Uintah Basin. One at Ouray and one at Whiterocks. The agency at Whiterocks was for the Uintah band of the Utes, although the name is not Uintah at all—they are known among the Indians as Paw Qwa Nuance (Lake Shore Indians) because they came originally from the neighborhood of the soft shores of Utah Lake.

Uintah—there has always been controversy about how it should be spelled. It seems that the preference is Uinta by those foreign to Uintah Basin. Those living in Uintah Basin prefer Uintah. I suppose the people in Uintah Basin were acquainted with the Ute language and their spelling of Uintah is more correct than the outsider who spells it Uinta. The name means River of Pines, or Water of Pines. A more correct spelling is Uintpah ,Water of Rivers. The fact is, regardless of how you spell it, Paw means Water in the Ute language of the Indians, or put the accent on it so that the word is Uintah—the accent on the 'tah' and not on the 'U. So the agency for the Uncompahgre and Whiterivers was established at Ouray and continued to be there until 1910 when the troops left Ft. Duchesne.

When I was a small boy I can remember the old agency buildings at Ouray. The school house, the dorm and the office buildings. There is only one building at the old establishment that still remains.

During the early days of the reservation, Berthoud surveyed there for a road connecting Salt Lake City, Utah and Denver, Colorado. The survey for that road came through Uintah Basin, and crossed into Ouray. It was at this time that the ferry boat was established at the same spot where the old fort used to be. In my day they called this the government ferry, because the Bureau of Indian Affairs took it over and operated it.

OURAY

Half slumbering, where the Green River whispers by, sits of the little half ghost town of Ouray, Utah. It was named after 'The Arrow,' great chieftain of the Uncompahgre people. The village, even today, has an air about it that historians feel when they first lay eyes upon the place. And rightly so, for this small Indian hamlet is one of the most historic spots in the entire State of Utah.

Eastward stretches the Smoky River (Indian name for the White River), through the hills and valleys almost to where the Rockies, backbone of the continent, rear their snowy heads. From westward runs the River of Blue (Indian name for the Duchesne River), beginning within sight of the Wasatch Mountains. It flows far, draining the Uintah Mountains on its way. The two long rivers meet with Big Water (Indian name for the Green River) within a mile of each other at the place we now call Ouray. Travel over long distances demanded wood and grass and water; rivers were the highways across an arid land. From this meeting of the rivers, great Indian trails led in four directions, branching wherever tributaries entered into the mainstreams. Men who roamed this vast region in the early days, sooner or later, came to Ouray, the hub of travel.

Today, Ouray lies far back in the eddy of modern civilization. Because history scribes have largely missed it, there are only a few who have an inkling of its past. But, long ago, this was one of the great crossroads of the west.

Here streamed the track of empire in the days of the fabulous mountain men.

Time and time again, this place, on the banks of the river, won prominence by events and visits of men. The things that history is made of only to slip back again, to its quiet dreamy ways.

What part Ouray played in the life of the Indian nations, though it must have been interesting, has vanished because the records were purely verbal. All we know occurred after the advent of the white man. And it was here the white man's life in Utah began.

Looking northward from the village, a distance of several miles, there is a high, rounded hill. Fathers Dominguez and Escalante, on their journey to Monterey, crossed the Green River at the old Indian ford near Jensen, Utah. Then they followed the trail southward until they came to that high, round hill. There, in 1776, they paused. From the hilltop, they overlooked the site of Ouray. They never went to the confluence of the rivers. From the hill, they turned westward; but records say they were the first white men to see this crossroads of the wilderness. It was important enough to them that they made a record of the pause.

* * *

Over the hills, from far away, came a long pack horse caravan. They rode to a beautiful grove of cottonwood trees on the left bank of the Green River about midway between the mouths of the Duchesne River on the one side and the White River on the other. Where the trees grew in a circle, with a natural clearing in the center, the brigade set up its camp.

Entienne Provost, the roly-poly fat man with a high, clear ringing voice, was the leader of the company. This was in the year of 1824. From here, Provost set out in quest of 'plew,' for the trade in beaver skins was still in its zenith. Out in Utah Valley on either the Jordan or Provo River, Provost and some of his men were tricked by a Shoshone chief. All except Provost and one of his men were killed. After the disaster, Provost and his man fled to the headquarters he had established on the Green at Ouray. It was from him that Provo, Utah and the Provo River take their names.

Around the bend of the river above Ouray came a line of river men and the barks they used were of a peculiar construction, for they were round and made of buffalo hides stretched over wooden frames. 'Bull boats,' they called them. They had begun their voyage where the Green River crosses the Buffalo Plains. Down Flaming Gorge to Brown's Hole, the gateway of Ladore, past the mouth of the Yampa River, through Split Mountain and Hell's Half Mile, to the smooth water a few miles above Jensen they floated. Then on down to the confluence of the Duchesne and the White Rivers at Ouray.

These were the first river men ever to make that journey. One wonders who among them had the experience to bring those peculiar craft through some of the roughest white water in the world. Perhaps, and this is pure speculation, the man who knew how to run the cataracts was Dennis Julius. He is pretty much of a mystery. in western history. In fact, we wouldn't know him at all, except that he carved his name in the ledges, mostly along the Green and Colorado Rivers, showing he traveled these rivers by boat. Was he a voyageur from Montreal or Quebec who had canoed the fast Canadian rivers? We don't know.

This boating company was led by William Ashley of St. Louis. He established headquarters at Ouray while he did a little exploring. It was for him that Ashley Valley and Ashley Creek were named.

Ashley came to the site of Ouray in 1825. When he arrived, or shortly thereafter, an overland company from Santa Fe appeared. It was commanded by one of the five Robidoux brothers. Just which one, it is hard at this late date to determine, although most believe it was Antoine, who came to be known as "The King of the Fur Trade."

UTAH'S FIRST CHRISTMAS

Into the valley of "The Great River of the West," the long caravan came. The people camped and tents were pitched in a big circle sheltered by giant trees.

One night it snowed. The falling flakes, festooned the bare limbs of the trees and gathered on the bushes round about. The watch fire burning in the center of the circle, cast its flickering light on the glistening snow. The soft colors came and went as the flames of the fire rose and fell.

When new snow falls, the world lies hushed and stilled. So it was this night; heaven, earth, and all living things apparently paused with bated breath throughout the hours of darkness. They waited, it seemed, for the coming of a great event.

As daybreak came, the storm had blown away. The sun rose in a clear sky, casting rays of splendor over a land covered with unsullied white.

The people stirred. The smoke of breakfast fires rose above the valley. Distantly, came the tinkle of tiny bells; the ponies moved about grazing and the herd bells on some of the horses rang, making pretty music on the winter air. Happy voices sounded, for this was to be a day of celebration. The voices spoke in many languages: French, English, Spanish, Ute, Shoshone, and Comanche. Each person spoke in his native tongue, but this was a universal holiday, one in which all people joined.

Before the day was very old, preparations were made for a feast. There would be barbecued buffalo and venison, cakes made of sweet dried buffalo berries mixed with suet and cornmeal. There would be other delicacies dear to the heart of Mountain Men and Indians.

From the big, main tent, the leader of the camp came with his pack. He was a rotund man. His cheeks were red. He was bearded and dressed in furs. In his high-pitched voice, he called the children to him. To each he gave a bauble: a string of glass beads to this one, a small mirror to that one. All around he went—laughing, "Ho, ho, ho," as he passed out his gifts. Each child clasped his present close, ran to show mama, wide-eyed, breathless and very happy.

The day wore on, and finally, the food was ready. But, before they ate, the people knelt in the snow in front of the tall, wooden cross. The fat man led them in prayer to God Almighty in remembrance of the Great Lord, Jesus Christ. After prayer, they sang a Christmas hymn. Then they feasted.

This was the first time Christmas had ever been celebrated in the land that later became the state of Utah. It was held where the Duchesne and the White Rivers flow into the Green River in a locality now known as Ouray, Utah. The people were members of a fur brigade. The fat man, their leader, was Entienne Provost. The date was December twenty-fifth, in the year of our Lord, one thousand eight-hundred and twenty-four.

THE OLD ADOBE FORT ON THE GREEN

Opposite the mouth of the Duchesne, on the left bank the Green River, less than a mile below the Ute Indian Village of Ouray, Utah, are the ruins of an old fort. There are no signs or markers to show where it is. Nor is it identified on the pages of history. Yet, it is what remains of one of the earliest settlements in what is now the State of Utah.

The walls were made of adobe. The high waters of many spring times have melted the bricks into grass grown, symmetrical heaps of clay. At its location, the waters of the Green and the White, in years of high water, inundated the old place.

To the careful eye, the plan of the fort can still be traced under the debris and ruin wrought by the passing years (see sketch). It was approximately 95 feet long by 78 feet wide. At the northeast and at the southwest corners were circular towers, like the towers of a castle. Against the walls on the inside, were the rooms for quarters and storage. The center, in the style of mountain men, was open and free of roofing. A whole pack train could shelter within its walls.

Who built the old fort?

To answer this question, one must follow men whose trails have now grown dim with passage of time. There are legends, stories, cross-trails and confusions, old letters, journals and even some writings on the rocks over which one must pore to get at the final conclusion.

One reads stories of Ft. Robidoux and of Ft. Winty (Uintah). Some say, at the mouth of the Winty; some say, on the fork of the Winty. It was these stories, mentioning these old places, which caused a college professor of Western history to search all one summer in the Randlett area for old Ft. Robidoux.

The trails first became tangled due to the modern-day and the long-ago names of the rivers. In the days of the mountain men, the Whiterocks River was known as the Winty (Uintah). The Duchesne River, where it flows into Green River at Ouray was also called the Winty. The confluence of the Duchesne and the Uintah is near Randlett. But, in the old days, it was the Uintah that flowed on, now it is the Duchesne.

The people of the area, the old-timers along the Green, even the Utes, call the place 'Old Fort Kit Carson.' And not without reason, for in his autobiography, dictated to Blanche Grant, Kit says:

"In the latter part of October, 1833, we started for the mountains to find the trappers. We followed the Spanish Trail that leads to California until we struck White River; took down the White till we struck Green River. We crossed Green River to the Windy, one of its tributaries, and there we found Robidoux. He had a party of some twenty men that were trading and trapping. The snow was now commencing to fall and we concluded to go into winter quarters. We found a place that answered every purpose near the mouth of the Windy. We passed a pleasant winter."

Carson said he helped Robidoux that winter and in the spring went on to the Snake River to find another trapper's camp. He left before the ice went out of the Green. He would have spent five or six months at his winter quarters at the mouth of the Winty.

Mentioning Robidoux by name, Carson spoke of his activity as if it was at the mouth of the Winty, but never did he speak of a post anywhere in the area. It is only reasonable from this to assume that Robidoux, at this time, was carrying on an itinerant business, as were most of the old traders and trappers. It seems that if Robidoux had a fort on the Winty or even in the area, Carson would have stayed there or would have mentioned it.

There is no doubt that Carson spent the winter of 1833-34 in the Uintah Basin. Nor is there any doubt that he constructed his quarters near the mouth of the Duchesne on the Green. But the tradition that what we know as 'Old Ft. Kit Carson' was the place he built for his winter sojourn is, without doubt, incorrect. The place is too big and elaborate for Carson to have built for his winter stand of five or six months. Besides, the walls were built of adobe in a heavily timbered area. Carson, if he followed his past practices, would have built with logs. There is charcoal in the debris, indicating that perhaps the place was burned. But, if so, this probably came from the roof which would have been of wood.

Warren Angus Ferris spent the winter of 1834-35 in the Uintah Basin. At least part of the time, he was around the mouth of the Duchesne (Euinta) and the White. Ferris was a graduate civil engineer. He kept a good journal and even went so far as to draw and leave to posterity a good, working map of the area. In neither his journal, nor on his map, did he indicate a post like the one disclosed by the ruins at the site. Not only this, but neither does he show a fort on the Whiterocks location of Ft. Robidoux.

The map shows three log cabins on the Green, above the mouth of the White and near the mouth of the Euinta (Uintah) now called the Duchesne. In his journal, Ferris tells of his party living in log cabins and tents made of hides. He lived for awhile in a tent. He moved into a cabin, but didn't like it; so he moved back to the tent again.

Ferris was literate and careful. It is almost a certainty that had any trading post existed in 1834-35, Ferris would have shown it on his map and mentioned it in his journal. It is more than probable that the three cabins shown on Ferris' map at the mouth of the Euinta and mentioned by him in his journal, were the winter quarters Kit Carson built.

In late 1838, the fort was there, although it had been abandoned. Meek, a man who had been at Ft. Davy Crockett, in Brown's Hole, on the Green, when telling of the events of 1840 to Mrs. Frances F. Victor, said: "The horses were found on an island in Green River. The robbers having domiciled themselves in an old fort at the mouth

Stone inscription near Westwater tells of the passing of Antoine Roubidoux.

of the Uinta."

So, who built the old adobe fort?

Along the D&RG Railroad between Price, Utah and Grand Junction, Colorado, there is a railroad place known as Westwater. Traveling north from Westwater, along a branch of the Old Spanish Trail, for about 15 miles, a sort of cave or natural shelter is reached. There, chiseled on a ledge close by, is this inscription: "Antoine Robidoux Passe Ici Le 13 Novembre 1837 Pour Establire Maison Traittes a la Rv. Vert ov Wiyte."

Translated into English the inscription says: "Antoine Robidoux passed here November 13, 1837, to establish a trading house on the river Green or White."

The trails are tangled again. Robidoux supposedly already had a trading post in Uintah Basin in 1837: it was Ft. Windy or Ft. Robidoux, on the Whiterocks River. The fort on Whiterocks was established in 1831 or 1832, they say. Therefore, the seven in the inscription must have been meant for a one. The ledge was cracked and eroded, the "Wiyte," must be "Winty." Besides, Robidoux was French; so why, if White River was meant, wasn't the French word for white (blanc) used?

The inscription, however, is clear; it is a good one. There is little doubt about what it says, especially if one does not have a fixed idea as to when Robidoux first established a permanent trading post in Uintah Basin.

French-American Antoine Robidoux was a leader of voyagers— explorer, trapper, trader, soldier, founder of cities, but somewhere the writers missed him. Kit Carson, Jim Bridger and others became famous, but Robidoux, who equaled them all, gets only a few disparaging remarks from a religious fanatic on the pages of history.

It was Robidoux who built the old fort on the Green.

It was built in 1837. But the life of the establishment was very short for it was vacant in late 1838, according to Meek's story to Mrs. Victor. The first year of heavy snows would bring high water in spring. The fort, at its location, would be flooded and would have to be abandoned. This is why Fremont found Robidoux at Ft. Winty on the Whiterocks in 1844.

Once more the trails are hidden and crossed. Could this old fort on the Green be the first, white, year-round settlement in what is now the State of Utah? Yes, it could, but there are conflicting claims the limit of space will not allow recounting here. Claims which, as time goes by, will be resolved by further investigations. Eventually, someone will untangle and follow the tracks of the old mountain men. When this is done, we shall know the historic spot where the first white man built to stay, in the State of Utah.

It can only be said, at the present state of the record, that if the old fort on the Green was not the first, permanent, white establishment in Utah, it was early enough to be of great historical significance and should be known and preserved.

ESCALANTE-DOMINGUEZ TRAIL

There were ten men who made the exploration two hundred years ago. The course they took led them into regions where only two of them had ever been before. The journey that they made was remarkable and rivals the treks of others we have read about in the annals of our country. It equals the trip of Lewis and Clark to the great western shining water. It surpasses the trip that Fremont made because they set off into a country hostile and completely unknown to the leaders of the pack.

What amazes me most is the apparent hand of God in the selection of each volunteer who made up the party. Each man was a specialist in his line and without him there could never have been success.

Let's take them one by one.

Father Dominguez, the leader and the boss. He was a "Criollo," a Mexican born and bred....

...Two hundred years ago, in 1776, two Franciscan friars, together with their companions, set out on a historic journey which was to take them across a wild and unknown country, the roughest in the west. These were the first white men and with them, the first black man ever to set foot in our beautiful State of Utah.

When the expedition got well started, there were ten men in all and their aim was to find a route around behind the lands of the hostile Indian nation, the Hopis and Apaches. They were to go from New Mexico, to Monterey, California. And although they never succeeded in this mission because the season grew too late, still, they made one of the most remarkable treks in history.

With Monsignor Stoffel, I followed the Dominguez-Escalante trail, step by step, turn by turn, league by league from the Colorado line to Utah Lake. Inevitably in such circumstances, one forms a picture in his mind of each man in party. He might be wrong for there were no descriptions and no pictures of them, nevertheless, there they stand right before your eyes.

Father Dominguez, Mexican born and bred, young—not yet thirty, well educated, lucid, quiet but authoritative, a good orator. He stands medium height, dark and swarthy, quite handsome. He is kindly, religious, and devoted entirely to the Father and the Son.

Father Escalante is very young for the pastor of a church. He is pure Castillian, so his hair is light, his eyes are blue and he is the tallest of the lot. The light blue cassocks that the fathers wore made him appear even taller and more slender than he actually was. He was well educated, too. He had a gift with a pen; for few can say so much, so accurately, in so few words as he was able to in his journal which we can follow even today.

Don Miera, by now forty years old and supposedly retired. This man was a soldier, a little grizzled around the edges and graying. He was a mathematician and map maker skilled in many things. There is no doubt that he was responsible for the accurate courses and distances set out in Escalante's diary. He was from Burgas, Spain. A Castillian, too, he was probably light complected because up there the Teuton blood runs strong.

Into a land where only Indians had ever been before, went an expedition led by white men. That was over two hundred years ago, the year of our country's birth.

Each individual of the party was an extraordinary man, when you consider them one by one. There was Father Dominguez, the leader, a high authority in the Franciscan Order of the Catholic Church. Father Escalante, young, intelligent; such a good scribe that even today, you can follow the trail day by day, league by league from the descriptions and data he put down with his pen. Don Miera, a grandee of Spain, and a soldier born and bred. Miera was highly educated, a cartographer, responsible, we suppose, for the remarkable accuracy of the courses and distances given in Escalante's journal. Then there were the venturesome Dons, high in the civilian government of New Spain; these were Don Pedro Cisneros and Don Joaqieun Sain. After them in rank came Olivores, Aguilar, Lucero, and the Miniz brothers. Andre Miniz, though holding no rank, was exceptionally intelligent; he had learned the difficult Ute language. He knew his way in the wilderness and among the Indians. It is probable that he and his brother Lucrecio were so well versed in Indian ways they acted and used a part of their habiliments, adopting from each culture, the best, most useful items for such a journey. As they rode no doubt their clothes were half and half.

As the outfit proceeded on beyond the last outpost of Abiquieu, they picked up two more men: Juan Domingo, a black man; and a mixed blood Indian they called the Coyote. No doubt, these two men were slaves, but since the Franciscans were against holding humans as chattels, these two men were taken along—not for the excuse they gave that they might cause trouble if they refused their company but because they wished to set them free.

As the explorers left the Sabuguavas, a band of the Ute Indian Nation, they added two more to their band: a boy in his early teens they called Juaquin; and as a guide, a young, full blood Ute Indian whom they named Silvestre. It was the Ute, Silvestre who led them from the last outposts of civilization to the shores of Utah Lake in what is now Provo, Utah.

As Monsignor Stoffel and I followed the Dominguez-Escalante trail from the Colorado line through Utah to the shores of Utah Lake, I was continually surprised and astonished by the skill and knowledge of that guide whom the fathers called Silvestre.

You see, Silvestre's Indian name was 'The Talker.' The Lake Shore People, the Paw-guau-nuance, said they had three chiefs. Besides these, there was a man who had great influence among this people. This man, they said, was Silvestre. Putting everything together, I have concluded that Silvestre, young as he was, was a Shaman, a medicine man. If this is so, then he was a Skyreader, a Vision Dreamer, a healer, a prophet and a master of the magician's art. He could understand the boom boom of the drum; could read smoke and messages tied in the knotted string. All of the medicine man's skills and knowledge has been handed down from father to son for generations. So this Ute, Silvestre, was a learned man. I'll admit today, that much of the Ute culture has vanished. I can find no one now who reads the drum, the smoke or string. All who did have long since passed away. The young ones never learned it in these latter days. The old ones died and carried many of their secrets to the grave.

But as Monsignor Stoffel and I followed the trail, the father laid out the route in courses and distances on the map using a compass, the odometer, and his fingers for conversion of miles to leagues. While I, Ute like, 'Silvestred' the land. In other words, from high places I scanned the terrain seeking out the most logical way to go.

When we started on our search with my Blazer, I thought I knew the Uintah Basin country as good or better than any man alive. I knew the deserts, the streams and their courses, the hills and hollows, every place where the expedition went was as familiar to me, I thought, as the palm of my left hand. I was surprised. As well as I knew my country, I found that Silvestre knew it better.

As we went painstakingly forward day by day, I found places where I thought, looking ahead, "Right here Silvestre pulled a boo-boo. He should have gone that way, not this way." And then when I got high and could see, I finally trembled. Silvestre was right and I was wrong. I think his name should have been Ouray (the Arrow), because if ever there was a man who could pick the shortest easiest route between two points, it was Silvestre. When he failed to do this, I had to read between the lines to find his reasons, but the thing is, I found them.

Now, let's follow the trail and I'll show you. He came down Douglas Creek Canyon, striking the White River a little above what is now Rangely, Colorado. The most direct route to the Timpanogas from there was down the White River to the place where waters meet, now called Ouray, Utah. He could cross the Green River at Ouray at the Big Island Ford, where the island parts the river in two. Then he could go up the Duchesne River on the same trail he finally took. But he chose to leave the White River and go north across Dead Man's Bench and down Cockle Burr to the water that is now the famous old "K" Ranch. It caused him to have to make a dry camp and the horses, that night, were restless because they were thirsty. As it turned out, he went a long way around losing many miles on his journey.

Why did he do that? I was puzzled. Then it dawned on me; he was in hostile Indian country. Those they called the Comanches were acting up and raiding. The vicinity of Ouray, since it was a great crossroads of the west was dangerous, always had been. Among the old Utes of that day, it was called the Bloody Ground because here raiding warriors could lie in wait, raiding the unwary. Silvestre decided to avoid it. He went north so he could use the ford of the Green a few miles above Jensen, Utah. Then he could follow the trail around the base of the Uintah Mountains, the same trail that Fremont used many years later. The fords across the rivers, that time of year, were easy. He could go over the Duchesne River, pass into the Kamas Valley, strike the headquarters of the Provo River and go down the stream to Utah Lake, the home of Silvestre.

They finally camped for two days at La Vega de Santa Cruz on the banks of the Green River. Here for some reason not disclosed in the journal, Silvestre changed his mind. They made an easy ford of the Green then headed south by southwest.

Why did Silvestre change his mind? Well, one of the nights while they were camped on the banks of the Green, the guide slept apart from the rest of the party. In the night, either Miniz or Joaquin, heard their guide talking with other Indians. In the conversation, unclearly heard, ambush was mentioned. This brought suspicion down on Silvestre's head. They thought maybe he was planning to betray them for their horses. But the suspicion was unfounded, as was later shown. Most likely, what really happened was that Silvestre's friends warned him that night of a danger on the Fremont Trail, probably a large war party of Comanche or Sioux. He decided to avoid them so he turned south.

They explored Brush Creek, the Sunshine Ranch and Ashley Creek and beyond. On the other side of Ashley Creek, near the foothills of Asphalt Ridge, the trail forked. The east branch led along an apparently easy way, it was flat land near the river. The west branch turned to climb the ridge toward Collier's Pass. Here the guide paused and hesitated, increasing the father's suspicions of him. There is no doubt he was checking all the signs. There were tracks on the road ahead. He was listening to the blue jays, smelling the air for smoke, noticing a thousand little things a white man wouldn't see. Finally he chose the western branch.

As we crossed the edge of Ashley Valley, following the compass and the map, I was unbelieving because the way Silvestre chose....

This is the story of a Ute Indian who in 1776 guided a legendary expedition led by two Franciscan friars, across a rough and rugged country unknown to western men. They left old Santa Fe of New Spain and on to the shores of Utah Lake.

The actual head of the party was Fray Francisco Atonasio Dominguez, a Mexican born and bred. With him as second in command was the young Fray Silvestre Velez de Escalante, from a northern province of Old Spain. Escalante was the scribe who left behind the excellent journal by which, even now, you can follow day by day, league by league, the route of the historic journey.

After the above religions, were Don Miera y Pacheco, an army captain, an engineer and cartographer, a Grandee from a northern province of Old Spain.

Besides the three named above there was Don Asneras, Don Sain, Celibares, Angular Lucero, Sucrecio Muniz, and above all the Ute speaking interpreter Andres Muniz.

Later, when the trek got well under way, beyond the border outpost of Abiquierez, Coyote who was a mixed blood named Helipe, and Juan Domingo, a black man, joined the march. They proved their worth on a later day. And last but not least, were the two Ute Indians, close relatives probably. One of these was just a boy in his early teens, Joaquin, the fathers named him. And the other was a young man in his early twenties whom the fathers called, Silvestre.

Silvestre, we found as Father Stoeffel and I followed the trail last summer, impressed us with his remarkable knowledge of the country, his faithfulness, and his skill in taking the expedition forward.

The Yutas of the Timpanogas gave Dominguez a buckskin upon which four figures were depicted, three of whom they said represented chiefs and the fourth was a man of great influence among his people. This fourth figure, they indicated, was the brother of the chief of chiefs. The fathers, including Muniz who should have known better, evidently did not understand what they had been given. They considered it a token of goodwill or a present. In fact, what they had was a passport, a guarantee of help and safe passage anywhere they might go in the lands of the whole Ute Indian Nation. It was the chief of chiefs intent, and his hope, that the fathers would use it to return quickly to them so that they could be taught the wonderful message of the Gospel.

Silvestre's Indian name was 'The Talker' (an advocate with the spirits, good or bad) This, coupled with the fact that he was a chief, indicates that possibly he was a Shaman, in common parlance—

a medicine man, an Indian priest. If this was so then he was a sky reader, a vision dreamer, a healer and a prophet. He would be a master of the magician's art. Besides all this, he could read the boom-boom of the drum, smoke talk and the messages of the knotted string. Added up, this would mean that Silvestre was a very intelligent man, that his skills and knowledge had been handed down from father to son for generations and he had been taught constantly since he was a boy of young and tender years. His father must have died and this left Silvestre, the chief Shaman of his band.

So now we follow the trail of the exploration guided by Silvestre, set out accurately in courses and distances, evidently by Miera and written down in a diary by Escalante who also describes the terrain.

At first Muniz knew the way from New Mexico to Colorado as far as the country of the Sabuagwas, after that they found Silvestre and he took over, so now....

They traveled north over mountains, across rivers and valleys. Finally, they went over a mountain at Douglas Creek Pass along a well worn trail descending down the canyon and striking the White River a little above Rangeley, Colorado.

It was here that Silvestre made his first decision. He knew he could go down the White River to Ouray, Utah. There was a good ford where The Big Island split the stream in two. In those days, it was an easy crossing because the river was about evenly divided so they crossed one channel then the other.

In 1776, of course the place was not called Ouray, it was known as The Place Where the Waters Meet. The White River coming from the east; the Duchesne River flowing from the west; and Willow Creek running out of the Bookcliffs, met the Green River within a mile or two of each other. In the days when water, wood and grass were so necessary to travel in an arid land, here at this spot, where the rivers came together, was a great crossroads of the west. But it had another name, too. The Indians also called it The Bloody Grounds, for here there had been many encounters between bands— the different tribes who, by design or accident, met at this hub where the main trails went out like spokes on a wheel. Definitely, with the people the fathers called Comanches on the loose, this was dangerous ground. So Silvestre was not willing to lead his charges through that way but was determined to avoid it.

The guide told the fathers that from here they would leave the White River, continue north across a stretch of land easy to travel but without water. It was too far, he said, to make it in one day. They must camp one night in a dry camp; it would be best to split that trip. They would stay on the White River until noon, allowing the horses to graze and rest. After allowing them to drink their fill, they would begin the trek across the desert. It was a hard segment of the trail but they made it, finding water at the foot of Blue Mountain at the site of what is now the famous old "K" Ranch.

After crossing the desert, the explorers rested one full day, to take care of the meat of a buffalo they had shot. Then they went to the banks of the mighty Green.

From the ford of the Green, about a mile above this camp, there is no doubt that Silvestre all along had intended to travel the northern trail, the same one Fremont used several decades later. This leads around the base of the Uintah Mountains, crossing many streams on the way. It finally passes over the summit near the beginning of the Duchesne, drops into Kamas Valley to the headwaters of the Provo, then down this stream to Utah Valley. But something at the camp on the Green changed the guide's mind.

One night, as they rested at the Green River, Silvestre slipped away and slept apart from the others. Either Muniz or Joaquin checked up on him and heard snatches of a conversation as Silvestre talked with another Ute who came in from somewhere. It was in that conversation, the eavesdropper heard "ambush" mentioned. Next morning, whoever the listener was warned the fathers, telling them to be on que vive. And they were, although they didn't show it.

But the suspicion, as it later turned out, was unfounded. Silvestre was worthy of their trust. Nevertheless he did talk to an unknown Indian. My conclusion is, he was given information which caused him to avoid the Fremont Trail and turn south along the Buffalo Trail, down the Green River, then turn west up the Duchesne, in the process keeping clear of the Bloody Ground.

As I stood in Ashley Valley with Father Soffel and we checked, time and again, which way the trail was tending, by map and compass, I couldn't believe it. To our left was a broad river plain which appeared to be easy to travel around the eastern nose of the Sierra, but here we went straight for Collier's Gap, in the high Asphalt Ridge. It was my opinion then, although Soeffel didn't agree, that the Ute guide was afraid or didn't know his business. When we came to the summit, I swallowed once then swallowed twice. The first time for my embarrassment and the second time for my surprise. Far below us, we could see miles and miles down the river. Here it flows around the loop of Horseshoe Bend and twists into the mighty turns of the Stirrup. When you follow the river, that is if you could, you would go for mile after mile around the turnings getting nowhere, but I could look down the way Silvestre went and it was as straight as a ruler to the campground where the explorers stayed that night. Not only that, but up high you could cross the arroyos where they are no bigger than irrigation laterals but as they flow they have washed great chasms impossible to cross down below. There is only a narrow ribbon along which you can go.

I have lived in Uintah Basin, man and boy, all these years. Not only that, but I have traveled it, to all the deserts, mountains, valleys and streams. I didn't believe there was a man alive or dead who knew it better from north to south, from east to west, than I did. But when we finished the Escalante Trail, I'll have to admit Silvestre beat me. He was not the bear who went over the mountain to see what he could see, he already knew what was there. Yes, the hand of God must have led the fathers to him.

They forded the river easily a few miles above Jensen, Utah, crossed Brush Creek, then Ashley Creek and headed south, southwest. At last they came to where the trail forked, one to the left and one to the right. Here Silvestre paused and hesitated. The white men's suspicions of him grew. Of course, he could see what the white men never did at this point. There were Indians on the trail ahead, some on horseback and some afoot. Were they ambushers waiting to attack somewhere? In the padre's party were between thirty and forty horses, each one of them, in 1776, worth their weight in gold to Indians. So Silvestre checked for telltale signs. He smelled the air, looked for smoke, listened for blue jays, watched for animals. Each of them told him something. At last, after he had satisfied himself, the guide moved forward taking the right hand fork.

When Silvestre reached the summit of the ridge, they could see where the Indian band ahead had waited for a time without turning their horses loose. They had been watching their back-trail. It was either a poor party because the fresh tracks showed some were on foot, or part of their pony herd had been stolen, or they had captives. If it was the latter, then they expected pursuit and were watching for them. If not, then they were watching the white men, whom they had seen across the river the last day or two. Perhaps it was curiosity that kept them observing these strange men in peculiar clothes and pale skins. Possibly they had heard of people like these but had never seen any before.

As the march continued down a long, dry arroyo to the first bottom of the river, they found fresh tracks of the people who had camped there for quite awhile, then continued on. Silvestre said those people were Comanche in pursuit of some Utes whom they had seen while hunting buffalo.

THE INCOMPARABLE UTE

The mists of time have faded all the legends. From the trails, the pony tracks have vanished. But a scribing pen on paper has left a story of one of history's most remarkable explorations of the North American Continent.

It is a journal. It tells the tale of two Franciscan Friars, Fra Dominguez, the leader, and Fra Escalante, his companion. With Don Miera, a grandee of Old Spain, Andre Muniz, the Ute speaking White man and two others, adventure bound they set out in 1776 from Sante Fe to find a trail through the back country to Monterey.

In their passage, they went over mountains, across valleys and deserts viewing scenes and panoramas that no white eyes had ever seen before.

As they went, they wrote down, day by day, league by league, their itinerary so remarkably accurate in courses and distances and descriptions that even today, you can follow their trail exactly in their footsteps.

In the beginning, the wayfarers dedicated their endeavors to the Holy Mother Mary and her husband Joseph, asking them to intercede for them throughout their dangerous journey. From that time on, they depended on the Heavenly Father to guide them knowing that as he willed, so it would be.

Like the Seven Cities of Cibola, there was a story among the Indians about a lake far to the north where peaceful, happy people dwelt. Toward this storied place they set their course.

By the casting of lots, or was it the hand of God? They were led to a band of Utes. Visiting among them was a young, strong intelligent Ute whose home was on the shores of the fabled lake. With gentle persuasion and some valuable presents, they prevailed upon this Ute to guide them as far as his homeland.

So remarkably capable was this Indian that it is to him I dedicate this story.

The Fathers gave their guide the name Silvestre; but his Indian name was Pa-gai-its (The Talker). This would indicate that he was a medicine man. He was a vision dreamer, a weather caster, and a healer. He knew the language of the drums and of the smoke. He could read the messages of the strong and was a master of legerdemain. He would have ranked as a chief.

Silvestre was a member of the great Ute Indian Nation. The Fathers called his band the Lagunas, after the lake they lived by. But their Indian name was Paw-guau-nuance (Lake Shore People). Among themselves, they are still known by that name.

As Silvestre left the Sabreaganas, they warned him that the Comanches were on the rampage. He knew that to pass this group of White men, with thirty or forty head of horses, through the Bloody Ground, as Uintah Basin was then called, would take all his wits, skills and know how. Smilingly, he led the party out on their long trek.

There was only once that Silvestre's choice of proceeding was questioned. Don Miera insisted on going a different way than Silvestre had picked. The result proved to be arduous and never again in all the long miles was Silvestre's decision questioned.

At last, they dropped down Douglas Creek Canyon and struck the White River just above Rangeley, Colorado. Now, they were on the threshold of the Bloody Ground. They must go for many miles, using the greatest caution, across a region of deadly peril.

Silvestre had a choice of two ways. He could go down the White River to The Place Where Waters Meet (called Ouray today). There are three good fords across Awat Paw (Big Water) at this place. But since Willow Creek, White River and the Duchesne enters Green River there, it was a great crossroads of the West. For this reason, it was most likely the company of explorers would run into hostiles there. If he crossed safely, Silvestre could go up the Duchesne, eventually joining the trail he finally took. The other way he could go was across a desert to the most northern ford of the Green in Uintah Basin, follow the trail around the base of the mountains, later to be known as the Fremont Trail. Then cross over the pass to Kamas Valley. There he would catch the headwater of the Timpanogos River (River of the Great Stone Person, now named the Provo) and descend it to Utah Valley—and home.

Checking the trails for signs, Silvestre chose the second course. He told the Padres that on the morrow, they would cross a wasteland without water. It was impossible, he said, to go from water to water in one day, so they would split the time. They would stay on White River that night and until noon the next day. Then they would set out across the barrens, make a dry camp at night, and find water late in the afternoon of the second day. It came out exactly as the Indian said. As the sun sank low down the sky on the second day, they found lots of water and good grazing at the foot of Blue Mountain at the present site of the "K" Ranch.

They shot one of the few buffalo in the region and rested a day to care for the meat and rest their animals. Then they rode on and camped in a grove on the left bank of the Green. At this place, they spent two days. While they were there, Silvestre slipped away and slept apart from his companions.

One of the mysteries of the journey happened here, because as he slept apart, one of the party eavesdropped on him. The suspicious person, whoever he was, heard the guide talking in Ute to another Indian. While he couldn't hear the whole conversation, he did hear the word 'ambush' spoken several times.

When this report was given to the Padres, they mistrusted Silvestre. They thought their guide might be leading them into a trap where their horses and mules could be stolen. They watched him very closely.

Next day, they went up the river a mile and forded it. Silvestre turned south, away from the Fremont Trail. On this day, too, they noticed that Silvestre for the first time wore the serape they had given him at the beginning of his service with them. Upon noting this, their fear of treachery grew. But they dissembled their feelings completely, so Escalante said. Later on, in his diary, Escalante was meticulous to explain that their fears about Silvestre were completely unfounded.

It is more than probable that Silvestre met another Ute at the camp on the Green. This man had told him not to go the Fremont Trail, for already, his party had been seen. Their intentions, they guessed, was that an ambush had already been laid for them. This is why Silvestre, after he crossed the river, turned south. In this way, he foiled his ambushers.

The trace he followed to the south was known to Silvestre as 'The Buffalo Trail.' It led from the buffalo plains of Wyoming, into Brown's Hole, over Diamond Mountain and on to Ouray. The way passes around the shoulder of 'The Buckskin Hills,' turns southwest and proceeds toward Asphalt Ridge. As you reach the south side of Ashley Valley, the trail forks. Approaching as Silvestre did, from the north, the easiest way to go seems to be the left hand fork because it leads down an easy incline to the river and apparently along the bank. The right hand fork climbs up a gully to the summit of Asphalt Ridge.

At the fork, Silvestre paused and hesitated. Escalante wrote that the guide seemed to be confused. But the Priest was wrong. Silvestre waited for a sign either from his friend of the campground scouting ahead or from something in nature he could recognize but the White men couldn't. To explain, an old Indian said to me once, "The trouble with White men is unless they are Indian trained, they go only by what they actually see and hear. An Indian will go not only by what he sees and hears but also by what he should see or hear and doesn't.

If you are in blue jay country and you don't hear his cry as you approach, you better move cautiously and find out why the bird is silent. It might save your life."

So Silvestre waited. He got his sign and took the right hand fork, climbing up Asphalt Ridge to Collier's Gap.

I questioned his decision. Why leave the easy going to the left and take the rough ascent to the right? Like Miera, I questioned the guide's selection only once, for, from the summit, I could see why he went the way he did. Far below us was the Green River. It turns almost a full circle around Horseshoe Bend then enters into the twisted channel of the stirrup straight. Before us, in the badlands, was one hidden pass and then another. The old trail, which you can still see, goes through those passes, straight as an arrow, back to the river at the campground of Las Llagas. Five miles for twenty, I would take that anytime. It dawned on me that as well as I knew my country, Silvestre knew it better.

Along the trail, Silvestre saw tracks of a sizable party. Some were on horseback and some were on foot. Several had remained on the summit watching the back trail but when the Spaniards got there they were gone.

These people had remained at the river for quite a long time. Silvestre, checked around. He said they were Comanches and were in pursuit of Utes who had stolen some of their horses on the buffalo plains.

How did Silvestre know this? Well, he probably found a string on a tree limb and read it; for the writing of the string was universal like the hand sign language.

The Comanches were here, they knew of the Spanish. From here, Silvestre must use all his cunning or disaster would strike.

Camp was made at Las Llagas de San Francisco and Miera. The old soldier set up a scheduled guard system to watch over the camp.

Early next morning the Muniz brothers, Indian trained, scouted the trail ahead. Upon their return, they said there was no apparent danger. So the Spanish company set out.

Silvestre, followed the Buffalo Trail for quite a distance, watching. He knew there must be some who would think he was going to Ouray; at that place they could set their trap.

But Silvestre thwarted those plans, for abruptly he left the Buffalo Trail. He moved cross country, west-southwest, across Brough Bench where there is no trail but is easy going.

It was here we found Silvestre's overlook. It is the high, ledgy point where Silvestre pointed out to the fathers the confluence of the White and the Green. From this place the guide had a good view for spotting signs of hostiles.

They went down a little unnamed stream to where the Duchesne and Uintah Rivers meet. They lost no time now, they traveled fast and camped that night on the banks of the Duchesne (Rivera de San Cosme).

Next day they set out on the most perilous stretch of the Bloody Ground. In truth, Silvestre knew there was pursuit. They saw the smoke signals at the foot of the Sierras which the guide could read; the Spaniards have been spotted and their location given.

The guide, knowing pursuers were behind him, fairly ran all day. But even so, he took precautions: he followed the river keeping in the trees and thickets, he wouldn't travel the open, easy going to the south. He passed through wild roses, had to ford the river several times, not in an attempt to hide but to keep in cover if there was an attack.

The Indian knew his party had three rifles, tree bows with arrows, knives, tomahawks, and axes. Perhaps there were other weapons, even if the Padres were against them. The Spanish company was not an easy mark. In fact, they were formidable if they had cover when attacked.

Nevertheless, the Ute hurried onward, on this day. They

eschewed the siesta, so dear to a Spaniard's heart. As night fell, they were at the campground of Catarino de Lena, on the Duchesne River about a mile above the town of Duchesne. This has been one of the longest days travel of the entire exploration.

The Ute knew that tomorrow he would be drawing near the guarded, eastern ramparts of his own people; there would be safety. He still had one of his greatest problems to solve. In the morn, they set out going over the west bench and down onto the Strawberry River. Silvestre chose to follow the river around 'The Circle.' (It is under Starvation Lake today.) It was rough going. They were in the river bottom, then up on the ledges where they lamed a horse. At last, the Ute left the river turning up La Golendrina (we call it Rabbit Gulch). At the forks, they took to the left up the deep, narrow defile of the Sink. The wind beat down the Sink like water down a funnel and it was cold. Escalante wrote they nearly froze all day.

To the south, an easy trail went through the axis of The Circle, up a short draw to Libione Flat, to Dead Ox Flat and on to the present site of Fruitland.

Why did Silvestre pick the hard way? Father Stoeffel and I, who followed the trail cogitated. Finally Father Stoeffel, and then I, came up with the answer. At the time the Fathers came through here, it was in the midst of the pinenut harvest season. This was a pinion forest. It would be overrun with people harvesting their winter's nut supply.

In going where he did, Silvestre chose one of those legendary 'hidden ways.' He couldn't be seen because you have to stand on the very rim of the Sink before you know it is there. The rock walls deaden all sounds.

When the Spanish explorers came to the head of the Canyon, they had left the pinion forest behind them. That night, the party camped on Red Creek about a mile above present Highway 40. The grass was good and there was plenty of water.

At daylight, the explorers made the last lap across the ill-reputed Bloody Ground. They dropped onto Currant Creek, climbed the Sheep Trail, rounded the corner of the mountain and went up Deep Creek above the Narrows. They camped at the head, in one of the most beautiful campgrounds of the whole journey. Better than that, they had crossed the land of danger and were nearing Silvestre's home.

As they went across Strawberry Valley, climbed Strawberry Ridge and dropped down, Silvestre was in a hurry because he was nearing home. The timber was so thick, Miera could not take his bearings. So today you can't tell exactly where they went.

On Diamond Fork, smoke signals showed all over announcing the coming of the Fathers. That night at the forks of Diamond Fork and Spanish Fork Rivers, Silvestre, knowing they were being watched from the shadows, spoke to his people. He told them who he was and who his companions were. He explained that the Padres were men of Big Medicine and that they came in peace.

Next day, from a high overlook, the Padres saw the beautiful Utah Valley. In the distance, they saw the lake. They realized it was not a myth, for there it was; its waters shining in the sun.

In a day, they met Silvestre's people and found out the guide was a chieftain. They found out, too, that to cross the Bloody Ground infested by Comanches—without mishap and without a battle—was a miracle.

When it came time to part, presents were exchanged. The Big Chief gave the Fathers a strip of buckskin with pictures drawn upon it. In some dark archives of New Mexico, Old Mexico, Spain, or even in England, there might be hidden that piece of buckskin. If it could be found, it would be considered by those who could read it, a great historic document.

You see, although Escalante's diary doesn't mention it, the old chief said this when he gave it to Dominguez. That buckskin was a gift seldom given; it had great significance. It was a passport. It guaranteed safe passage forever to the man who possessed it. It was good in every land controlled by the Ute Nation or its allies. It is probable that even the Comanches, the Hopis, the Navajo, and the Apaches would have honored it.

Sorrowfully, Silvestre parted from his charges as they prepared to leave his homeland. From that time on, he stepped back into the shadows—faded forever from the pages of recorded history.

All we can say is that the party of the Fathers, at some unknown rendezvous with fate, would have vanished from the scene had they not had with them the guiding hand of the man they called Silvestre. He led them steadfastly, true, direct and as sure as an arrow shot from the bow of a master. Silvestre was the master who led them safely through all danger.

Note: Both preceding articles are similar but because each contains additional information concerning Silvestre, we decided to use them both.

NINE MILE ROAD

THE ROAD

Nine Mile Canyon.

The main theme of this story is not a person or any animate thing—it is the story of a road. Along its course, the tides of the history of a region ebbed and flowed. What happened along its winding way is as enthralling as the tales they tell of the road to Santa Fe or those on the Oregon Trail. As you travel its twisting miles, you see the points where events occurred, which as the years passed, became a part of the folklore of a people.

The story deals with humans, 'tis true, for this road was the track of an empire. Over the serpentine route came presidents, generals, soldiers, cowboys, Indians, outlaws and settlers. It was the road that stage coaches and freighters traveled for it was the artery over which came the mail and commodities to keep the people of Uintah Basin, in eastern Utah, well and happy.

The Basin is a great land-locked valley completely surrounded by snow-capped peaks. It's an area as large or larger than some of the fifty states of the Union. To get in or out of the big "U" country, you must cross its rivers, climb over several mountain ranges. You must traverse its deserts, where the summer sun shines down pitilessly and the winds of winter blow across the barren wastes. Today, the journey is easily and swiftly made. But yesterday, the miles came hard, especially when the rivers ran wild in flood or the snow lay deep on the mountain passes.

In the 'Early Days,' the Basin had within its confines an Indian reservation of many thousand acres; Ft. Duchesne, a post of the United States Army; and beyond the boundaries of the reservation, to the eastward, a white settlement in Ashley Valley.

Later, when the reservation, the final home of the three northern bands of the Ute Indian Tribe, was opened to the white homesteaders, there were other towns—Roosevelt, Myton, Duchesne, and smaller centers, laid out and settled. The Basin became the dwelling place of thousands of those pioneers we read about in history.

The Indians, Ft. Duchesne, and the whole white population was served by the pass known as the Nine Mile Road. It stretches over mountains, up and down canyons, across deserts and rivers, from the nearest railroad at Price, Utah, one hundred, twenty miles to Ashley Valley, its northeastern terminal, serving all the points in between.

There were many roads into Uintah Basin but the most glamorous, historic, certainly the one which has become a legend is this old Nine Mile Road.

When the automobile and motor trucks came, bringing with

The old Stage Coach going through Nine Mile Canyon.

them new roads and maintenance equipment, the Nine Mile Road faded into obscurity; for newer, faster highways were built, taking the place of the old. But the old Nine Mile Road never died completely; its route has been changed some and it has been improved, but you may still, if you wish, travel its entire length. The hustle and bustle are gone. Nevertheless, the legends and memories linger. Only ranchers and sightseers travel it now, yet the ghosts of other days are still there.

I suppose no one knows, for certain, how Nine Mile Road got its name. Nor does anyone know for certain how that picturesque abyss, Nine Mile Canyon, through which the road passes, got its name. It is quite certain that either the road was named for the canyon or the canyon was named for the road. Wherever old-timers meet and Nine Mile is discussed, the mystery of the naming is considered but no one seems to know the answer.

The stream that flows in the canyon is not Nine Mile Creek.

It has an old-fashioned, quaint sounding name, the Minnie Maud, which infers that perhaps the canyon was not always known as Nine Mile.

The canyon is longer than nine miles. There is no significant nine mile stretch from any definite point. No spring or presently known object would give rise to the name. There are several theories of naming but only one, in my estimation is based more upon fact than fiction. It goes like this:

The U.S. Army wanted fast communication from Ft. Duchesne to the outside world, so while building Ft. Duchesne, the Army also built a road and a telegraph line to Price, Utah, the nearest rail point. As time passed, soldiers concluded the new road was the best all-season route into the Basin and used the road exclusively for all army freight. In the spring and after hard rains, however, there were places along the way where the depth and quality of mud was unbelievable. Mules mired to their bellies, wagons to their boxes and wheels built up gumbo like a honey bee's hind legs in pollen-gathering time. Many of the officers at Ft. Duchesne were veterans of the Civil War and had taken part in McClellan's Peninsular Campaign in his attempt to take Richmond. In that campaign, in far off Virginia, was a 'Nine Mile Road.' A whole Union Army Corps bogged down in the mud there during one of the movements of 'The Seven Days.' As a party of soldiers moved along, going from Ft. Duchesne to Price. they, too, bogged in the mud. An officer said, "This is as bad as the Nine Mile Road."

The chance remark stuck and from then on 'The Nine Mile Road' was the name used by the army. The civilians quickly appropriated the army designation.

In the years before the Army built the road, there were a few people in the Canyon, mainly outlaws, using it as a hideout. Most of the settlers in the canyon came in after the Army built and named the way in. The canyon, probably known as Minnie Maud Canyon, assumed Nine Mile Canyon, taken from the Army's designation of the road.

The opening of the Ute Indian Reservation to white settlement, had such a profound effect upon the Nine Mile Road and the country it served, that 'The Opening,' came to be a point in time from which all events in the Basin were measured.

The old-timers would say: "That was two years before the opening," or "That happened two years after the opening." 'The early days,' to indicate a time before the opening and, 'In later days,' were also used.

The story of the Nine Mile Road, covers times before and after the opening. Consequently, these old terms seem the best to define the how, when and where of events in Uintah Basin. They will be used in this narration the same way the old-timers used them.

When the bulk of travel into the Basin came along Nine Mile Road, a mail contract was let, bringing all U.S. Mail over its route. Mail was left at the Bridge, Ft. Duchesne, the Strip and Vernal bi-weekly. After the opening, the mail service became a daily service to all settlements along the line.

The speed of the mail coach made it necessary to change horses along the route. For this purpose 'Stations' were established by the stage company approximately twenty miles apart where fresh horses were kept. Here, tired horses were taken off and rested while fresh horses were hitched on and the coach continued on its way.

Twenty miles over this kind of terrain took a half day for the mail and a good long day for the freighters. At each station was a dining room where hungry passengers could eat and sleeping accommodations, if anyone desired them. There were also campgrounds where freighters and others stopped for the night.

To take care of the needs of campers, the stations usually had a general merchandise store, feed yard, and in some cases, saloons and card rooms.

From Price, going to the Basin, stations were located at: Soldier—the top of the grade going up to West Tavaputs Plateau (The Land of the Sun); Lee's Station in Nine Mile; Frank Alger's in Nine Mile; the Wells in the Wells Draw; the Bridge, where the road crossed the Duchesne River which after the opening became the town of Myton; the Strip, near where the village of Gusher is now; the Half Way Hollow; and then Vernal, the end of the line.

You can still follow the old stage road and the track of the army mule. It began in Price, Utah at a small frontier hotel. The mail coach left there at about seven o'clock A.M. each day, outbound for the country of the warlike Utes. It ran northeasterly across the foothills and sagebrush flats, until it came to a small stream flowing rapidly down from the mountains. It turned north at the stream, entered a canyon and followed it uphill to the summit of the mountain pass.

To a point, the coach traveled at a fast, jingling trot, leaving behind a long plume of dust. Then, as the horses leaned into their collars against the grade, the pace slowed to a fast walk. The uphill climb grew steeper and steeper as the mountains grew higher on either side. The road narrowed as the canyon narrowed. At last, there was only a dugway, a final 'pitch,' and the climb was over.

At this point the mountain breeze met the traveler. A wide expanse opened before him. This expanse is a mountain park, known as Whitmore Park. In the summer, it is a place of green grass, sagebrush, quaking aspen, cool water and pine trees. In the winter, it is covered deep in snow. To the north is a backdrop of high, snow capped peaks; to the left the park stretches away out of sight in the distance; behind are the slopes of the mountains dropping down into Castle Valley, the site of Carbon County coal mining camps and Price; to the right is the head of fabulous Nine Mile Canyon.

In the old days, on the south side of the park, was Soldier Station. When the mail arrived here, it was noon. The table in the dining room was already laid for dinner in anticipation of the arriving, hungry passengers. There were no short orders; the meal was strictly cook's choice. The diners ate what was placed before them. The food was plain frontier fare, but it was well prepared, and above all, there was plenty. A meal cost fifty cents for adults, twenty-five cents for children under twelve.

Any traveler, whether riding the stage or not, could eat at the station, but he had to be there at meal time. There were no meals between meals, unless you were a friend of the cook's.

Most people, with their own outfits, going in or out of the Basin, prepared their food at the campgrounds, it was only the affluent who used the station dining rooms. To some, eating at the station was a treat like the modern day family's eating out nights, which come only occasionally during the year.

To stage passengers, there was one hour at the station to eat, rest, freshen up and prepare to travel on.

A short distance beyond the station was the campground. It was usually empty during the day, but as the sun sank low, the campers began to pull in to prepare for the night. The campground would fill as the evening wore on, there would be freighters, light rigs, horsemen, and pack strings. Every kind of outfit known to travel in those days, stopped for the night.

In Whitmore Park, in the early days, a British Syndicate operated a cattle ranch. There were American cowboys and an American foreman to handle the cattle, but the general manager, the man who paid the wages and the bills, was an Englishman.

They say, this Englishman came to the station twice a week for his meal. He was accustomed to buy one, perhaps two, drinks of 'red eye' at the bar. He'd talk awhile with those he knew, then ride back to his cabin several miles distant in the park.

The Westerners, seeing the Englishman ride, laughed at his style, for he rode like the European Aristocracy. The Westerners said this was riding 'hard hinder.' Be that as it may, he was not exactly a dude, for he had spent time as an army officer in India with some famous outfit like the Khyber Rifles. He could ride and shoot with the best.

According to the story, he got many letters from London. Quite often a letter came slightly scented and perfumed. When one of these special letters came, he didn't wait until he got home to read it; he secluded himself and read it then and there. When he had finished, he sat rapt in thought. He gazed far out over the horizon, dreaming, it was supposed, of Piccadilly Circus, the Thames, the Chimes of Big Ben, and Mayfair.

Once the mail brought this man a picture. It was of a pretty lady, standing by a carriage, in front of Buckingham Palace. This caused much comment and gave rise to the mystery of who this man really was. Was he a lord of the realm, exiled from his native land? Was he a disgrace, living in the wilderness as a remittance man? Was he what he appeared to be, a man working for his living? It's probable no one will ever know, for his record is lost in the limbo of time.

The cattle syndicate lasted for only a year or two, then it sold out. The snow was too deep in Whitmore Park in the winter. No cattle ranch could prosper there.

When the syndicate ceased operations, the British overseer went away. Those who knew him, wished him well. They hoped he had gone back to London, where he apparently longed to be, rejoined his lady and lived a long and happy life thereafter.

Winter's snow was heavy in the Park. When the wind blew, it piled the snow into deep drifts. It is said that a four horse team and two wagons could be buried alive by the snow in less than half an hour if caught in the open while a gale was blowing. At these times traffic snarled, until the wind died and a road could be broken through the snow. Freight outfits broke the way by doubling and re-doubling teams of horses on a wagon. The lead team had to be changed every fifty to one hundred yards; this kind of floundering progress was horse-killing work.

The worst winter, of any on record, came after the opening in the winter of 1909-10. That year, it took twenty-six days for a company of wagons to go from Vernal to Price and back. The shelves and bins in all the stores in the Basin became empty and bare. There were shortages everywhere.

Spring broke late that year, but when it came, riders were sent out summoning the homesteaders with wagons and teams to go to Price for food and necessities. The warehouses at Price were bursting at the seams with orders which could not be delivered. The regular freighters could not catch up or fill the needs of the depleted country. The homesteaders came. The roads were filled with traffic and in three weeks, the lean year was over.

There are still stories told of that never-to-be-forgotten winter when famine stalked the land. To many, the mention of Whitmore Park will still cause shudders. Old-timers tell how stores rationed the food supplies, how neighbor helped neighbor, how clothes were borrowed and lent, how no one died for lack of food, nor froze because of the lack of warm clothing. But, they say, nothing can describe the relief and joy when wagons, in long lines, arrived loaded from Price.

John McLain went down to the Green River to fish one summer day. He used dynamite to blast the holes and eddies to catch a big supply of fish quickly. As he was preparing a powder charge, a blasting cap went off in his hand, mangling it to shreds. John wrapped his injury in a burlap bag to stop the bleeding, mounted a mule bare backed, and rode to Francis' Station, now Nutter's Ranch. At the station he was loaded in a buckboard, accompanied by a friend. They started for the closest doctor at Price.

When he got to Soldier Station, McLain could go no farther. Loss of blood, pain, and exhaustion made it imperative that he rest awhile. His friend and the station operators knew McLain would never reach Price alive.

As the evening shadows fell, Company 'K,' 28th U.S. Infantry, came marching into the campground at the station. This outfit was commanded by Captain C. W. Abbott Jr., assisted by Lt. V. A. Drum, who became a general in World War I. In addition to these officers, there was a young, contract surgeon, Dr. Dade, with the troops.

When it was learned a doctor was with the soldiers, he was called upon to help John McLain. The doctor took one look at McLain's wound; he knew there was only one way to save the sufferer's life—amputate. But there were no medicines and no instruments along; these were waiting at Ft. Duchesne. At the station there was a long, oil cloth covered table, sharp butcher knives, and two regular meat saws. Dr. Dade decided to operate with what he had.

While the knives were being whetted and all preparations were being made, McLain was given whiskey. When everything was ready, the patient was drunk as a hoot owl. He was placed on the table with four husky soldiers to hold him down.

With Kate Bowen, the station cook, acting as operating room nurse, the doctor began to cut. The whiskey helped, but it could not do more than slightly dull the pain. Everything went rapidly and well until the surgeon began to use the saw. When the saw began to work, McLain could stand it no longer. He threw off the soldiers holding him, and cussed everybody in sight, including Kate Bowen, the cook turned nurse.

The surgeon said, "Lie back down there, you coward. Let me finish your arm or they'll be digging your grave in the morning."

Poor John McLain, lay back down on the table. He shoved his injured arm out and said, "Saw it off, you damn butcher, but be quick about it."

The doctor was quick about it. He finished the job and McLain lived to a ripe old age. His story became known wherever he went. He was the man who, while drunk, let an army doctor cut his arm off with a butcher knife and a meat saw. John, when chided about this, always answered, "Yep, be damned if that kid didn't damn near kill me. It hurt so bad, but he saved my life."

John Baumgaertel, first sergeant of Company 'K,' who helped hold McLain down that night said, "Infantry was infantry in those times. Nowadays I don't know why they still call them infantry. They don't walk anyplace, they ride. When I went to Ft. Duchesne, we got off the train at Price, shouldered our field packs and rifles and walked every step of the way. Yes, and we carried our drinking water, too. We went as far in a day as the freight wagons did. If we had been force marched, we could have gone as far as the stage did. They don't make infantry like that anymore. It's too bad, too bad."

What Sergeant Baumgaertel said about the infantry hiking between Price and Ft. Duchesne and visa versa, is true. It is borne out by the record. The speed of the infantry as compared to freight outfits is true also, but his boast about the speed and distance of a forced march is not verified.

Soldier Station was not a long stop for the stagecoach. One hour and it was on the way again. The road crossed Whitmore Park, went down a dugway, and dropped into the head of Nine Mile Canyon. This canyon is like a narrow, winding trench, cut into the mountains by the water. It is a pleasant ride; its scenic grandeur is breath-taking and splendid. To the right and left, except where side canyons come in, are sheer mountain ledges, reaching up almost to the blue of the sky. As it goes downward, the canyon becomes deeper and finally, at its mouth it joins the Green River in the mighty gorge named Desolation Canyon by Major Powell, its first explorer of record. The great sculptress, nature, had carved the great rock walls of the defile into hundreds of spectacular pieces. There are masques, cathedrals, fortresses and pinnacles of gigantic proportions. It is enchanting; its massive beauty rivaling the Grand Canyon itself.

In the early days, before the army built its road, there were six men who had ranches in the canyon. Ed Lee had two places, one which later became Lee's Station and a lower ranch at the mouth of Bull Canyon. Matt Thomas ran cattle in both Argyle Canyon, a fork of Nine Mile, and in Nine Mile itself, although he had no permanent camp in the area. Joseph Thompson settled near the mouth of Argyle, then along Nine Mile Canyon. Thompson had two daughters, the apples of his eye, he named the creek after both of them. He gave it the quaint sounding name, 'Minnie Maud Creek.'

Mr. Argyle ran cattle in Nine Mile and in the fork which bears his name.

William Warren settled in the canyon near the mouth of Argyle. It was he who guided the army engineers over the trail which they later built into a road.

Far down on the Green River, at the mouth of Nine Mile, in the early days, was an outlaw hideout. No one knows when the outlaws first went there, but it was a hangout for the Wild Bunch. Butch Cassidy, Harry Longbaugh, Matt Warner and others used the place on occasion. It was chiefly a rustlers' center. Cattle were stolen, driven there, butchered and the meat sold to the coal camps in Carbon County. Many stories are told of well mounted, well armed, mysterious men, who rode the trails of the area, apparently going to or from the camp down below. The outlaws left when the settlers came.

The bulk of the settlers came in after the army built its road. Most of the old original places remain unchanged; the aura of the 'Old West,' still lingers there. It is like stepping back in time seventy years, to travel Nine Mile Canyon today. There is something subtle and mysterious in the atmosphere of the great chasm, brought on I suppose, by its terrain, its colorful recent history and its history of ancient days. It is a wholly captivating and pleasant place.

The Anasazi, that ancient, vanished race of Cliff Dwellers dwelt in the canyon. High in the ledges, their houses can be seen. They are built of rock masonry, on shelves, far up from the canyon floor.

Except where vandalized by thoughtless modern man, the houses are in almost as good a condition today as they were on the day their builders left them.

There are petroglyphs, signs, symbols and writing on the rock ledges, carved there in succession by the Anasazi, the Utes, the Spaniards, the Mountain Men and by the people who passed that way in subsequent times.

The stage came rapidly down the canyon for it was cool and pleasant, the road was downhill and here it could make excellent time in good weather. It arrived at Lee's Station in mid afternoon, stopped for thirty minutes to change horses and went on into the lengthening shadows of the echoing ledges. The ride down the long canyon was by far the most pleasant stretch of the whole journey.

It was all downhill now. The evening coolness was coming on and along this stretch, the mail made excellent time. It arrived at 'The Old Brock Place' early in the evening. Brock never owned this place while the road was in its hay day; it had been purchased by Pete Francis who ran the station.

Pete Francis was a Mexican and no one knew his antecedent. His real name, before he analogized it, was probably Pedro Francisco. Pete had built his station and also a small log saloon where the freighters, cowboys and the outlaws from down below were wont to gather. Sometimes the carousal went far into the night.

One night a party was going on. Freighters, local cowboys, and strangers no one knew, all gathered at the log saloon drinking. There was a fight that night, the true facts of which have never been clear. At its end, Pete Francis lay dead, shot to death by someone. Dave Russell, a local cowboy, was accused and convicted of the shooting. However, it has been said that Russell was too drunk to shoot anybody that night, that it must have been someone else. Some say, Pete Francis had financial connections with outlaws down at the north of the canyon; that either he turned informer or otherwise pulled a double cross and the outlaws shot him. Whatever the truth might be, the fact remains that Russell served time because he confessed to the shooting.

After the death of Pete Francis, the place was purchased by Preston Nutter who made it his home until the day he died. Preston Nutter was a cattle baron from Clarksburg, West Virginia. He became a legend in his own time. His cattle operations were known in all the regions of the West. Nutter's Ranch was as famous as those great ranches of Texas and the southwest. It is said, he never knew how many acres of land, or how many head of cattle he owned. He was a very remarkable person who rode tall in the saddle in a rough and rugged land in a rough and lawless day.

At the opening, Katherine Fenton, a young school teacher, was on her way to the land office in Vernal to file her claim to reservation land. As she came to Nutter's Ranch, the wheel on the vehicle she was riding broke. She would have to wait until the old wheel was fixed or a new one could be obtained from Price. If she waited, she would not be able to reach Vernal on the day set out in her notice and she would lose her priority to the land she wanted.

Preston Nutter, on hearing Miss Fenton's story, hitched up his fastest team. He drove the young lady to Vernal, getting her to the land office on time. This started a romance which ended in marriage two years later. Katherine Fenton became Mrs. Preston Nutter.

The Old Brock Place, after Nutter purchased it, ceased to be a stage station and campground. The stop was changed to Frank Alger's Ranch nearby. It was here for many years that 'Martha' plied her trade. Martha was an Indian woman who was the cook at Alger's Station. Like so many people and things in Nine Mile, she became a legend in her own lifetime. She was the best cook the westerners ever knew. There was no one who could equal her roast beef, gravy, or apple pie. When special guests were on the road, like the Governor, Teddy Roosevelt, General Sheridan and others, the guides made it a point to have at least one meal at Martha's. In time, her fame spread, not only along the frontier road, but over the entire west, to Salt Lake, to Cheyenne, to Santa Fe. Although she was offered many positions in the big hotels of the cities, she turned them down to stay in Nine Mile.

Leaving the last station in Nine Mile, the road went on downstream for a few yards, then turned north and headed straight for Indian country. It was desert; there was no stream, no spring between the Minnie Maud and the Duchesne River far away.

The road, from Brock or Alger Station, went a few hundred yards farther down the canyon, turned north and entered Gate Canyon. Later the Army, state, and county joined together and built a road the shorter way. It went all the way to the mouth of Gate Canyon.

Gate Canyon is as well known and famous as Nine Mile itself, but for different reasons. It is the most dangerous of all the dangerous stretches of the road between Price and Vernal. Its lower reaches is a causeway hemmed in on both sides by high, insurmountable ledges. It runs twisting and turning like a crooked flume. Once in the bottom, there is no way out except up or down the road. Near the mouth of the canyon for several miles, it is like a spout on a giant funnel, draining a vast region above. Gate Canyon is dry for its entire length. But during the hot summer months of July and August, cloudburst strike the mountains at the head of the canyon and a wall of angry water comes roaring down with the speed of an express train. It is said by those who know, that the water in the causeway will rise fifteen feet in a matter of seconds. Woe be unto him who is caught by it in a narrow place. It has killed animals and men.

In the early days, there was a rock arch that spanned the causeway. Under this arch, all the traffic up or down the canyon must pass, hence the name 'Gate Canyon.' The water had worn the rock under the arch into ledgy steps over which the vehicles bumped and jarred. In time, the jarring wagons began to crumble the base of the rocky span. It was feared the bridge would fall, killing those beneath it. Miners were hired to knock it down with dynamite. 'The Gate' no longer exists, except in the name given to the canyon.

The way to the summit twists and turns upward, for it must follow the course cut by the water. In many places, the passage turns back upon itself, leaving points outthrust into the center of the canyon. It was at one of these outthrusted ridges that the Wild Bunch planned to rob the Army Paymaster.

When Ft. Duchesne was an Army post, the paymaster came from headquarters in Salt Lake City, to pay the troops. He always carried a cash box filled with enough gold and silver coins to pay the men in cash. He rode the train to Price, where he was met by a cavalry escort, and rode an Army ambulance from there with his cash box to Ft. Duchesne. The trouble was, no one knew exactly when he was coming except the officers at the post.

Some men from the cavalry escort got drunk in Price and let the cat out of the bag. They were part of the Paymaster's escort. Someone from the Wild Bunch was drinking with the troopers that night. He hied away to his friends camped close by to bring the news.

The Wild Bunch knew Gate Canyon as well as any men alive. They picked their spot and laid their trap. There is a place in Gate Canyon, where the road turns and goes east for about two hundred yards at the foot of a low ledged point. It swings abruptly around the point, doubling back upon itself, and runs west under the ledges at the base of the ridge for about two hundred yards, swings then and goes north. There is no way to the top of the low ridge from the road in the bottom of the canyon for sheer ledges bar the ascent. The top of the ridge can be reached where it joins the mountainside to the west. It was here the outlaws planned to perform their coup.

There were five men, Butch Cassidy, Harry Longbaugh, Dave

Lent, Eliza Leigh and Matt Warner, each an expert rifleman with a Winchester repeating rifle. They would hide their horses, mount the ridge, find cover and wait for the Paymaster. As the ambulance and escort reached the turn around the point, one man, stationed on top, would begin firing. The Paymaster and the troopers, to reach safety, must go up or down the canyon for the far side of the gauntlet was also barred by sheer ledges. It was two hundred yards in plain view, either way the soldiers went. With riflemen like these waiting for them, the soldiers would all be brought down before they could reach cover and safety. The ridge was only about fifty feet across on top, so all fire could be concentrated on one side if need be.

The robbers took to the road in the nighttime. Riding hard, they were in Gate Canyon by daylight. The horses were hidden and the outlaws mounted in the ridge. The long wait began. The morning ended. The afternoon wore on and now the time was near. About four o'clock in the afternoon, after many outfits had gone by, the Paymaster showed up. He had six troopers to guard him, two out front and four behind, besides the lieutenant, the driver, and six cavalrymen. This would be easy, the easiest haul the Wild Bunch had ever made.

The soldiers came on, unaware of their eminent danger. They went east to the point and as they swung around it, Harry Longbaugh, raised his rifle to fire. At this moment, from up the canyon, came the sound of peculiar music. Harry Longbaugh, glancing up the road saw, swinging around the bend, a whole company of U.S. Infantry marching out from Ft. Duchesne. Too many soldiers, even for the Wild Bunch. They lay in their hiding places and all that money went safely on to the fort. The music they heard was a soldier with bagpipes, playing to relieve the tedium of the march.

Matt Warner, who became a useful, law-abiding citizen of Price, said in later years, "When we saw the infantry, we just lay there in the rocks, making not the faintest sound and let all that money go up the road. I have never known whether to figure we were lucky or unlucky, I guess it depends upon the way you look at it."

The old road goes on its dry, hot winding way and steepens as it goes. At last, it passes through pinion pine and juniper trees and another summit has been reached. From this point, the whole Uintah Basin lies below. Far across the great valley to the north, looking ethereal and transparent in the sky, are the snow capped Uintah Mountains, the loftiest mountains in the State of Utah. They run east and west, the only east-west mountain range in the United States. To the east is the trench through which the Green River flows and beyond, the mountains of Colorado. To the west is the transversal range of the Uintahs, obstructing the way to Heber Valley and the Great Salt Lake.

During the opening, the homesteaders came in long, plodding lines, reaching for the new rich lands they had heard about. From the peaks at the head of Gate Canyon, on a clear day, the road could be traced for almost its entire length across the big, wide country by the clouds of dust rising on the air from the hooves and rolling wheels of people moving in, looking for land and homes. From here the worst of the trip is over. All the high mountain passes are behind, the way is all downhill to the Indian country.

The wagon road drops down into the head of Smith's Draw, which as time went on, by common usage, came to be known as 'The Wells Draw.' This too, is desert country, there is no natural water in the draw, except in wet weather.

Before 1891, the southbound stage met the northbound stage in Smith's Draw at a place called Castle Rock. The meeting was at midnight, if the schedules of both coaches were on time. The first driver to reach the rendezvous, built a campfire and put the coffee on to boil. When the other stage arrived, a midnight lunch was eaten. Passengers and mail were exchanged. The coach from Nine Mile went back to Nine Mile; the coach from the Bridge went back to the

Bridge. A barrel of water was carried by each outfit to water the horses at this point.

In 1891, Owen Smith dug a well in the draw at a place almost exactly halfway between Vernal and Price. It was also about half way between the Duchesne River and the Minnie Maud. Smith dug his well like a mine shaft and at one hundred and eighty feet, he struck water. It was not good water, but it would do to water livestock. Water for human consumption would have to come from someplace else.

Where Smith dug his well, he established a station. It became the busiest and most colorful station along the whole length of the Nine Mile Road. It was an oasis in the desert. All traffic stopped there for one reason or another.

Water was drawn from the well in a huge wooden bucket pulled by a horse on a 'whim.' There was a valve in the bottom of the bucket and the water poured from it into the troughs. Later, Hamilton installed an engine and a pump on the well and drew the water quicker and better.

There was a charge for watering here, not by the gallon, but by the head of livestock. There used to be a sign nailed on the corral post, setting out the toll: Horses 50 cents per team; 30 cents per head; cattle 30 cents per head; sheep 15 cents per head; dogs free.

There were four stagecoaches on the road each day. One left Price northbound every morning; one left Vernal every morning going toward Price. Because it was halfway between Price and Vernal, the only overnight stage stop on the line was at the Wells. Both the Price bound and Vernal bound coaches stopped here for the night. Each morning they left, one going on to Vernal, the other on to Price.

At the Wells station, there was a large dining room, big enough to handle twenty people at a meal. There were sleeping accommodations for all comers, although there might be several to the room.

There was a complete general merchandise store selling food, clothing, and hardware. There was a livery stable, a blacksmith shop, a feed yard, and a saloon. They say, you could buy anything at the Wells that you could find in town.

Grazing livestock on the public domain was big business. Big sheep outfits used the Wells, because of the water and the supplies they could obtain. Cattlemen from the Basin drove their cattle to market over this route and stopped at the station to water their herds.

The campground was large, stretching down the draw for a quarter of a mile or more. Day after day, there would be from fifty to a hundred outfits camped here for the night. In the evenings, around the fires, the campers used to gather after all the chores were done. There was always the storyteller, always the harmonica, sometimes the violin, and many times good voices. When the weather was good, the campground rang with music, laughter and song. This was not restricted to men; there were women and kids camping, too. They enjoyed these times of merrymaking, adding their gentleness to a rough trail. It was very pleasant to hear the sweet strains of old songs like Lorena, Aura Lee, Genevieve, Pretty Little Primrose and others, floating over the barren hills of the desert country.

Sometimes the well could not supply the demand and went dry. At these times, there were waits until the well filled again. When this happened, the activity at the troughs went far into the night, even until morning.

The names of famous Americans who stayed here adds luster to the history of the place. General Sheridan, General Crook, Teddy Roosevelt, Maud Adams, Lucy Gates, Reed Smoot, William Spry, Julius Baumberger, all slept and ate here at one time or another.

No story of the Nine Mile Road would be complete without the coyote. He was near every campground along the way. When the human voice quieted, the coyote chorus began and from far away. His peculiar yapping and mournful howl filled the air. As time went on, his voice became almost a lullaby to the wilderness dweller. It is true he was a varmint; he caused loss and trouble to all who had chickens, sheep, or calves. Even so, now that he has almost completely vanished from the scene, those who knew him, speak of him with nostalgia. He is part of those good old days memory has painted with a golden hue.

There was a dog at the Wells named 'Bob.' He belonged to no man; his affections attached to a stage horse named 'Baldy,' who returned the affection in full measure. The dog and the horse traveled together, ate together, and slept together. Every time Bob was fed, his food had to be carried to the stable.

Baldy's schedule was twenty miles a day. One day he went from the Wells to the Bridge; the next day he came back to the Wells. Bob always went along.

It was easy to shoe the horse when his feet got tender, but this dog was something else. He sometimes limped as he ran. A cowboy made Bob laced boots out of soft boot top leather. He thought he had the problem solved. But, the trouble was, Bob could not scratch his fleas efficiently with his boots on. The station operator solved this; he took Bob's shoes off or put them on when he harnessed or unharnessed Baldy.

Sometimes, some joker would ask, "Does the horse belong to the dog, or does the dog belong to the horse?"

The station operator, a wit in his own right, would answer, "Well, I don't know. All I can say about this 'belonging' business is that they 'belong' together."

Then there was 'The Volunteer,' a stage horse who loved the Wells better than any other place on earth. He was willing to travel forty miles a day to get back to a dry barren land with only poor water to drink, all because he preferred it.

The Volunteer made the run in the forenoon from the Wells to Alger's in Nine Mile, arriving there about noon. At about four in the afternoon, the coach from Price, en route to Vernal, arrived at the Nine Mile station.

Frank Alger had the horses staying at his place well trained. He never tied them in their stalls. When it was time to harness them for the mail, he whistled to them and the horses came to him to be harnessed.

The Volunteer was entitled to rest overnight before he went back. He ate and rested until the northbound coach arrived, then at the whistle, he came out to be harnessed. He never came out for the southbound mail. To test him, he was shuttled to other stations along the line. He seemed to know the Wells bound stages and always volunteered for them, but never for one going the other way. The tip-off was that at the Wells he wouldn't report for any coach at all; the hostler had to lead him out to be harnessed.

When the stage line ceased to operate, the Volunteer was left at the old place in the desert he loved so well. He died there, one summer day, in his old age. His bones lie whitening someplace out there in a spot he chose, in a draw where he always longed to be.

The water for human consumption at the station in the draw was brought by the mail coaches. The stage from Price filled a fifteen gallon barrel at the Minnie Maud. The coach from Vernal filled a fifteen gallon barrel at the Duchesne River. This water was delivered to the station for drinking and cooking purposes. All the water for utilities was supplied by the well.

The old Wells Station is gone now. Nothing remains of the buildings except a few tumbled down rock walls where the corrals once stood, a few broken posts, and some tangled wire. The well is there, covered. Still the timbers hold and water could be drawn, if needed, from its musty depths. The automobile and rapid motor transport has made its use unnecessary so it has faded into oblivion and ruin. The draw has not changed. It is there as always and the marks of its past can still be seen as you drive slowly along the road.

In the old days, the run from the Wells to Indian country was all downhill and easy if the weather was good. The stage made good time to the Bridge and it arrived there about noon. The freighters camped one more time for the night before they came to the Duchesne River. There was a greasewood flat on a low bench below a place in the road called 'The Pitch.' This was called 'The Dry Camp.' There was no water, and wouldn't be, short of the Duchesne River.

To prepare for the Dry Camp, freight wagons carried water in barrels, for both horses and men, to be used at this place. It was usual for the freight wagons to have barrels on the outside of the wagon boxes resting on strong platforms built for that purpose in the manner of all wagons crossing dry country since the days of the westward marching pioneers. The barrels were filled either at the Duchesne River or at the Minnie Maud depending on which way the outfit was proceeding.

The Pitch was a steep road up a dugway and then along an ascending ridge, where the road pulled out of the Wells draw, which veers off to the east, leading away from the direct route to Myton. The Pitch wasn't so bad in good weather, with rested horses. But if the road was wet or snowy, outfits had to double to make it to the top. To double meant to take all the horses from two outfits and hitch them on one to make the pull up and out.

At the Dry Camp, in the morning, with rested horses, the freighters tackled the Pitch. If it was necessary, teams were doubled until the last wagon was up, then they continued on their journey.

From the top of the Pitch, the road runs down a ridge and drops into a small hollow, called 'Snake Holler,' named either from the number of rattlesnakes found there, or because it turns in wide regular turns like a snake track in the sand.

At the mouth of the Hollow is 'Pleasant Valley.' Where the name for this came from is, indeed, a mystery, for it is a dry, hot desert valley. In the old days, it had no green except shad scale, greasewood, and rabbit brush. It is said that at the Opening, everybody who filed in Pleasant Valley was a bachelor. There were no women in the whole, wide expanse and this was very pleasant, hence the name, 'Pleasant Valley.' This, no doubt, is a joke. Most of these places were named by the government surveyors who laid them out by quarter sections. Some surveyor, it is supposed, looked out over the valley and in his minds eye, thought how this place would look when the canal, then in the planning, brought irrigation water to make things grow in this valley. What he saw was pleasant, so he put the name Pleasant Valley on his map.

THE WELLS

*The Wells was a welcome oasis between the Duchesne and the Minnie
Maud. This picture as it appeared in the old days, the Butch Cassidy era.
The operator the was I.W. Odekirk, standing on the left.
This photograph was given the author by the late Lawrence Odekirk who
also told too much of the history and legends of this desert oasis.*

Away out in the middle of nowhere is a place where only memories dwell; the rest is wrack and ruin. But once, long ago, it was a
bustling place beside the stream of empire moving west to settle a
new frontier.

In 1886, the Army built Ft. Duchesne on the banks of the Uintah
River and while they were building their post, the soldiers constructed a wagon road to the nearest rails at Price, Utah. This was the road
most travelers used as they rode to the Uintah Basin.

Between the Minnie Maud in Nine Mile Canyon and the
Duchesne River, there was not a drop of water. Nearly fifty miles,

the road wound through the heat and the dust of the desert and the only drink for man and beast was in the barrels the outfits carried. For men on horseback and light rigs, it was not so bad but for the freighters, it was different; too much of the heavy loads had to be barrels of water.

Owen Smith, with an eye for wealth, could see a gold mine in plain water. He measured the distance between the two streams and by Smoky Ledge, he sank his mine. Eighty, ninety, a hundred feet, he dug his hole. But it was still dry and dusty in the bottom.

One day, discouraged and about to give up, Smith rested from his labors. A friend stopped to chat awhile. In the course of the conversation, the friend said,

"Out in Carbon County is a water witch. Why don't you try him? If there is underground water anywhere in this draw, he will find it for you."

One day, two days, five days in all, the diviner worked. Then, as the sun was setting, the wand went down in certain terms and stayed there without a waver. The water witch drove a stake. Then he said to Owen, "Under here is an underground stream. It is deep, near two hundred feet, but if you dig to it, you will have plenty of water. If you do as I say and the water is there, you will owe me five hundred dollars. But if I am wrong, you owe me nothing. Send the money to me at Price."

Owen Smith dug. At one hundred and eighty two feet, the underground stream came gushing. Smith had his liquid gold.

Owen built a station by his well. Besides selling water, he had a store, a feed yard, a blacksmith shop, a small hotel, and a restaurant.

Somehow, the tale got around that Smith never paid the diviner so those plying the road dubbed him "Owing Smith." Now, the tale was a lie, for Owen, in fact, had borrowed the money and paid the man in full. It was the first of his debts he liquidated. When the story finally seeped in to Smith, he took his receipt, framed it under glass and hung it in his place of business. If somebody said, "Owing Smith," he would point to it and say, "I'm Owen Smith all right, but be damned if I'm owing anybody. Now, how would you like me to prove it to you? With this receipt or with fist or gun or with that there singletree?"

Naturally, the story ended, except as a humorous yarn, told around the campfire.

This watering place on the road to Indian country, by common usage, came to be known as "The Wells." It is on of the storied spots of Utah. Its history, as you have guessed by now, has all the flavor of the early western scene. Soldiers, cowboys, outlaws, Indians, homesteaders, the great, the near great and just plain people, all were here, played their brief roles, stepped off the stage and into legend.

Smith's desert station was not only about halfway between the Minnie Maud and the Duchesne, it was also about halfway between Price and Vernal. Since the distance between the two terminals was too far to go in a day, The Wells was the only overnight stop for the stage line carrying mail and passengers over the Nine Mile Road. Both the inbound and the outbound coaches stopped for the night under the big, brown ledge.

Because the stage stopped, so perforce, did its passengers and the list of distinguished men and women who sojourned at this supposedly lonely outpost is endless. Lucy Gates sang one night after supper dishes were cleared away. Tommy Birchell, the cowboy baritone; Charlie Stewart, the whistling sheepherder; Ralph Cloninger, the Salt Lake player, all went through their paces by lamplight for the assembled residents and wayfarers. And it was all for free. Almost every night, there was some sort of entertainment.

Reed Smoot, William Spry, Don B. Colton and other high government officials slumbered in the rock walled rooms adjoining the long dining room.

One day, five heavily armed men rode into The Wells. They

bought water, hay, and grain for their splendid mounts and had supper in the dining room that night. As darkness came, they went across the canyon and spread their bedrolls under an overhanging ledge. Next morning, Jim Hamilton, then the owner and operator of The Wells, called to them in time for breakfast but they were gone.

A curious drummer (salesman) inquired, "Who were those pistol packing cowboys who ate here last night?"

Jim answered, "That was Butch Cassidy, Elza Lay, Harry Longabaugh, Harvey Logan and a kid they call McVey. Those are the ringleaders of the Wild Bunch."

Hamilton, telling about this incident later, said, "I told the truth, but hell, I could see that drummer didn't believe me. Come to think of it, that was the last time I ever saw Butch Cassidy."

Around the point below, came the rattle and jingle of cavalry on the march. Their guidon identified them as Troop "D", Ninth U.S. Cavalry. That night they camped at The Wells. They were moving out after twelve years of service at Ft. Duchesne.

This was the famous "Blackhorse Troop," of the Ninth Cavalry. They were all black men with black accouterments, mounted on coal black horses. 'Show Troops,' the army journalists described them and they were good at their calling. But this was April 1898 and they rode on to fame in the annals of American fighting men. At Kettle Hill, in the battle of San Juan Hill, the Ninth was among those who charged afoot without waiting for orders, up the slopes with the Roughriders, behind Teddy Roosevelt, taking the Spanish fortifications up on top. This, contrary to popular belief, was a waspish, deadly little battle against a sharp-shooting, courageous foe. The 'Show Troops' had proven they were also ready, willing, and able to fight.

With the Blackhorse Troop, on the way to Cuba that day, was a young, black sergeant. Benjamin O. Davis, the grandson of a slave, climbed up the ladder to become the first black general officer in the

United States Army. General Davis died in November, 1970, at the age of ninety-three. He had a long, distinguished career including service on the staff of General Eisenhower in World War II. He will go down in history as a great American.

When the Ute Reservation was opened to white settlement in 1905-06, the Nine Mile Road was lined with outfitters. Men on horseback, families in covered wagons, buckboards, surreys and rigs of every description were on the move to the brand new towns of Uintah Basin. They say, you could stand on a high peak at the head of Gate Canyon and trace the old stage road all the way to Vernal, sixty miles or more, by the dust churned up by hooves and wheels. All or most of these paused at The Wells. Sometimes there were as many as fifty outfits camped for the night on the campground.

The remark was made that at a place like The Wells, the news of the world must have come late. But an old-timer cried, "Not so! Not so! We had a telegraph line and later a telephone and something else besides; The Salt Lake Tribune, caught the fast express that high-balled on the road to Denver. When the sun went down and the stage pulled in, we got the paper on the same day it was dated. During the Spanish American War, it was as much as the stage driver's life was worth, to leave Price without those papers. It was one of the brags of Bracken and Lee, that their stageline had no equal for service. And this was so, the record will show, that the automobiles never equaled it until the roads were paved and they got that new-fangled snow removal equipment."

Well, it's all gone now. The ruined rock walls and the old campground are all that remain of The Wells. The automobile changed everything. But Nine Mile Road still goes almost exactly as it did in the old days. It is not the mainstream, it was in the yesterdays, but to the historian, amateur and professional, this is good, because as he drives the route, the aura of the Old West still lingers. He can feel the past, the fiber and bone of American Heritage.

THE MOFFAT RAILROAD

"You know, Mr. Stewart, when Jim and I first came out here to settle on the Uintah-Ouray Indian Reservation, and we came to rest at last on this place which is our home, we sat in the middle of a sagebrush flat, in a covered wagon. We had seven boys, seven horses and seven dollars. We were eighty miles from the nearest railroad, the odds were eighty to one that we couldn't make it. But Jim kept saying, 'We got to get up and keep going, Maudy. The Moffat Railroad is just around the corner. When it gets here, we must be ready. Then everything will be going our way.'"

So it was with every Tom, Dick and Harry; every Mary, Jane and Molly. In a few months at least, in a year or two at most, they would have a train running almost by their door. So, they waited. But no iron trail with its fire wagon came, then or ever.

You see, in the early days of the settling of Uintah Basin, they had only one road that could be used to get into and out of the Basin in all seasons. The rest were all plugged up with snow from early fall until late spring. The only lifeline the Basin had to the outside was the old, storied Price to Myton road through Nine Mile Canyon. Basinites needed a railroad desperately and so they hung on wishing and dreaming all the while. Somehow they lived—sometimes without sugar for their coffee, if they had the coffee.

But the dreams Basin people had—that most any day now they would hear the choo-choo of a train and the deep-toned whistle of a steam locomotive—were not just idle dreams. Once, twice, three times their dreams almost turned into reality and here it is:

David H. Moffat, the Rocky Mountain railroad tycoon had a consuming obsession. He wanted to bore a tunnel through the Colorado Rockies, the longest tunnel in the world at the time. He wanted to build a railroad between the booming Denver, Colorado and the booming Salt Lake City, Utah. It would be the shortest route between the two cities and also between the east and west coast. The proposed line passed directly through the Uintah Basin.

Moffat went to work, he had to raise a lot of money somewhere. He raised some money in the west but not enough. He raised some money in the midwest, but again, not enough. Then he said to himself, "Why not contact the greatest railroad mogul of them all, Jay Gould of New York City?"

Gould and Moffat met. Facts and figures, too numerous to mention, were covered. Gould, quick to make decisions, said, "We'll go! We will meet you in Denver ten days from today. There we will draw up the papers, sign them, and be on the way."

Moffat walked out of the office stunned but elated.

Moffat and George Gould, Jay's brother, met in Denver. All details were settled. There remained only the signing of the papers. The lawyers said, "It is noon. If you gentlemen care to have lunch, eat, and come back at two o'clock, the papers will be waiting for you."

They left to eat lunch, Gould affable and Moffat beaming. At lunch, Gould received five wires delivered to him in rapid succession. Upon reading the last one, his face fell and with tears in his eyes he said, "Mr. Moffat, I regret to tell you we shall not be able, at this time, to help you build your road on the new route through Utah—just your tunnel." The clock on the wall ticked off one thirty P.M.

It was over. No words of explanation, just commiseration. The mystery remains to this day. What was the cause? Why did Jay Gould pull his money down? No answer, even today.

* * *

Postscript

My Dad and I were coming down Wells Draw with a fast little

team and a buckboard, the fastest means of travel in those days, we thought. Then, around the point below, came one of those roaring, snapping contraptions leaving a trail of dust behind it as long as the tail of one of Nutter's peacocks. By the time we got our horses quieted and back on the road, the "thing" was far up the road and around the next bend. It was one of Henry Ford's new automobiles.

At first, these automobiles were looked upon as a joke, a toy, a play thing meant for damn fools or daredevils. But they were like a baseball hitting you in the eye when you weren't looking; you didn't see it, but in the end, they were the answer to Uintah Basin's need for a rapid transit system.

As times have changed, with fast cars, giant trucks, and good highways, we don't need a railroad anymore. We couldn't or wouldn't use it if we had it. The Uintah Basin is on the move at last.

But to those who lived then, who can forget the good old days when no sugar, no coffee, patches and a good pair of horses were the order of the day.

THE STRIP AND FORT DUCHESNE

THE WHISKEY TENT TREATY

Chief John Duncan taken at the time the
Uintah Ute Indian Reservation Agreement was signed.

In northeastern Utah, clustered in the desert sand, about three miles east of Ft. Duchesne, was the most lawless settlement the annals of the west have ever known.

Shakespeare wrote, "All the world's a stage and all the men and women merely players. They have their entrances and their exits; and one man, in his time, plays many parts."

So be it, but this is not the story primarily of the actors, this is the story of the little town, the stage itself. Behind the footlights walked and played the people of those by-gone days, in a setting so unusual and turbulent, it sounds like fiction. It is, nevertheless, the truth and the characters, real. There are rich men, poor men, beggar men, thieves, doctors, lawyers, Indian chiefs, and yes, a few animals who step onto the stage, play their brief roles and vanish into the wings to be seen no more.

The place lived only a short time. It came and was gone in a quarter of a generation. But while it lived, it was so unique and tumultuous, it has become a legend of the west. "She died with her boots on," is a fitting epitaph for the little settlement on the desert floor, indicating its demise was sudden and complete because it vanished, leaving nothing behind to mark its place but the blowing sands, a black cut in the hills—and the legends.

So intertwined are the affairs of the town with those of the old St. Louis Mine, that the history of one cannot be told without telling the history of the other. Because the whole thing began with gilsonite. The stage was set when white-men became interested in the black ore and wished to make it their own.

On October 3, 1861, Abraham Lincoln proclaimed that the Ute Indian Nation should have a reservation in the eastern part of the Territory of Utah. The Indians were to have as their very own, for as long as water runs and grass grows, all the lands draining from the tops of the mountains into the Uintah and Duchesne Rivers.

Angling through the country from northwest to southeast, is a

Chief Old Tabby of the Uintah Utes.

small, insignificant elevation, called from time immemorial, by local residents 'The Sand Ridge.' This is the eastern boundary of the Indian Reservation because it divides the drainage of the Uintah River from that of the Green River.

About two miles west from The Sand Ridge, running slantwise in the sand rock, lies a vertical, fissure vein of a rare hydro-carbon, a black mineral, of a type found only in the Uintah Basin and nowhere else in the world. No one knows when this hydro-carbon was discovered, nor by whom, but the first man to prove its worth was Samuel Henry Gilson. It is from him that the name for the ore, "Gilsonite," comes.

Gilson made the finest paints, varnishes and lacquers in the world from gilsonite. Besides the painting products, Gilson found that an unmatchable insulation could be made from the mineral. It was impervious to sun, water and eroding chemicals. The pilings of historic "Saltair," a resort on the Great Salt Lake, were treated with Gilson's insulation. As soon as the excellence of Gilson's products became known, the commercial value of the hydro-carbon ore, on the markets of the world, became assured.

Bert Seaboldt, a man from many parts and of many pursuits, was hard on the heels of Gilson in experimenting with the ore from Uintah. When the two men met, they compared notes and pooled their interests. Bert was a man of action, so after the establishment of Ft. Duchesne, he slapped location notices on the Carbon Vein, later known as the St. Louis Mine, and was ready to begin operations. He erected a tent city on the mining property and started to dig ore.

Now, the heavy hand of the government fell. T. A. Byrnes, the Indian agent, rode to Seaboldt's camp and said, "Unless you are taking steps to get the hell off this land by sundown, the troops from Ft. Duchesne will be here in the morning to help you. You are trespassing on Indian land."

Seaboldt took the necessary steps to move by sundown, but just because his activities had been hampered, didn't mean his enthusiasm for gilsonite had been dampened. He checked and re-checked the Surveyor General's office, in an attempt to find an error. He even did some surveying himself, but his efforts were futile. The rich, black vein belonged to the Ute Indians.

R. C. Chambers, a lawyer, expert on mining law, was called in but he could find no legal loophole. Chambers concluded, "If Seaboldt and associates were ever to acquire the carbon claims, they would have to be taken out of the Reservation by act of Congress."

Into the gilsonite picture walked two more men of stature— McIntosh, a Park City mine owner with ample funds and Charles Nagel, later U.S. Secretary of Commerce, a politician of excellence. Both agreed to help Bert Seaboldt and Sam Gilson in their endeavors. Suddenly the wheels of Washington began to turn.

On May 24, 1888, an act of Congress was passed and signed into law. It provided that seven thousand acres of the Ute Reservation, which included land covering the gilsonite mine, would be purchased by the U.S. Government for the then fabulous price of twenty dollars per acre. As surveyed, the purchased tract of land was in the shape of a rough triangle and consisted of nothing but sand, hills, ledges and desert.

The act provided further, that the transfer could not be made unless the Utes ratified the action of Congress by signing a treaty. And this was not to be the usual form of a treaty where Awat Towatch (Big Men) sat around the council ring to smoke, discuss, think and finally put their names on the paper, thereby binding their people. This time, the treaty must be signed by a majority of the adult, enrolled members of the Ute Tribe, living on the Uintah Reservation.

What a time to attempt a treaty with the Utes! In the summer of 1888, the war drums were throbbing in the mountain valleys. Faces of the warriors were smeared with war-paint. There had been pitched battles with Colorado stockmen when the Indians had gone up the White River to hunt in their ancestral hunting grounds, a privilege reserved to them by treaty. Sheepmen and cattlemen had been trespassing on the Reservation; their herds had devoured the grass where Indian pony herds grazed. Prospectors were digging for gold in Rock Creek without permission. Everywhere the Red man looked, the White man was intruding into the last green land the Utes had left on earth. Only the common sense and forbearance of the older heads of the Tribe, prevented a suicidal break in the peace, setting the Reservation ablaze with gunfire.

Despite the adverse conditions, the ratification treaty was to be attempted. But, how could the Indian signatures be obtained? None of the Ute people would receive a cent when they signed the documents; all of the money would go into the tribal account to be paid out later in the form of annuities. Without immediate, tangible reward, how could a majority of the scattered tribe be assembled in the stipulated places at the stipulated times?

Those concerned, sat down together to lay out an acceptable procedure. The Commander of Fort Duchesne, the Indian Agent and Sub-Agents, and Bert Seaboldt were there. The discussion went on for a couple of hours without making much headway.

Harry Clark, a sub-agent, had said little in the meeting. But he had listened and finally he spoke up: "Hell, men! I can bring every Indian on the Reservation to any spot you tell me to if you will turn your heads the other way while I do it."

"How do you intend to do this, Harry?" the agent asked.

"Give them whiskey," was the reply.

The proposal had merit, but to supply liquor to an Indian was against the law. Would it be possible, just this once, to relax the rule? If responsible government officials, acting in their official capacity, were to supply and dispense the liquor, would this be a breach of the law?

Lawyer Chambers went over the directives and other documents. His opinion was no law would be broken if the liquor were distributed officially.

The commander said, "I can use all my troops to patrol the area and keep the peace. But I can't justify funds to purchase liquor for Indians."

Seaboldt volunteered, "I'll donate all the whiskey you need."

The die was cast. Two days in September, 1888, were set for the treaty signing. The mine property was designated as the place. The Agent insisted that the Indians see what they were selling, so the treaty ground was to span the Carbon Vein.

Hank Stewart, Newt Stewart and other Indian-speaking white men, plus ten or more mixed bloods, all on Seaboldt's payroll, rode over the reservation, talking the treaty up to the Utes. Besides these people, there were the Indian Police and other agency employees who urged the people to be present for the ratification.

One day, an old gray, bent Indian woman came to see the Ute land the white men wanted to buy. Seaboldt met her, with Hank Stewart as interpreter. She wanted to look over the triangle that, by this time, had been marked out with tall stakes.

"Do you see the stakes?" she was asked.

"Yes, I see the stakes and many other things," she replied. "Once my people owned all this mountain country. From the village you call Denver in the east to the big lake of salt in the west, from the buffalo plains of the north to the land of the Navajo and Apache in the south was ours. It took many days to ride across our country. You could not see across it, even from the highest mountain.

"But, today, I stand on this little hill and I can see all the land we Utes have left. You white men have taken all the rest. Even so, you come to me and you ask, 'Will you give me some more of what you have left?' I look and I see that what you want is worthless. Ponies cannot live here. This ground will not grow corn or squash or melons. Only the prairie dogs and rabbits use it and they can move someplace else. I will tell my people to sell it to you because $20 an acre is too much for it. But, I will never agree to sell you any more at any price." The old woman turned and rode away into the dusk.

Seaboldt remarked, after the old woman had gone, "I don't know why we wasted our time on that old squaw, she can't do much to help or hinder us."

"Don't judge the Utes by other Indians you have known or read about," Stewart replied. "Among these people, wise women often speak big words and her people listen. That is Ta-tatch (Bishop) Sowiette's (slim belly) widow. I would say that old woman just agreed to deliver to you the votes of the whole Uintah Band. And she can do it too."

Three days before the big meeting day, Harry Clark had two big tents pitched in the sand beside the gilsonite vein. All the proselyting was over, all the promises made. All that remained to be done was wait.

The waiting at the treaty ground was not in vain, for the dust began to rise on all the trails and roads leading toward Ft. Duchesne. The Indians were coming.

Like hordes of Ghengis Kahn, they came—men, women, children, horses, and dogs—to set up camp by the big tents in the desert. The big tents, later became famous as Oopaw Kahn (Whiskey Tents), because it was here, for the only time in the Indian's memory, that he could drink firewater in the presence of God, man, and the devil, without being hauled off to the guardhouse to answer for his sin.

At last, it was the dawn of the first, 'Treaty Day.' The big tents were entirely surrounded by the camps of the Indians.

Hank Stewart said about that encampment, "At sunup, I rode to the top of that high hill yonder. I sat there looking down on the big Ute Indian camp. I was looking at more Indians in one place than I had ever seen in my life before. I knew I would never see anything like it again. This big camp was pandemonium: axes ringing, children yelling and crying, men and women shouting over the barking and yipping of hundreds of dogs. Moving here and there among the tents and teepees were Indians in their bright colored clothes and blankets. It was going to be a big day and they were dressing for it. I thought to myself as I watched, if there is any trouble here today, all the soldiers in Ft. Duchesne won't be enough to take care of it."

The great chiefs, Tabby (Child of the Sun) and the young John Duncan, with Ta-tatch by their sides, beat the drum and assembled their people to them. John Duncan spoke for the three of them.

"Today, we sell all the land inside the stakes you can see, driven in ground. It is no good. We would have given it to the whites if they had asked for it. But they are willing to buy it for enough money to keep our people for many moons; we will sell it. They want the black stuff, too. They know how to use it. Let them have it! Besides the money, they will give us whiskey. I am surprised. The white man has always said it sends us crazy. But, today, he says we can have it. Drink it if you like it. And get drunk too, if you want to. But don't make any trouble. The bluecoats will be here from Ft. Duchesne to keep order. We don't need them. If any of you cause trouble, you will answer to your chief or to the council. This is a big day and a big gathering. We hope you all have a good time. But keep in mind what we say: No trouble. We have spoken."

At 7 a.m., Harry Clark and his clerks arrived from Ft. Duchesne with the instruments to be signed. Following them, came a wagon with kegs of whiskey loaded in the back. Behind the wagons came two troops of the famous old 9th U.S. Cavalry. The promise to the Indians would be kept; there would be whiskey for them at the tents and soldiers to police the area if anyone got out of hand.

The final preparations were made, the heads of whiskey barrels were knocked out and tin cups, holding at least a pint, with hooks for handles, were hung around the rim of the barrels.

The tent flaps were thrown open and the people streamed in. As each Ute approached the signing table, he was told, "Put your name or thumbprint right here. Then get yourself a cup of whiskey."

They came in at one end of the tent and moved out the other. The signing went rapidly.

Just before noon, Ta-tatch came. She thumb-printed the treaty, took a small sip of whiskey, mounted her white horse and rode toward her home at Whiterocks. This was the last autumn for her because, during the winter, she passed on to join Sowiette in the Happy Hunting Ground.

Both Tabby and John Duncan came, signed, got their whiskey and went out.

By evening, the signing was almost done. Harry Clark counted the signatures and said to the Commander and Seaboldt, "According to our reckoning, we already have more than enough signers to make the treaty good. Do you want to fold your tents like the Arabs and silently steal away?"

Seaboldt responded quickly, "No, Stewart says some of the people won't get here until tomorrow. I'd hate to disappoint them. We'll stay open one more day, as we promised. Oh, by the way, don't be too stingy with that whiskey, we've got plenty."

All through the night, both cavalry and infantry guarded the whiskey tents and the camp area. The report shows that after ten o'clock, the camp was as quiet as a tomb. Only the dogs moved about or made any noise. The promise by John Duncan, that tribal retribution would catch up to wrongdoers, evidently had the desired effect.

By noon of the second Treaty Day, the signing was done. But Bert Seaboldt never withdrew his whiskey. He said, "Stay open until dark. Let them finish it; there isn't too much left anyway."

And finish it they did. The night of the last Treaty Day was quite a party. Even so, there were no adverse incidents requiring either tribal or official discipline. Hank Stewart said, "With all those people and all that whiskey, I'd have bet there was hell to pay. You can't get as big a bunch as that together, either white, black, or red, give them that much whiskey and get away with it. There had to be some trouble somewhere. But there wasn't. We got away with it; I can't figure it out."

The big encampment came to an end as the last of the Utes took the road home. It was all over, but it has lived on as a legend of the Big U Country's history.

And gilsonite, the cause of all the commotion? No sooner had the treaty been ratified than Gilson and Seaboldt put location notices on the carbon vein and opened the first gilsonite mine in the world. The mine ran until 1904 and closed; its rich, black ore 'held in reserve,' by the company that owns it for some future operation.

The mine, too, has become a legend of Uintah. There is nothing left of the old diggings but a deep black cut in the ground and ledges, the blowing sand, and the memories.

THE STRIP

This is a picture of The Strip, later known as Moffatt.

Now, a situation arose, so bizarre and incredible, it seems to be a figment of the imagination. Title to the triangular piece of land had been conveyed by the Utes to the U.S. Government. It could not be a part of the public domain as it was within the confines of an Indian reservation, yet the Indian Service had no jurisdiction over it. The military had no power of enforcement because it was not a part of the military reserve, nor was it on an Indian reservation. Since it was federal land in fee, the territory of Utah and Uintah County had no police power there. The U.S. Marshall had jurisdiction if a federal law was broken, but there were no federal laws covering the common varieties of crime. The triangle, off the mine property was literally lawless. It was a place unique in history. Nothing like it has ever been known before or since.

Astute men, understanding the legal implications, started a settlement on the excluded land but off the mine property. It was built along both sides of the main wagon road that wound the crooked, dusty miles between Price and Vernal, Utah. The town was never plotted nor was it formally named. By common usage, it came to be known as 'The Strip.' It was small, having only two saloons, a general merchandise store, a telegraph office, a barber shop, a restaurant, a livery stable and stage station, a hotel, a dance hall, and a few other establishments run by shady ladies. Liquor flowed freely and gambling was the rule of the hour, day and night. The sky was the limit. There were few permanent residents, but since the place was where the action was, it never lacked patronage and visitors. The result of all these things taken together, spawned a town as wild or wilder than Tombstone or Deadwood. Certainly, considering its size, no place in the west ever matched The Strip. As towns go, it was simply and actually, an outlaw. The life-blood of the little settlement came from the mine, travelers, stockmen and the soldiers of Ft. Duchesne.

The Strip was a gathering place for people of every ilk. Outlaws, Indians, gamblers, cowboys, sheepherders, freighters, miners, and travelers stopped there for business or pleasure. Butch Cassidy, Elza Lay, Harry Longabaugh, Dave Lant, Matt Warner and many other riders from the 'Wild Bunch,' sojourned at the Strip. Here, the outlaws could visit, drink, and play with impunity because they were immune from arrest. It was only coming and going that they had to keep their eyes peeled.

The old-timers say, you got only what you wanted at the Strip. You could have trouble, a drunk, a woman, a game of chance, or all of them together. On the other hand, if all you wanted was a meal and a bed, you could have that too, without hindrance or molestation. Nevertheless, the stories told about the place rival the histories of many more famous places in the annals of the old west. There were outlaws who came but bothered no one. Gun battles were fought in the streets. Poker games were played for high stakes. This town by the ledges was as wild as the old west was ever reputed to have been.

Dakota, Badger, and Sergeant

The yarns about The Strip are not all about outlaws, gunfighters, and mysteries. Some deal with other characters fully as interesting, if not quite so bloody. Such was the threesome: Dakota the man, Badger the dog, and Sergeant the ex-army mule.

Dakota, the man, had a down east, cultured accent and when in his ups, which wasn't often, he recited Shakespeare, like a Junius Brutus Booth. He was suspected of having been an actor or a professor of the arts, but no one ever found out; for, at that time and place, it was impolite and downright dangerous to attempt to delve into a man's antecedents. He called himself "Dakota," and that's all anybody knew about him.

Badger, the dog, was half wolf-hound and half bull-dog, a sort of monstrosity in the canine world. Hen Lee, the saloonkeeper used to feed Badger plenty of raw meat to keep him in fighting trim. The dog fought anything, tame or wild, for a living.

But Badger's biggest act was to pull live badgers from a partly sunken barrel in the back yard of the saloon, and kill them. At these badger fights, the crowd gathered, whiskey flowed and money was bet with a lavish hand on the outcome of the battle.

One day, Badger had fought and killed a particularly fierce, big, male badger, but he had paid a price. He was bitten, slashed, clawed, wounded and bleeding. He half crawled, half walked to the shade of the saloon. There he lay alone, to bleed, to lick his wounds, and to recover if he could.

Dakota had been there throughout the whole contest, and had neither bet nor said a word during all the gory event. But now he borrowed a wheelbarrow, loaded the dog into it and trundled him home to his boarded up tent. Dakota doctored the dog with skill. In due time Badger was around with Dakota, scarred but as chipper and spry as ever.

Hen Lee watched the dog and one day decided to reclaim his

property. He went to Dakota's tent, knocked on the door and received the usual invitation to "come in." Lee, a tough, hard man himself, said later, "When I opened that door and walked in, I was looking straight down the barrel of a cocked thirty-thirty and into the face of a snarling, mean-looking dog. I saw the situation quick. I turned right around, walked out the door and nary a word was spoken. After I got out I hollered back, "Dakota, you just got yourself a damn ugly dog."

Sergeant was a condemned army mule, and as was the custom with the army, condemned animals were sold at public auction to the highest bidder. It was easy for prospective, civilian buyers to find out from the soldiers what was wrong with the animals the army offered for sale.

Such was the case with Sergeant. Civilians were told the mule had become absolutely intractable, in fact, he was dangerous to handle.

If an animal was condemned, offered for sale, and there were no bidders, then the critter was led off behind a hill and shot. Now, the shooting very seldom happened, but in the case of Sergeant, this was almost sure to be his fate.

On the day of the sale, Dakota and Badger showed up at the auction bright and early. Each sort of dozed the time away, until finally Sergeant was led out, eyes glowing, nostrils flaring, breathing defiance to the whole world. When bids were called for, Dakota called out, "Fifty cents." It was the first and only bid for Sergeant. Dakota and Badger bought Sergeant for the price of 'four bits,' and went leading him home. The surprise was that, in the association of his new partners, Sergeant became the best, most peaceful mule anybody ever had. When asked how this had come about, Dakota replied, "Why, he never was a bad mule. All he ever wanted was his discharge. You see, his enlistment was up several years ago."

Dakota, Badger, and Sergeant, made a living as "Predator

Control Specialists." It seemed they very seldom killed the predator, they merely ran them off and they never came back. In those days the state didn't pay the cost of predator control, the stockmen paid for this themselves. Each occasion depended upon a bargain agreed upon between the parties. When Dakota came to terms, he invariably said to the stockman, "I'll tell you if we can take the job as soon as I have talked the deal over with my partners," meaning, of course, Badger and Sergeant.

One morning, Dakota pulled his tent down. He, Badger, and Sergeant disappeared into the morning mists. They were never seen at the Strip again.

Baco

Baco, a Ute Indian boy, who frequented the Strip, went to the Indian University at Carlisle, Pennsylvania. He graduated, excelling in dramatics. Under the name of Baco White, he became a famous actor on the legitimate stage before the days of the motion pictures. His acting roles in 'The Squawman,' an old, famous play, skyrocketed him to fame and fortune.

Baco White, played in all the great cities of the east and then his company went overseas to London. For six months, Baco performed on the English stage, which included a command performance before the King of England.

Strangely enough, 'The Squawman' was set in Ute Indian country, Baco's home. It is no wonder that Baco could add realism to his role as one of the villains of the play. He had known the country and its people since childhood.

But, in the end, Baco came back to the Ute Reservation to die, struck down by the Great White Plague, consumption. He lies buried near the Strip, under the ledges above his home, beside the bones of his father, Little Joe. This was the place he chose as his final resting place. Buried with him is his small "medicine bag," he carried in all his wanderings. Around his neck is his beautiful bear claw necklace, an emblem of a warrior of the Utes. Despite Baco's education and his success in the white man's world, he never forgot or forsook the ways of the Indian. He rides now in the Happy Hunting Ground of his people.

Bob Ricker

Bob Ricker was from Kansas and while there he had learned the holds and bars of the professional wrestler. He came west and wound up in Southern Utah rustling cattle and stealing horses. He never became as famous as the McCarty's, Cassidy, Logan and the rest, but in his latest occupation, he rode with some the famous 'Wild Bunch' and was accepted by them.

The time came when he slipped and the law began looking for him with a pair of handcuffs. He decided to change pastures so he took the 'Owl Hoot Trail' over the Bookcliffs heading for Brown's Hole. On his way he stopped at the Strip.

Tom Nichols, the saloonkeeper, gave him a job behind the bar as a bouncer. Ricker wasn't very big but he knew holds that subdued a quarrelsome cowboy in short order. He was doing all right, but he wanted to do better. He cooked up a scheme to sell whiskey to the Indians.

As has been said before, selling liquor to Indians was taboo, even in the outlaw town, because it violated federal law. Therefore, the Indian Service and the Army had the right to enforce the Anti Indian Liquor Law.

In spite of the warnings of older hands, Ricker went forward with his scheme. At nighttime, he stashed whiskey in various hiding places: in hollow logs, in cracks in ledges, under rocks and in grain sacks. When an Indian wanted to buy he would contact Bob. Bob would say, "Give me ten dollars and maybe I can tell you where a pint of whiskey is." The Indian paid his money and was told where to find his bottle. Never, at anytime, did anyone ever see Ricker make the delivery. He was getting plenty of trades and his business boomed.

The commander at the post had a simple way of forcing information from an Indian. He had him picked up and jailed in the guardhouse while he was still drunk. When the Indian sobered up he was told, "When you tell us from whom you got your bottle, we will let you go free, but until you do, you will stay right here in your cell."

The Indians stuck it out for several days, always long enough for the seller to get out of the country, then he told all he knew.

One of Ricker's Indian customers got caught in this kind of bind. He held out for five or six days, but Ricker didn't run. He stayed, thinking the delivery couldn't be proved. A squad picked him up and there he was, in the guardhouse at Ft. Duchesne. As he laid there he thought, "My trial will be in the Federal Court in Salt Lake. I am wanted down south for rustling, everybody is bound to know where I am, so I gotta get out of here."

The guard brought Bob's supper every evening after dark. Bob was lying on the bunk with his shoes off, apparently asleep. He looked small and harmless, so the guard opened the cell door and stepped inside. What happened next was so fast the soldier never knew what struck him. He was down and out on the guardhouse floor almost instantly. Bob lost no time, he took for the open in his bare feet. Somehow, with the soldiers beating the brush and riding all the roads and trails, the escapee made it back to Tom Nichols' saloon.

Tom knew that his place was no haven for the boot-legger, so he gave him a pair of boots and sent him on to Tom Taylor, the foreman at the St. Louis Mine.

Ricker was well liked by all the men on and off the Strip, and Taylor decided to help him. He went to the bunkhouse and called for

George Stewart, a young shift boss at the mine. "George," Taylor said, "get a blanket and hide Bob in a good place down in the mine. The soldiers are looking for him and they'll be around here in a minute."

Stewart led Bob down the ladder and hid him somewhere in the mine's black maw.

Sure enough, the troops from the fort rousted the whole Strip and came to the mine and rousted it too. But, Bob was safe wherever he was hidden because no one found him.

One night, after the hue and cry had died down, Ricker's horses, Mack and Cosby, were led to the mine shaft. Ricker came out, mounted and rode away. He made it to Brown's Hole and then to Baggs, Wyoming.

Ricker was "raising hell" around town and was killed by a shot gun blast as he tried to break into a saloon after closing time. He lies buried somewhere in the Baggs Boot Hill.

The Dutchman

One blustery day in early spring a stranger rode into the Strip. He asked where he could find Butch Cassidy, but of course, the code of the west prevailed and he got no answer. He took a room at the local hotel and lingered day after day, talking little but listening much. He spoke English well, they said, but he had an accent which betrayed his Teutonic origin and so, as time went by, and since they had no other name for the man, they coined one for him. He became known as the 'Dutchman.'

Every morning he groomed his horse to perfection and rode out along the roads to exercise his mount and in the process to train him. He sat in his saddle in a manner strange to western horsemen, but it was plain he was no novice, for what he could do with a horse was beyond believing. His back, as he rode, was ramrod straight but there was grace in all his movements. Time after time, for the benefit of onlookers, he put on a show, putting his stallion through its paces. It performed all sorts of maneuvers for him apparently without guidance from spur, rein, or hand. It was admitted that for showy horsemanship, none at the Strip had ever seen his equal. The curious would ask how he trained a horse so well. He would willingly reply, "I use no spur, no whip. You see a horse moves away from the leg but he moves to the hand and this you must always remember."

The foreigner had a way of walking, a way of standing, and a way of talking that betrayed him as a military man of spit and polish. Somehow, as he wore it, the plain western garb making up his habit, turned into a uniform of silver buttons and golden braid. His manners were impeccably courteous to those about him but unbidden familiarity was extremely distasteful to him.

Nor was it only on horseback and in the saloons that the stranger's quality showed to such perfection. One night he went to a dance in the dance hall and his manners toward the women were charming. His conversation was witty and in perfect taste. His bow was beyond description, but it certainly gave pleasure. He made even the dance hall ladies feel like ladies. The reels, quadrilles and polkas did not entice him, but when the small orchestra broke into one of the famous Strauss waltzes, he picked the best female dancer in the hall and went whirling away with the beautiful Viennese waltz. In a minute most were on the sidelines watching.

It became apparent though as time went by, that all was not a bed of roses for the Dutchman; he was on guard against someone. Each day the stage pulled in, he scrutinized from a window each passenger that alighted. He noticed every rider coming into town along the road. He had come to this little lawless town to hide, but even here, he did not feel safe.

There was plenty of speculation about the foreigner. Was he afraid of the law? Was someone he feared on his back trail? What was the story behind this man? It was Elza Lay who, many years later, finally cleared up the mystery.

One day, Elza Lay came to town and as he visited here and there, he made no effort to conceal who he was. During the course of Elza's call, the Dutchman approached the outlaw and there was a subdued conversation. When Lay rode out in the morning, the Dutchman rode with him. Thus it was that the charming man from over the sea became a rider of the Wild Bunch. In spite of the fact that the Dutchman rode with the outlaws, there is no record that he ever took part in any robbery. If there was ever a charge against him, it could only have been for aiding and abetting.

After many years had gone by and Elza Lay's outlaw days were over, in the 1920's when the early days of Butch were but a memory and the Wild Bunch had become a legend, only then, did Lay break his silence and clear up the mystery of the Dutchman. Like all the stories of the Strip, the denouement is incredible, but the record shows that it is true. Lay said:

"I never knew who the Dutchman really was, that is, I never knew his real name. We just called him Karl or Dutch and let it go at that. He rode around with us for about two years and we liked him because he was a very decent fellow. You know how it is when you are off for months at a time in some forsaken hole hiding out. There isn't much to do but shoot, play cards, ride horses, and tell yarns. Well, at such times this Austrian nobleman, because that is what he was, used to tell us of the life he had back home in Austria. He described the gay parties and balls held in the Emperor's Palace in Vienna. He told us of the princes, the princesses, the Grand Dukes, the Dukes, the Barons and the other noblemen of the empire. He said he had spent a winter in Russia as an emissary's aide to the court of the Czar in St. Petersburg. He described the Winter Palace and 'The Seasons,' in St. Petersburg, how the balls and parties went on every night throughout the whole winter and he described the gay glitter of the dances, the operas, and the ballets. He said, 'In Russia, you slept all day and played all night.' He described the yearly event, in

Vienna, of the Prater Drive, how everybody who was anybody turned out for the two mile long drive down the Hauptallee. The carriages and harnesses were painted and polished until they sparkled in the sun like diamonds. The horses, he said, were curried and groomed to perfection and he believed they were the most beautiful horses in the whole world.

"He told us about his majesty, the emperor Franz Joseph and his empress Elizabeth. Franz Joseph, he said, worked so hard that he never had time to spend time with his family and so they were erratic. The Crown Prince was named Rudolph and he was just a little wild and hard to handle. Rudolph had many affairs with ladies in and out of court circles. But when he met and fell in love with the Baroness Marie Vitsera, it was all over. He insisted he should marry this young girl. Of course, Franz Joseph wouldn't listen—marriages of princes and princesses were made for the benefit of the empire. A marriage of the prince to a commoner such as Marie could not be.

"The Dutchman, as you know, was assigned as a companion to Prince Rudolph. He was a companion in name, but in reality he and several others were bodyguards to the Prince. Considering the Prince's behavior, this duty came to be more in the nature of a nursemaid than anything else.

"Well, Rudolph never wanted to be emperor when it came his turn and when he found out he had to be and that he couldn't marry the Baroness Marie, he lost his head in a sea of despondency.

"'One night,' the Dutchman said, 'a servant of one of the Prince's companions came riding hard to my home. He delivered into my hands a hastily written note. It said Prince Rudolph and the Baroness Vitsera had committed suicide. My life was now forfeit if the Emperor's police found me. I must flee to save my life. I lost no time. I ordered my best horse saddled and brought to my door. I got all the money and easily carried valuables the house contained, then I mounted and rode away fast into the night. I made it out of Austria and to comparative safety.'"

"The Austrian told me," Lay said, "that the Emperor had a long arm, long enough to reach him even in America. "He will do this even if the true story of the Prince's death is out, because now he will want revenge against those he feels had failed him and the empire. I'll never dare to go home until the old Emperor is dead."

The last time Elza saw the Dutchman, he had a small layout in Price River Canyon below Castlegate. He supposed that in time the hue and cry over Prince Rudolph's death died down and the Austrian went home.

But Lay said, this stranger who rode into the Strip that day long ago, was a rider of the world renowned stallions of Vienna, the finest show horses in the world. Horses were his big love, he spent hours with them. It was from the supervisor of these stallions that he had learned the expert of expert ways to handle horses. It was this Austrian who had taught the big, brown horse that Lay had ridden at the Castlegate payroll robbery. The characteristics of Long Brown, after the Austrian was finished with him, will be covered in a later chapter.

At the Strip, a rider approached one time, who did not ride in the western fashion. He posted as he came and when the Dutchman saw him he recognized the European military style. Immediately the Austrian was on his guard, armed and waiting. The stranger alighted and went into one of the saloons, the Dutchman followed. Listening quietly, he recognized the clipped English accent and seemed to relax. In the course of the day, the two men met. Each recognized the other for what he was, a member of Europe's aristocracy, two men of the same ilk, one from Austria, the other from England. For a couple of days they were fast friends. The stranger who rode in that day was Lord Robert Scott Elliott, a member once of that famous dragoon outfit, made famous by the charge of the Light Brigade at Balaklava, although he was too young to have taken part in that encounter. Lord Elliot apparently had a hidden past too. He was one of those men roaming the States as remittance men.

The Bandit Horse of Uintah

At the Strip, John Caldwell ran a livery stable and tended to the relays for the stage line. His natural bent was horses, any kind of horses, but preferably race horses. John acquired a long lanky brown colt from the Whitmore Brothers of Price, Utah. As the lean colt grew, Caldwell trained him patiently day by day. He found the horse was not so fast for a short distance—a quarter or half mile—but if the race went for a mile and a half or better, the tall brown was practically unbeatable. Time after time, in special matched races for long distances, the Caldwell horse proved his mettle and not once was he ever beaten. The racer became famous in Uintah. He was called "Long Brown," and wherever he ran, the people from the Strip and Ft. Duchesne backed him to their last nickel.

One morning in the fall of 1896, Caldwell, as usual, went down to the corral to care for the stock. The gate was closed and fastened, all the other animals were there, but Long Brown was gone. Someone had stolen him during the night. Caldwell was not an even tempered man and so his indignation flared into a mighty rage. He armed himself to the teeth and went in search of his race horse and the thief who had stolen him. But the hunt was to no avail. Long Brown had vanished into the blue. Somehow the whole episode had the stench of that master wide-looper, Joe Walker, rider of the Wild Bunch.

There always had been a tacit agreement between those living on the Strip and the members of the Wild Bunch that no one on the Strip would ever be molested by the outlaws and in return, no man on the Strip would ever inform the law as to the comings and goings of the outlaws. Only two or three times was this understanding violated by either side and this happened only in an emergency. So, if Long Brown was taken by any member of the Wild Bunch, it would have been only for a very special purpose. The facts would soon come out, everybody thought, but the mystery of the disappearing horse deepened as the months went by and no trace or rumor of him surfaced. It was much later that the probable answer came.

At Castlegate, Utah, the Pleasant Valley Coal Company, paid its miners twice a month in cash. The sum was large, danger of loss was not overlooked so paydays came at irregular intervals announced by the paymaster after he had the money in his hands. On payday, the proper sum was sent on the train from Salt Lake City, arriving at the destination about noon to be paid out that same day. Butch Cassidy and Elza Lay, had known about the payroll for a long time and had discussed the possibilities of stealing it, but it was not until the summer of 1896, that they decided to pull the job. Because of the circumstances surrounding payday at Castlegate, a successful holdup would take careful planning. First, it had to be done in broad daylight. Second, the money had to be taken from the midst of a crowd. And last, the escape must be made down the narrow chute of Price River Canyon. After they had decided on the holdup, Cassidy and Lay began laying plans for the robbery down to the smallest detail.

Since Castlegate was situated in a deep canyon, the only route for the getaway had to be along the main road either up or down the canyon. The bandits knew the best way to go was down the road because this pointed them towards Robber's Roost, their safest sanctuary and the distance to the first break in the mountain wall was shortest that way. It was three or four miles from the holdup site to the first opportunity to leave the narrow defile. Those three or four miles were crucial. If there was pursuit from behind and if a posse from Price arrived in time from down below, the brigands would be bottled up between the two forces and there was no escape up the rough ledgy mountains. The first lap of the getaway route had to be covered quickly if success were to attend their efforts. Therefore, the horses, to cover that distance should be the very best obtainable. They must be swift and they must have endurance. They searched carefully for horses to meet their requirements. Cassidy found a little

catlike, sorrel mare for his mount and Lay picked a big, brown geld-
ing to make the run down the canyon to their first remounts.

Tom, Billy and Fred McCarthy had held up the bank at Delta,
Colorado. Billy and Fred went in while Tom held the horses outside.
The holdup was successful. The robbers came out of the bank loaded
with money. All went well until the outlaws mounted their horses
and tried to ride out of town. At this point, W. Ray Simpson, an
expert rifleman, shot Fred and Billy out of their saddles, only Tom
got away. The trouble was, Billy and Fred had all the swag and even
though Tom was free, he had nothing to show for all his work and
grief. But suppose the horses had been trained to run on without
their riders? If the boodle had been tied to the saddles, Tom at least,
would have had the loot his gang had so dearly paid for.

With the McCarthy disaster in mind, Butch and Lay, with Karl,
the Austrian horse trainer to help them, converted the big, brown
charger into a bandit horse. When they were through with him, he
would make off with the dough regardless of what happened to his
rider. As things turned out, the outlaws didn't need the special quali-
ties they had spent all winter drilling into the big horse, but they
were there if things had come off differently.

When spring broke in 1897, the outlaws rode north to case the
job and finally make their play. The Austrian, under the name of
Karl Heibauer, leased a small layout at the north of Spring Canyon.
From this place as headquarters, Lay and Cassidy, rode to Castlegate
everyday. They checked and re-checked all pertinent aspects of their
proposed operation and while doing it got everybody used to their
hanging around.

The next payday came on April 21, 1897, and the money to meet
it was sent down from Salt Lake City, as usual, on the express car.
The train carrying the payload was due to arrive in Castlegate right
on the dot of 12:40 P.M.

Cassidy and Lay knew the schedule of every express train on the line. And long before this train arrived that day, the two rode up to the front of the store, over which the company maintained its offices. They were ready and waiting but, from their manner, it would have been hard to guess that they were about to commit one of the most daring stick-ups in the annals of the west.

The train began to whistle from up the canyon, signaling its approach. But still there was no indication from the two holdup men that they had anything unusual in mind. Butch sat on an empty box slowly puffing a cigarette and Lay stood leaning lazily against the wall. Like everyone there, they were watching the train pull in slowly and stop at the depot.

E. S. Carpenter, the company paymaster and two other employees, Phelps and Lewis, came down the outside stairs from the offices above and walked rapidly to the depot some seventy yards away. Knowing the difficulty of an escape from this fastness, Carpenter had dismissed the possibility of a robbery at Castlegate. If there was ever to be a theft, he thought, it would be farther up the mountain before the train dropped into the canyon. Anyway, there was nothing this day to arouse his suspicions as he walked down to get the gold and silver.

In a few minutes, Carpenter and his companions, got a brown valise and two white canvas bags from the express office and started back toward the store.

This was the outlaw's cue. Elza Lay, seemingly in no hurry, untied the horses and casually mounted the big, brown horse, holding the reins of the little mare in his hands. Butch Cassidy still sat on his box, twirling the rowel of one spur with his fingers. Nipper, Elza's little black dog, aroused at Elza's movements, got up from where he had been napping, stretched, sat down and looked inquiringly up into Lay's face. Everything looked peaceable.

Carpenter and Phelps came to the foot of the stairs and started to climb. Cassidy, quick as light, stepped up behind them, shoving a gun in Carpenter's ribs and said, "Hold on men, I'll take those bags."

Carpenter dropped the valise to the steps. Phelps started to turn in protest, Butch struck him over the head with his gun barrel, knocking him cold.

Lewis, behind Carpenter, Phelps and Butch, knew this was a holdup. He thought he had a chance to do something about it, but as he started to step forward, he heard the sound of a pistol being cocked behind him. He looked over his shoulder straight into the muzzle of Elza Lay's gun. He dove for the door of the store.

Butch handed the valise and one bag up to Lay, then he picked up the bag Lewis had dropped, and stepped toward his horse. The little mare, sensing a crisis, was frightened and began acting up. She kept shying away so Butch couldn't mount her. Finally, 'The Big Brown,' calm and cool, crowded the mare into the wall and Butch, taking the reins, mounted in one swift jump.

It was all over in seconds. The desperadoes, with the money, were off in a swirl of dust before bystanders knew there had been a robbery. There was no awareness of anything wrong until Carpenter shouted, "Robbers! Robbers! Stop those men—they have just robbed me."

The outlaws were away, out of the crowd, but the mare was hard to handle. Butch, in his efforts to control her, dropped his bag of coins, holding only silver. All the gold was with Elza Lay on the Big Brown.

Back in Castlegate, Carpenter, ran for the telegraph office, but, when he got there the line was dead. Joe Walker, at exactly the right moment, had cut the wires somewhere between Castlegate and Price.

Carpenter wasn't beat yet, he had the locomotive uncoupled from the cars and with two riflemen on the platform, the engine went driving and whistling down the track toward Price.

The outlaws heard the whistle screaming behind them. They

knew pursuit was coming in the form of a fast passenger engine. The celebrated luck of Butch Cassidy did not desert him. Before the locomotive came around the bend in sight, the horsemen reached a line shack by the side of the road. They stopped behind it while Carpenter and his cohorts went rolling by. At the shack, all the money was put into a seamless sack and tied on to Old Brown.

Things had quieted now and so the two horses ran side by side down the canyon. The little black dog, striving mightily, brought up the rear, losing ground steadily. They reached the first re-mounts at the north of Spring Creek, covering the ground in record time and here the Austrian had fresh horses all saddled and bridled. The gold was transferred from the brown horse to a big gray, then they rode up Spring Creek and on the road to Robber's Roost. Butch shouted back, "Take good care of those two horses, Dutch, we have to return them to their owners."

The Austrian waved his hand in assent.

The small, black dog, arrived in time to accompany his boss on the long trail to safety.

Down below Price, Joe Walker, met Butch and Lay. The booty was taken by Walker who rode for his cabin up Green River at the mouth of Chandler Canyon. Cassidy and Lay rode on to decoy the pursuit toward Robber's Roost. It was their belief, that even if they were apprehended by a posse now, it would still be hard to convict them of the holdup if they were caught without the loot. It was at this time the discussion occurred about the dog. Butch opined that maybe they should kill Nipper and hide the carcass because he was a dead giveaway.

Elza said, "Ah, come on Butch, the dog won't make any difference, not with your ugly mug to identify."

Butch replied, "Yeah, I guess you're right, but if that little feller goes much farther, we better give him a drink. He must be nearly choked to death."

Lay dismounted, dished in the top of his hat, poured it full of water from a water bag. The dog lapped it up. When Lay re-mounted he had the dog under his arm and remarked, "This little guy can do with a rest. I guess I'll let him ride for a ways."

When Carpenter reached Price, the sheriff of Carbon County was informed of the theft of the payroll and the news went out to neighboring towns over the wires. But all the places were the same; there was too much time-consuming organizing before posse-men got on the way. The robbers were never intercepted, although everybody knew they were heading for Robber's Roost.

Cassidy, Lay and the dog, after picking up more fresh horses at Peterson's Spring, rode onto the San Rafael about seven P.M. that night. They were safe from further pursuit.

Walker, without any difficulties, made it to his cabin at Chandler Canyon. When the hue and cry died down, he leisurely rode to the Roost with the payroll money. It was divided there among those entitled to a split.

Until Castlegate, Butch Cassidy and his Wild Bunch were practically unknown. But this robbery was so bold, so spectacular, that the men who performed it immediately sprang into national prominence. Butch Cassidy, with Elza Lay beside him, and those who rode with them, became the most notorious outlaw band of their day. They were famous almost overnight and were ranked with the James', the Daltons and earlier desperadoes.

The Dutchman stayed at Spring Creek a week or so after the holdup, then vanished from the scene. He was not known in Utah again. It is probable that he deemed it safe to return to his home across the sea with his share of the stickup money.

John Caldwell, at the Strip, was awakened one morning at daybreak by an old familiar whinny. He thought to himself, "That sounds like Long Brown, but it can't be. That horse has been gone for months." About the time John had convinced himself that he had been dreaming, the whinny came again. Caldwell jerked his trousers on, pulled on his boots and hurried to the corral. There stood Long Brown, fat and sleek; his coat shone from his careful grooming. On his feet were brand new shoes, he had just been expertly shod. Long Brown had been returned by those who had borrowed him months ago. Not only that, he had excellent care during his absence.

But, when Long Brown was ridden, it was found, he was not the same horse he had been when he went away. Now, he was a bandit horse. Trails and roads meant nothing to him. If his rider wasn't careful, at the slightest excuse, he took off cross country. He leaped washes, ditches, brush, and fences like a trained steeple chaser. If he lost his man on such a chase, he ran on like nothing had happened and never stopped until he drew up at his home place. He would walk or jog up the road, but if a horseman approached him from behind, he was off like a shot. When he was out of sight, in buck deer fashion, he circled out for cover and stood without sound or movement until the stranger passed by; then he went quickly in the opposite direction. His racing days were over because he always flew the track and went whirling away into the wild yonder in spite of all his jockey could do. There were only one or two men at the Strip who ever wanted to ride that crazy outlaw horse.

The mystery of the big mount didn't remain a mystery long, after the details of the Castlegate holdup came out. Putting two and two together, all men knew that the distance runner had been borrowed by the bandits, trained for their purpose and had been ridden by Elza Lay out of Castlegate, carrying the booty from the robbery. After the job was done, the horse had been returned to his rightful owner.

As the news spread, Long Brown became a celebrity. People from everywhere, as they passed through the Strip, came to look at the horse that had played such a stellar role in the famed payroll stickup. Caldwell had offer after offer from men who wanted to buy his bandit horse. But he always refused, commenting, "I won't sell him to no stranger. When he goes, it will be to someone I know will treat him right. He ain't no good to me anymore, but still, I like the big, long cuss."

One day Matt Curry, the trader at Ouray, made Caldwell an offer and the horse was sold. Matt kept Long Brown at his trading post as a curiosity. He used to say, "Why, he's the best damn hoss ever was bawn. He used to be an outlaw but he's gone straight for yeahs now. There just ain't any equal to that old crittah."

Long Brown kicked the bucket one day at Ouray in his old age, long after the Ute Reservation was opened for white settlement. There were quite a few, including Indians, who paid their last respects to the famous horse. Matt had him buried there on the river bottom, to keep the coyotes away, he said. The mound marking his grave is still discernible in the willows and grasses of his favorite grazing ground.

The Millionaire

St. Louis, the great city on the banks of the Mississippi, in times past, had reached out its long wand of industry and touched the Uintah Basin time and time again. It set its mark on the country first, when the fur trade swept across it and left the names of "Ashley" and "Duchesne." There is a strange affinity between the giant of the Mississippi and this mountain fastness. Always, St. Louis, when it tries, breathes life into the great landlocked valley of the Uintahs. Where the Duchesne and the Uintah flow, "St. Louis" is a name of magic.

And now, once again, a St. Louisan strode into the picture. He was Adolphus Busch, a man of gigantic proportions. A man so large, in fact, he is classed as one of the greatest of the industrial American tycoons.

Busch, of Jewish origin, was a close friend of Murphy of the "Emerald Isle." Murphy was a St. Louis paint manufacturer. Adolphus Busch, among other things, was a brewer, producing that famous brand of beer, "Budweiser," of the Anheuser-Busch Brewing Company.

Murphy passed on to his great reward, leaving a surviving wife behind and Busch worried about her finances. Seeking to help the widow of his dead friend, Busch bought into the paint manufacturing business.

Gilsonite, the stuff of the best lacquers and paints, came to the notice of Busch. And he wanted the Carbon Vein, owned by Seaboldt and associates. Of a sudden, a deal was made and the mine became the property of the Gilson Asphaltum Company, organized by Busch and Mrs. Murphy. The ore was used in paint manufacturing all over the world.

The mine was named after the hometown of the owners, 'The St. Louis Mine.'

Money had come to gilsonite and to the outlaw town in no-man's-land, The Strip.

Tabby Weep

Tabby Weep (meaning born at Mid-day), the Ute Indian gun-hawk, frequented the Strip. He was reputed to be the fastest, deadliest man with a pistol in the State of Utah. Even members of the Wild Bunch couldn't match his speed and unerring accuracy with the Colt 44.

One day, Tabby shot it out with three opponents in front of the general store. He was hit twice but walked away, alive, leaving the dead behind him.

There are many versions of this shoot-out. But Tabby's own story, told many years later, goes like this: "I went into town knowing I was heading into an ambush, a friend had told me. I met one of the men who intended to kill me. He was in the store. He owed me sixty dollars, so I figured to collect. I made him go outside in front of the store and lay the money on a big sand rock. I went to the rock to pick up the money. As I reached for the money, this other fella, who had followed us out of the store, pulled his gun and began shooting at me. I whirled, pulling my gun and shot. My bullet hit this man. He walked round and round then fell over dead.

"When I had whirled to shoot, I stood facing the store and some-one, I don't know who, started shooting at me from the store win-dow. A bullet hit me in the neck, knocking me down. As I fell, I fired at the head in the window and I thought I got him, because the head and the gun disappeared. I thought to myself, 'Two down and one to go.' I found out later I had missed the man in the window by an inch, my bullet was embedded in the window frame.

"I hit the ground and lay there a little dizzy, but then I thought, 'This is a hell of a place to be. Somebody'll shoot me like a sitting duck.' So I got up.

"The man I had taken the money from had run around the corner of the store. I figured he was there about to shoot me from cover, so I made for the corner. When I got there, the guy was running away. He had a coat on, unbuttoned at the front and as he ran dodging and jumping over bushes and rocks, he looked like a scarecrow in a high wind. I could have brought him down. But he looked so funny, I stood there laughing to myself until he got out of range. You know, I never told that before on that damn coward, but he is dead now and it won't hurt him.

"Well, it takes a long time to tell it, but it happened awful fast. I guess the whole thing was over in less than a minute.

"I spent eight years in the pen for that minute. The white jury didn't believe I shot in self-defense, so I haven't carried a pistol from that day to this."

Jones—The Cowhand

Jones, the cowhand, came to the Strip, to drink and play a little. He tied his horse to the hitch rail in front of Henry ("Hen") Lee's Saloon and went in. Time went by and finally Jones surmised it was time to return to camp. He stepped outside and his bay horse was gone. In the bay's place was a poor, worn out, straddle legged mount. Somebody had traded Jones' horse without his consent. The cowboy figured this poor tired horse was better than no horse at all, so he took it. But the animal was so fagged, Jones wouldn't ride, he walked and led it all the way home, cursing his high heeled boots every step of the way.

Sometime after daylight, Jones and the tired horse got home. When the cowhand took off the saddle, he heard a clink as something hit the ground. He looked down, then stooped to pick up a Bull Durham sack with one hundred fifty dollars in gold tied in it. This was payment for a fresh horse somebody needed to ride far and fast.

Jones used to comment, "The feller didn't need to pay any loot in trade, because after I rubbed that horse down, fed, watered and rested him, that was the best danged horse I ever owned."

The St. Louis Mine Disaster

It is quiet, the old St. Louis Mine where it happened. It is about a mile east of the little town called Gusher out in eastern Utah. The works were closed in 1905 and never opened again, so now it lies somnolently dozing in the sun.

Traffic on Highway 40 rumbles by but few who pass know the tale of what probably was the first and most spectacular exploding mine disaster in the history of the state of Utah.

On an October day in 1898, the air was as rich as wine and the sun shone down in all its autumn splendor; it had left behind its summers heat so it was one of those beautiful fall days where a man is glad to be alive.

There was laughter and gaiety that day when the "diggers" came out of the "hole" to eat their noon day meal. They were totally unsuspecting that before the sun went down all but one of them would be dead.

The shift was almost through, it was four o'clock in the afternoon. Then, the gilsonite mine exploded. There are no words in the dictionary to describe those fateful moments; so suddenly did the blast strike and so great its havoc, it is difficult to write and tell how terrible it was. Ten, twenty, sixty seconds, no one knows just how long it was, when the worst was over. But those brief moments left terror, death and destruction in their wake. To those nearby, as one man said, "It was like Kingdom Come."

When I called it an explosion, my uncle who was there, exclaimed, "You can call it an explosion if you like, but it really was an eruption."

It all started with a mighty deep-toned roar as if a thousand cannons had fired at once. The St. Louis was an "open cut" mine on a vertical fissure vein. Over the heads of the miners were several horizontal layers of timber. Only the shafts where the ore went out were free and clear to the surface. There were six shafts in a row, all connected underneath and they detonated, one by one. One, two, three, four, five, six, faster than you can count, the whole mine went. Those shafts acted as giant tubes many times bigger than naval guns. They vented the gilsonite charges down below—shooting rocks, timber, dirt, dust and smoke hundreds of feet into the air. It was thirty minutes, they say, before the debris stopped falling.

The earth rocked and shook and terrific gusts of wind like muzzle blasts swept across the land. "Put a tornado, an earthquake and a volcano together for sixty seconds," an old-timer said, "and you'll have what it was like when the St. Louis Gilsonite Mine exploded."

The Boarding House, only two hundred yards away, was swept from its foundation, everything came crashing down. The windows and doors were blown from their sockets, the chimney fell, the roof was askew but unbelievably the house still stood and did not catch fire. All other mine buildings were flattened to the ground.

At The Strip, the little outlaw town a mile away, all the windows were blown out, the goods on the shelves of the stores and saloons were shaken down, poker chips rolling, glassware breaking, contents streaming; a terrible waste some folks said.

At Ft. Duchesne three miles away, the buildings rocked and dishes fell from the cupboards. Every soldier was put on alert, because, for a few minutes, no one knew what had happened. Then, those who could be spared, were rushed to the mine to render what aid they could.

In Vernal, twenty miles away, the earth heaved and loose things rattled. A few ran outside sensing something terrible had happened. Looking westward they could see a great, black cloud rolling and tumbling high in the sky resembling what we know now as an atomic explosion. They knew then that the St. Louis Mine had exploded again. (There had been a lighter, smaller explosion in 1896.) The watchers' hearts were filled with dread for most of the men working at the mine were Vernal men.

Gilsonite is a volatile stuff; when it goes, it burns like gasoline. And so the mine caught fire, feeding the flames on the vein of ore. The shafts lower down acted as opened dampers and the draft, with hurricane force, blew upward fanning the bursting blaze. The shaft on top of the hill to the north was a giant blowtorch, roaring loud enough to be heard for miles around. The plume of flame shot a hundred feet into the air and great billows of black smoke climbed steadily upward, spreading as it went, until it blinded the sun. From the head of Gate Canyon, fifty miles away, travelers could see the fire by night and the smoke by day.

For days on end the fire burned. Then after hours and hours of labor, they put it out by building bulkheads to cut off the draft and smothering what was left with dirt scraped in from the surface.

And what of the miners down in the hole? They all died except my grandfather, Joshua Birchell, who survived by what seems to be a miracle.

Joshua Birchell and Andy Garnes, two close friends, were working in the mine not far apart. As they paused for a breathing spell, each man thought he heard a woman call his name. Joshua Birchell said, "That's Mil Jane (grandfather's wife, my grandmother). I've got to see what's the matter."

Andy Garnes replied, "That's Winnie Britt, she calls like that to tease me; it's not long til quitting time, let's stay and finish the shift."

But Birchell knew what he knew, some folks call it superstition. He dropped his tools and hurried away to reach the manway and the ladders. As he left he called, "Come on, hurry Andy."

But Andy stayed to die. Birchell barely made it before the holocaust caught him. He was battered, burned and bruised but somehow managed to reach the manway where he fell down and lost consciousness.

The hoistman up on top was a man by the name of Jenkins. When the worst was over, he ran to the shaft, looking down to see if there was anyone he could help. Jenkins saw Birchell move in the murk and smoke down there. He called for help and on the end of a rope, they lowered him down and he saved Joshua Birchell. Both men were pulled to the top, Jenkins all but gone and Birchell apparently dead.

They laid Grandfather there on the dump for dead. My grandmother, Millie Jane, came running. She knelt there by Joshua's side, holding his hand and crying.

They brought blankets to put Birchell on and cover him with. But when they started to draw a blanket up over his head as is usually done for deadmen, Grandmother protested, "Don't do that until I've washed his face," she said.

They left Grandmother alone with her man and her grief. Once when she glanced down, she saw Joshua's eyelids flutter and she heard him speak, "Mil Jane, Oh, Mil Jane," he whispered soft and low.

Millie Jane, clasped her hands and raising her eyes to the smoke filled heavens, she cried, "God, oh my God! He lives! He lives!"

Expressing her heartfelt thanks for saving her beloved.

My Grandfather lived to work again in the St. Louis Mine. When I asked him how he withstood the awful shock, the heat, the flame and the gas, all he would ever say was, "There was someone down there with me; although I didn't see Him, He was there just the same."

The other miners perished. As time went by and the fire was out, they searched for the men who died. They found them all, save two. Andy Games and John Anderson still lie buried somewhere in the old St. Louis Mine.

And old-timers say that on a night when the autumn moonlight pours, if you walk the old mine vein, you can hear two miners digging down below. If you look down and shout, "Hey there, Andy," the noise will cease and two eerie lights, dimly seen, will fade away and die. These are called the ghosts of the St. Louis Mine.

After all these years, besides the ghosts, if you know what you are looking for, you can still find a few of the marks left by the disaster. The rock walls of the vein where the fire burned so long, are blackened inches deep from the heat of the fire. Melted gilsonite strews the ground buried a little by blowing sand. And there is still some debris lying where it fell that day long ago. Aside from this, no one would ever guess that seventy five years ago, this deserted old mine, once rose in terrible anger to wreak ruin and death upon those who dared plunder its riches from the ground.

* * *

After "The Opening," when white settlement was begun on the Ute Reservation, conditions changed. A townsite, Moffat, was laid out which overlapped the old original town called the Strip. Regular law enforcement took over—the wild, free days were ended.

The little desert settlement faded. Buildings were moved away and others burned. There is nothing left now but the blowing sand and the whispering wind to mark the spot where one of the small, colorful places of Utah's last frontier once stood.

There are so many tales about The Strip, they would fill a volume. The ones written here are only those the writer could gather in the time available. Someday perhaps, the whole story will be written. When it is, it will be a real, ring-tailed western—unique, robust, and wild—fit to take its place with the histories of Tombstone, Santa Fe, and other such places of the old west.

Bob Hughes

Bob Hughes, a fast, but careless gun-hawk, occasionally visited the Strip. On one such call, a crooked card-shark, won all of Bob's money in a poker game. When he found out how it had been done, Bob vowed he would rid the earth of one tinhorn gambler. The news traveled ahead of Hughes, and when he walked into the saloon, a pretty dance hall girl, whom Bob liked, grabbed him for a party. Sometime, somewhere, during the evening, someone got Bob's gun and filed the firing pin down so short it would not fire the cartridge. In the late hours, Hughes got around to the poker table, the gambler cheated as usual. Bob called him, beat him to the draw, but when Bob pressed the trigger, his gun only snapped. The tinhorn gambler killed him. Before the sun came up, that gambler, it is said, took off for parts unknown on a fast horse. There was a fresh mound, behind a knoll though, that no one seemed to know about. There are some who say that Bob had friends who didn't like the deal dealt to Bob by the gambler.

FORT DUCHESNE

Fort Duschesne in its earliest stages.

The army post by the Uintah River, and the soldiers stationed there, played such a large part in the early days of the settlement of Uintah; it would be difficult to describe the atmosphere of any of the places in the Basin without including Ft. Duchesne in the scene. The fort has a story all its own and this is not intended to be a complete history of it. Written here is merely a brief outline, to clarify the picture of The Strip, as it existed in the days before the Reservation was opened for white settlement.

The Ute Tribe was a warrior nation, a match for the Sioux or any other better known tribe, especially in their mountainous homeland. They were blessed with unusually level-headed chiefs who had observed their brothers to the east decimated by wars with the oncoming hundreds of whitemen. Peace, therefore, was broken only when they considered it a last resort for the salvation of their tribe. But at times, the Utes had danced the war dance, had painted their faces with war paint and had set out to stem the great white tidal wave washing over the land they had owned for centuries. There had been the Meeker Massacre, the Thornburg affair, and the fire fights with stockmen. It was never safe to push the Utes too far.

Because the whites were crossing Ute preserves to settle Ashley Valley, just beyond the Reservation boundaries and because there were other affairs in the making, conditions were uncertain in the Uintahs. The government decided that, to take care of all eventualities, it would establish a military post on the Ute Reservation. The idea was not so much to subjugate the Indians as it was to keep the peace between the two races. It has often been said about those days before 'The Opening,' that you never knew in Uintah which side the army was on, the whiteman's or the Indian's.

In the summer of 1886, General Crook, 'the Peacemaker,' arrived in Ashley Valley with his command. He had come in from the Wyoming side of the mountains. His orders were to build a military post at the first crossing of the Duchesne on the Ute Reservation. There were two wagon routes from Crook's camp in Ashley Valley to the Duchesne. One, the shortest way, was known as 'The Deep Creek Road.' The longer one, was the main road and led through 'The Twist,' a narrow, crooked defile down a mountain then across the desert.

Crook intended to travel the Deep Creek Road but early in the morning, before the march began, an Indian, Captain Billy of the Indian Police, rode into camp on a brown horse. Captain Billy told the general that a formidable number of Utes were waiting in ambush in the hills along the Deep Creek route with the intent to massacre Crook's whole command. Crook changed his orders and sent his column by way of the Twist. At this time, Crook had only infantry, but with mounted flankers out to right and left and the wagon train sandwiched in between companies, the march proceeded. One old soldier said about Crook's Basin Expedition, "In my day, infantry was infantry. When we came to build Ft. Duchesne, we carried field packs, rifles, ammunition and canteens. We walked every step of the way over the mountains from Ft. Bridger."

That morning, Crook was ill. So after everything was moving nicely, the general dismounted and climbed into the back of an ambulance where he could lie down. He slept or rested for most of the journey.

In late afternoon, as the foot soldiers approached the Uintah River, they could see on the opposite bank, lines of hostile Indians, deployed for battle. In the report it says, there were at least seven hundred braves in those mounted lines. But, according to the Indians who were there, the number given in the report was exaggerated. They said, the number was nearer two hundred, fifty warriors, ready to do battle at that time and place, although, they admitted they used some young women and boys to run a bluff so that their number would appear larger than it was. Besides, the Indians said, they didn't intend to attack unless the bluecoats crossed the river. All they wanted to say was, "You can come this far but no further."

Captain Duncan, Crook's second in command, rode back along the line to report to the general. Crook walked down the road to see the Ute line of battle. Then he asked, "Is that the river between us and the Indians?"

"Yes, Sir, that's the river, General," Duncan replied.

General Crook took a flag, stuck the staff in the ground and said, "Dig in. This is the future Ft. Duchesne."

A paradox again, Crook didn't know that he was on the banks of the Uintah and not the Duchesne. He, therefore, located the fort in the wrong place. After the mistake was discovered, the construction of the place was so far along, nobody wished to correct the error.

Happenstance located the military installation in close proximity to the Triangle which two years later would, by act of Congress and an Indian treaty, become a no-man's-land and the General's mistake contributed greatly to the building of the bandit town of the desert.

Ft. Duchesne was established August 16, 1886, and two years later, in September, 1888, The Strip began its operations. Thus, whiskey, gambling and other things were brought to the soldiers at their lonely frontier station.

Fort Duchesne in early stages, 1880's. It was the home of the famed Blackhorse Troop of the 9th U.S. Calavry.
—Used by permission, Utah State Historical Society, all rights reserved.

THE SPANISH-AMERICAN WAR

There was no place in the whole United States, and its territories, that had such a special interest in the Spanish-American War as the little lawless town called the Strip. This was especially true after the news came in about the Battle of San Juan Hill.

T. R. Roosevelt had resigned as Assistant Secretary of the Navy and set out to organize a regiment of his own. He picked his men from the gun-men and cowboys of the west, plus a few socialites from the east. Among those volunteering for the First U.S. Volunteer Cavalry Regiment, later to be nicknamed, 'The Rough Riders,' were men known to the people on the Strip.

When Fort Duchesne was established on the Ute Reservation in eastern Utah, the white 21st Infantry had arrived on the banks of the Uintah River. They were confronted by a battle line of hostile Ute Indians. The infantry dug in, awaiting a possible attack. The day after the 21st Infantry arrived, the 9th U.S. Cavalry, an outfit made up entirely of black men, except for officers, came to reinforce the infantry. When the 9th arrived they brought 'The Gun' with them.

'The Gun,' as the people in the vicinity called it, was a Revolving Hatchkiss Cannon. In that day, it was the deadliest weapon in warfare. From time to time, the Hatchkiss was test fired on the firing range to assure its perfect operation; the test firings always had a civilian audience and its fame spread. At the building of Ft. Duchesne, positions for defense were established on the big flat hill on the east bank of the river to the south of the post. The Hatchkiss was dug in there. The old emplacement, though smooth and worn by the weather, can still be discerned. After the stockade was completed, however, everything was moved inside it.

Units of the 9th U.S. Cavalry remained at Ft. Duchesne for twelve years, when it was ordered out for combat. During that time, every man became known on the Strip. The famous soldier, Benjamin C. Davis, who, though a sergeant during his service at the fort on the Uintah, later rose from the ranks to become the first black general officer in the United States Army.

The quarrel with Spain had gone on for months and then the U.S. Battleship Maine was sunk in Havana Harbor. Like the bombing of Pearl Harbor at a later period, this meant war. Quickly, the news in 1898 caused a flurry at Ft. Duchesne. The troops there were classed as veterans of long army service, well trained and combat ready. It was anticipated they would be ordered out.

But the Gun went first. The telegraph order came, "Prepare the Hatchkiss Revolving Cannon for shipment, with all its ammunition, to Mobile, Alabama." There was no secret about it, the Hatchkiss was on its way to Cuba. The weapon began its journey and the people saw it go. They cheered as it took the long road to Price. At Price, when the cannon was put aboard the train, with its crew, there was a grand celebration, with flags and posters flying.

Hard on the heels of the orders to ship the gun, came orders for the 9th Cavalry. It was to move to a point of embarkation and proceed from there to an invasion of enemy soil.

As has always been the way of the army, the troops under orders to move were restricted to the post. But as with soldiers everywhere, the troopers of the 9th knew a way to avoid the sentries and make it out for a last good-bye, a last drink, before they left for the fields of combat.

The celebration in the saloons on the Strip went far into the night. It can be said, no man in uniform spent a dime for a drink that night. Everything was free to the soldiers. Sometime in the wee hours of the night, the provost guard showed up and the troopers were herded back to Ft. Duchesne. There were no desertions.

Next morning, despite some mighty hangovers, the 9th U.S. Cavalry fell out on the drill ground. Proudly, sharply they went on parade. Up the field the troops rode. With the band playing, guerdons waving, and flags flying, they came back in line past the receiving stand. There were cheers and shouts of enthusiasm as the troopers rode by. Finally, they passed out the west gate and were last viewed up Bottle Hollow on the stage road to the rails. This was the last the people saw of the 9th, but not the last they heard of them.

Somehow, since those stirring days of '98, the Spanish-American War has come to be looked upon as a mere skirmish in the history of the nation. The Battle of San Juan Hill, in many writings, skits, and plays, has been depicted as a sort of comic opera charge by green boys against an army of frightened foreigners who couldn't shoot and couldn't fight, but knew only how to run. What a travesty of justice for both sides this picture paints of the Battle of San Juan Hill. It was a small battle, as battles go, it is true. But to those in the lines, it was as wickedly deadly, fully as bloody considering the numbers present, as any engagement in which American forces have ever been involved. The unmatchable courage and bravery of the ranks who fought at San Juan, has been equaled only once before in history. That was at the Battle of Missionary Ridge in the War Between the States.

On or about June 21, 1898, the Americans had landed near a place called Daiquiri. The objective of the army was the city and harbor of Santiago. Speed was absolutely necessary because the harbor of Santiago was bottled up by a superior U.S. Fleet. The Spanish Army must be caught between the nutcracker of the fleet on one side and the U.S. Army on the other. The Spaniards must not be allowed to escape into other sections of the island where reinforcements could be delivered. He must be forced to surrender.

Santiago was protected by three elevations rising between it and the Americans. To the north was El Caney with the village of El Caney at its base, in the middle was Kettle Hill, and farther to the south was San Juan Hill. All these elevations were well fortified with trenches, breastworks, and artillery emplacements.

General Shafter, so obese he could not mount and ride a horse, was the field officer in command. General Shafter's excess flesh did not impair his thinking however. He quickly recognized the necessity for speed. It was this necessity which caused the general to order an advance without all the preparations called for by the book. He took a great calculated risk to win all or lose all. He ordered the advance on July 1, 1898—it was a courageous move.

The American forces moved out up the Royal Road. Although many of them were cavalrymen, they were dismounted and were going forward on foot. There had been no time to clothe the men in the new light, kaike uniform. Most of the men were fighting in the heavy, woven blue and on the feet of the cavalrymen were the regular cavalry boot. Sweating profusely in the humid, jungle terrain, the men went forward. It was a time consuming, rugged march because the Royal Road was only a cart track through the morass of the jungle.

The general had set the pattern of the attack. El Caney must be taken first; then the hills of Kettle and San Juan would be charged and won.

The men went forward, each unit assigned to its objective. The forces, due to the assault on El Caney, turned off to the right on their way to the village. The others went on toward the other two hills. Suddenly the Spanish artillery opened and it was good. The accurate fire struck the Americans. The casualties were terrific. To make it worse, the Spanish were using the new, more powerful, smokeless powder. There were no telltale puffs of smoke to betray their places to American counter-battery fire. But there was no pause, no hesitation—the Americans went on.

These horsemen who had spent half their lives mounted, riding the wide expanses of the western deserts, now walked in heavy woolen blue and cavalry boots through the humid quagmires of the jungle. To the base of Kettle and San Juan Hills, they finally came and paused there in full sight of the Spanish breastworks above. Then they waited for the order to charge.

The pattern of attack laid down by the general could not be broken. El Caney must be taken before the assault on Kettle and San Juan could begin. In the meantime the artillery and the long range mauser rifles of the Spaniards kept taking heavy toll. By ones, by twos, by threes the Americans were falling dead or wounded. It should have been a rout, but it wasn't; the attackers stood their ground.

The general, so obese and heavy he could not sit in a saddle, stood on far off El Pozo Hill and could not discern through the mists and confusion of battle just what was going on. So he held back his orders while his men were falling at the bases of their objectives.

Once before, at the bottom of Missionary Ridge, men had stood this way and finally, without orders had assaulted the heights above them. So it was now, someone in the Rough Riders, always a poorly disciplined outfit, wild and free, like the open ranges they came from, shouted, "Let's go up the hill. We can't stay here."

And up they went. The Hatchkiss Revolving Cannon from Ft. Duchesne, had been man-handled and dragged by its crew through the jungle and morass of the trails behind. Now it was in range of the Spaniard's trenches and began to chatter its deadly song. Enemy fire feinted a little. Teddy Roosevelt, the only man mounted on the field of battle, rode his horse, Little Texas, forward as his men began their attack. Suddenly, to his surprise, found himself out in front of all his men. Teddy knew a good colonel would have stayed behind the ranks of enlisted men as army tactics said he should, but it was too late now. He tied a polka dot kerchief to his hat as a banner streaming out behind and led his men forward.

On Teddy's way he ran into that old army outfit, the 9th U.S. Cavalry. Like good, well drilled soldiers that they were, they stood holding their ground waiting for orders to go forward while bullets cut them down. Teddy passed his Rough Riders through them. When he turned in his saddle to look back, he saw the 9th with grins on their black faces, charging up the hill behind him. Teddy grinned back and led them on for the trenches on the top.

Now, there was a jumble. The Rough Riders, the 9th U. S., and the 10th U.S. Cavalries were all mixed up together, yelling like banshees or Indians. The minions of Spain were in their prepared positions. It didn't take long. Puffing and sweating, the Americans had taken the crest of Kettle Hill. The enemy had either surrendered or run to the harbor of Santiago.

Over at San Juan Hill, the same thing had happened. The men, without command, had charged. But when Roosevelt occupied the crest of Kettle Hill, there was still fighting on San Juan. So T. R. led his men southward to the sound of guns. He was too late; when he got to the trenches of San Juan, they had already been taken.

It is well not to discount the quality of the Spanish defense. The enemy in this battle were brave, excellent soldiers. Their marksmanship was superb. They fought well to the very end. But they were running low on ammunition, were outnumbered, and besides, by all the rules of warfare, these Americans should not have been as reckless as they were. They should have retreated from the base of the hills. No well-trained European continental army in all the world could have withstood these screaming wild men, who came on with the force and speed and fierceness of a band of Indian warriors.

The remnants of the opposing force, those not captured, withdrew to Santiago. That was as far as they could go. With the U.S. Fleet bottling up the harbor and the U.S. Army at their backs and all around them, there could only be one answer—capitulation for the Spanish.

With the winning of the Battle of San Juan Hill, the war came practically to an end. In August, the peace was signed. The war had lasted four months. The Americans had won.

Back in Ft. Duchesne, the telegraph key chattered. It told of a fight at San Juan Hill in Cuba. The Rough Riders and the old 9th U.S. Cavalry had distinguished themselves in battle there.

When the papers came, telling the details of the Cuban encounter, it seemed to those on the Strip as if the fighting had been done by home town boys. The Strip people threw out their chests and gloried in what the troops they knew so well had done.

Even the revolving Hatchkiss Cannon had been in the fray and had become the most storied weapon in the world. Since there had been only one Hatchkiss in all of Cuba, the famous gun had to be the one from Ft. Duchesne.

Once again there was a celebration on the Strip. The papers were read and re-read. The stories were repeated to every newcomer who arrived. The lamplight faded in the morning sun before the party was finished. The boys from the little settlement on no-man's-land had won the war, they said. There was as much truth as fiction in it, too, when all was said and done.

THE TROOPER'S VALENTINE

In a small cove, in a barren waste, is the Valentine of the Trooper. It is not known for sure how it came to be there, but it is easy to make an educated guess. According to the date, the Valentine was made in 1890 by some 'Boy in Blue.'

The Indian trouble called 'The Meeker Massacre', had occurred just a few short years before. Twice since then, there had been skirmishes along the White River between the settlers and the Utes. There was fright and nervousness whenever the Indian bands went east to hunt in their ancestral hunting grounds near the upper reaches of the river.

Finally, it was ordered, that the Utes must be kept on their reservation in Uintah Basin and away from their old hunting grounds in Colorado. This, it was concluded, was the only way further trouble could be prevented between stockmen and Indians.

Fort Duchesne, in eastern Utah, was only four years old when a troop of cavalry rode out one day to keep watch on the Ute bands leaving the reservation along the age old trails to the east. The troop's mission—to turn all hunting parties back before they reached the domain of white cattlemen. The cavalry crossed Green River at Ouray and proceeded up White River, following the hunting trails. The outfit arrived in the proper area and selected a place in the wild country, sheltered on all sides from prying eyes and searching bullets.

On the southern side of the campsite, a high clay butte rises from the plain. Stationed on the top of the butte, a man with field glasses can see for miles in every direction. No movement by horsemen, up or down the river, can go undetected from watchful eyes on the high hill. This was the place selected by the soldiers for their guard duty that day, long ago.

It is supposed a constant watch was kept by the troopers from the crest of the hill. Two men at a time kept the weary vigil by day and by night. Two hours on and four hours off was the Army schedule for each man. They probably were there for many days.

Among the men who spent time on the hill, was one with a seeing eye and an artistic heart. As he looked down from his aerie, he noticed a peculiar, natural feature of the terrain. It was a small elevation the water and wind had eroded into the shape of a valentine heart. Not only was the elevation heart-shaped, but also, around its edge, was a white border, like paper lace.

When the off hours grew long and monotonous, the artistic soldier gathered some small black stones and with these he made an inscription on the valentine heart. It reads:

TROOP

U.S.C.

1890

Besides being in a secluded area, it is possible to walk by the inscription without noticing the arrangement of the rocks, consequently few have ever seen the valentine. You must look from above to see the message the soldier left and the best place to view it is from the top of the butte.

Who the trooper was that carefully set these small stones in place will never be known. He, most likely, has been dead for years now. But what he made can still be seen. Whatever else he gave to posterity, it is certain he left a valentine for us on the desert floor.

HONEY JOE LEE—SINGING SAM AND

THE BULL FROG

Stationed at Ft. Duchesne in the early days was Troop D, 9th U.S. Cavalry. This was the famous "Blackhorse Troop," all black men mounted on coal black horses. In addition to being some of the best fighting men in the world, Troop D was also showmen who could sing, step dance and were masters of the drill on parade.

Among the men of Troop D, was the Singing Trio. Honey Joe Lee, a broad chested, big man like a modern football player. Honey Joe had, unexpectedly, one of those high, Irish tenor voices. Then there was the baritone, a medium sized individual with a mouth as wide as all outdoors, "Singing Sam," his buddies called him. Last of all was the "Bullfrog," tall and thin like a beanpole, but a voice that seemed to come out of the very bottom of the rain barrel.

When these three men sang together, they brought the house down with their harmonizing. They knew all the popular songs of the day plus those old favorites that live on from generation to generation. Their audiences would laugh or cry or pat their feet in jig time, depending on the song they sang. Those who heard them used to say that, as a trio, they were unbeatable, fit to sing on any stage, in any show in the U.S.A.

The fame of Troop D's singers penetrated far and wide, even as far as the "Owl Hoot Trail." Butch Cassidy, leader of the Wild Bunch, the famous outlaw band, sent word to Singing Sam one day, that if his singers would sing the night of the 13th day of May at Tom Nichols' saloon on the Strip, he would pay them twenty five dollars apiece in good gold coin of the realm. Of course, for that time and place, the offer was very generous, better than any they had ever received because all they ever were paid were the coins thrown at their feet while the show was playing. Singing Sam sent word back that the singing troopers of Troop D would be at the place requested on the night designated.

Now, the trouble was, that when the daily roster was posted in the barracks, the trio had drawn guard duty for May 13th. Honey Joe, Sam, and the Bullfrog had trouble, but somehow they arranged substitutes to take their place so they could keep their appointment with the Wild Bunch, but they didn't tell the sergeant or the officer of the day. This, they thought, might give Butch's plans away so that someone would arrest him. When the time came, the three soldiers slipped out of the post and hired themselves to the pleasure palace up the road a ways.

The corporal and the sergeant of the guard penetrated the why and the wherefore of the ruse long before the night was through and to save the stripes upon their sleeves, they had no alternative but to report the whole affair to the C.O.

The C.O. was an understanding man it seems, because for some reason he couldn't find a detail to go immediately to retrieve the errant soldiers. Finally, sometime after midnight he sent one man to ride to the Strip and arrest all AWOL troopers.

So the soldiers trio got to sing for Butch—sometimes songs of their own selection but always the songs that were requested by the Wild Bunch. Out of all the pieces that were asked for that night, the only one they didn't know was 'Come, Come Ye Saints.' This was the only one that Butch himself had selected. It is a puzzle to answer why Butch should want to hear that favorite old Mormon hymn, but it must have been because as the boy, LeRoy Parker, he had heard the hymn many times and it brought back sweet memories.

Out of the night came the man the C.O. had sent to take into custody the straying soldiers. The whole thing was over before Butch knew what was going on, so he never had the chance to pay his debt.

In the next day or two, Butch ran into Jim Sprouse. Jim was on his way to deliver a load of grain for the army mounts at Ft. Duchesne, so Butch explained the situation and said, "Here, Jim, is seventy-five dollars. Find Singing Sam and give it to him."

When Jim got to the post, he found that Honey Joe, Singing Sam, and the Bullfrog had drawn stable duty for the singing episode at Tom Nichols' the night the Wild Bunch were there. The grain was to be unloaded at a granary near the stables, so Singing Sam, along with his cohorts, were not hard to find. Jim dropped the proper amount of gold coins into the hand of each singer, then he asked, "Do you know who sent you this money?" Singing Sam replied, "Oh sure, suh. We surmise it come from that honest outlaw, Butch Cassidy."

As he finished the story, Jim remarked, "In spite of the fort that Butch held up, and the bank and railroads he robbed, still, he was an honest man. Don't you see?"

Jim Sprouse, who in the early days was a freighter on the old Nine Mile Road, spent the last days of his life in Roosevelt, Utah. Although Jim was never an outlaw and lived a long, law abiding life, nevertheless, he met and became a personal friend of Butch Cassidy, the famed leader of the Wild Bunch.

One time Jim remarked in a group of younger friends around the coffee table, that Butch was one of the most honest men he had ever known. Naturally this statement was the cause of a great deal of laughter because most of the men in hearing distance thought that Jim was joking. But, Jim wasn't joking, he was serious and to prove his point he launched into this story which came from his first hand knowledge of the kind of man Butch Cassidy really was. The tale is not in Jim's words but is the way he told it in substance.

WONG SING

Eastern Utah is a country filled with legends. There are stories told of trappers, traders, outlaw gangs, gunmen, lawmen, Indian Chiefs, cattle barons, troopers dressed in blue, rich men, poor men, beggar men and thieves. And not the least of the legends is about a man from China named Wong Sing.

Just this side of a lane bordering on a desert of the Ute Indian Reservation was the establishment of 'The Chinaman.' Wong Sing was the main cog of the wheel. His affability, generosity, fairness, and absolute honesty, coupled with a strange business acumen, made Wong Sing's store into one of the most lucrative businesses in the whole of Uintah Basin. It's a mystery still how a man with a place, isolated from the main highways, and all the cities and towns, could develop an institution so successful. And therein lies the tale.

When I first walked into that store, I was just a small boy. The two things I remember most were the smiling man behind the counter with a cigar in his mouth, and the smell; there was the scent of new leather from the harnesses, saddles and bridles mingled with the odor of spices, coffee, bolts of cloth, peanuts and candy. For a kid from the deserts, the whole was a very pleasant odor.

When I first knew the place, there were two Chinese men working there. Wong Wee, the elder, and Wong Sing, the younger. The one a nephew of the other. Wong Wing, another Chinese, came at a later date after the retirement and death of Wong Wee.

From time to time, after my first visit, I was at the store at various intervals. Then, in the 1920's, I was at the place of business almost every day and the Chinaman and I came to be good friends.

To most, I suppose Wong Wee, Wong Sing and Wong Wing were enigmatic Orientals, reticent about most subjects except when they talked business. There were few, as was the 'Western Way,' who questioned them about their background or their past.

When I first was in college, I was young, brash and bold, I guess. I had taken a class in Chinese philosophy from Dr. Thomas at the University of Utah, so I began to ask questions of Wong Sing about his life. Surprisingly, he talked, in fact he seemed pleased to think I was interested. So he answered all my questions and volunteered other information. Adding what he told me to what the white people and the Indians knew about him, I came up with a rough picture of this Chinese man and his story.

Wong Sing began life in Canton, China. His family were not coolies (unskilled laborers), but were of the merchant class. He ranked next to the Mandarins. Except for the big farmers who owned their land, everyone else was below him. In Chinese, the surname comes first then the given name. This meant that Wong Wee, Wong Sing and Wong Wing were members of the numerous Wong family. A name to be reckoned with in China.

Being a Wong, and a merchant's son, didn't mean that he could take it easy. He started school so early he couldn't remember his age when he began to study. Endlessly, he poured over his subjects, learning to read and calculate. He said he still used the Chinese method of bookkeeping because he believed it was a more accurate method than bookkeeping in the West.

Canton was the city doing the most business with the West. There were English, German, French, Americans and other foreigners in Canton. These people used the money of their own countries when they went shopping. Therefore, Wong Sing had to figure instantly the rate of exchange for all the currencies. "Pretty hard," he said, "pretty hard!"

Wong Wee came to America first. He was at the building of the Central Pacific railroad. That company shipped in thousands of Chinese direct from China to do the back breaking labor of laying the railroad. Wong Wee, however, did not work as a coolie. He ran a shake-down restaurant at the various rail settlements.

When the Central Pacific and the Union Pacific railroads met at Promontory, Utah, the end of the rail towns were over. So Wong

Wee ran a restaurant in Green River, Wyoming.

From Wyoming, Wong Wee sent home for Wong Sing and offered him a junior partnership in his business. Wong Sing, who was then in Hong Kong, came.

There was trouble in China, mostly due to the beginnings of the Boxer Rebellion against the 'Foreign Devils.' So Wong Sing's folks transferred their interests to Hong Kong, running a warehouse where goods were stored going into and out of China. Hong Kong was a British Crown Colony and things were more stable there.

News trickled back to China of the great land of America where pure gold could be found in the streams or picked with hand tools out of the ledges. So when Wong Wee sent for Wong Sing offering him a junior partnership in his business, Wong Sing sailed as a cabin boy on a freight boat from China.

Arriving in Wyoming, Wong Sing found things had gotten rough for the 'Yeller Chinese.' In the coal mines of Rock Springs and everywhere they went, the coolies worked too long for too little pay. If they could feed and clothe themselves and save ten cents a day, they believed they were in clover. If they could save a dollar a day, they believed they were getting rich. The white men, even the Irish, couldn't compete with the frugality of the Chinese, so they resented them first and then began to harass them.

This was the situation Wong Sing faced when he arrived to help Wong Wee. Although Wong Sing adapted fast, putting on American clothes and cutting his que, still the white men continued their persecutions. You see, most authorities never helped a Chinese in trouble. They just laughed and said, "Hell, he's only a Chink."

On the military posts, things were different. Some of the officers and men had served in China. They respected the Chinese people. On the posts, the Chinese could get along pretty well if they could find something to do. Wong Sing and Wong Wee moved to a military post and started a cafe, really a small bar, in the post canteen. There wasn't enough work for both in the eating place so Wong Sing worked at odd jobs and gambled with the soldiers.

Wong Sing was a good gambler, probably as good as most professionals. He claimed lots of luck, but lots of rapid calculations, too. You have to know the odds of making a hand like a full house, a straight, a flush, etc., in a four, a five, or a six handed game. "Keep your head down and think," he said, "Sometimes I loose, most of the time I win a little in a game."

When Captain Randlett was ordered to Ft. Duchesne in the Uintah Basin, he brought Wong Sing with him as a houseboy. Sing said they came to Ft. Duchesne from the Colorado side, through Meeker and Craig and by teams with cavalry escort to Ft. Duchesne. They arrived in the Uintah Basin in the summer of 1894.

In Ft. Duchesne, the cavalry was black men, the infantry was white men, and there were Ute Indians. Race didn't mean too much so everybody got along well together.

After Wong Sing arrived in the Uintah Basin, he looked the land over. He wrote to Wong Wee who sold his restaurant in Green River and moved to Ft. Duchesne.

What was the mix that made the magic of Wong Sing's success? Never in his history did he hold a special sale. He never used any gimmicks. A fair sale of goods at a fair price in accordance with its quality was his motto. He didn't sell you things just to make money. He sold it to you for your satisfaction. Nor did it matter who you were— Black, Indian or White— it was all the same. The quality was good and the price was right. Always you got exactly what you paid for. His reputation for honesty was so great among the residents of the "Basin" that he became a lay-word. Many times you'd hear, "Why man, he is as honest as Wong Sing."

Being Chinese, there were strangers who would try to con Wong Sing. That was a great mistake because in the end those men wound up looking very foolish. His mind was like a steel trap and when he sprung it someone's head would roll. It is no wonder that people came from near and far to trade with him. Wong Sing, the honest merchant from China.

Nu-pah-gath-ti-ket

(Bottle Hollow)

The wagon road winds over the red hill, down the leaning slope, across the small valley and enters a narrow defile known as 'Bottle Hollow.' This natural causeway cuts through a small, low mesa from a valley in the west to the Uintah River bottoms to the east. It is only about a quarter of a mile long. Where it spreads onto the plains of the Uintah, stands old Fort Duchesne.

The little pass got its name from the 'Boys in Blue.' The enlisted men at Fort Duchesne were not allowed to bring hard liquor onto the post. These soldiers were hard-bitten men to whom whiskey was the staff of life. They had to drink somewhere. The hollow, next to the post, was a good place to cache 'red eye,' and to drink it. As time went by, the 'dead soldiers,' accumulated at this drinking place until there were hundreds. So the passageway came to be known as 'Bottle Hollow.'

It is hard to realize now, driving the old road, that this was once the track of empire. In days gone by, this was a segment of the main road carrying all the traffic between 'The Outside,' and the Ute Reservation, Fort Duchesne, and the entire Uintah Basin. A mile or so to the north rumbles modern Highway 40, and what was once the mainstream lies almost forgotten, wrapped in its aura of bygone days.

There are many stories about this place. Most of them have been lost in the limbo of yesterdays. But if they could be found and written, they would add many pages to the colorful history of the West.

The narrow pass is a haunting place because of its tongueless past. Down its length the painted warriors of the Utes once rode, their feathered head-dresses waving in the breeze. Along this way flew the maroon and white pennant proud, with the big red "7" on its centerpiece, and the regimental band played the war song, "Garry Owen," as the legendary 'Seventh U.S. Cavalry' of 'Little Big Horn' fame came riding here long ago. It was under the command of Captain Benteen. He was a man whom Western history will never forget, for he extricated himself and his command from the massacre of 'Yellow Hair,' on the distant river of the 'Greasy Grass' in Montana.

The heavy-laden freight outfits creaked and groaned in the deep, rutted wheel tracks of this road. The stagecoach jingled and jostled, carrying its mail and passengers through this pass, to places far away.

After 'The Opening,' the homesteaders came with their wives and children and milk cows. All traveled down the hollow on their way to the 'Land Office' in Vernal.

Today, the old road can still be traveled. The rocks still lie on the hillsides to throw back echoes, as they did in times gone by. But one day soon, the wheels of progress will make one more turn. And what was, will fade into oblivion. Then, a much needed Ute Indian Project called Nu-pah-gath-ti-ket, meaning Indian Lake, will begin. Bottle Hollow will be dammed. The defile and the valley behind it will fill with water. Never again will things be the same; the bulldozers and heavy equipment will change the old things into new—uncovered and moved and drowned. Once again, an old landmark will pass, with its ghosts, into the past. Only the memories of it will live on.

OUTLAW STORIES

THE OUTLAW CITY

It is hard to reach the old outlaw town in a canyon of the Bookcliff Mountains. There never was a wagon road so you can only get to it by leaving your vehicle by a big, brown ledge and walking the rest of the distance along a deep-worn packhorse trail.

When you get to the village, you will find it one of the most lonely places in the world, for it is forlorn and deserted now, and has been for many a year. Isolation has saved most of the buildings from the usual vandalism, but nevertheless, they are slowly falling down from the ravages of time. In addition, beavers have damned the creek down below and turned the site into a swamp which helps the disintegration.

As you explore the houses one by one, you recall the stories the old men tell about this place and about the people who lived here. Part of the tales deal with the famous outlaw band, "The Wild Bunch", who as the years went by, rode into legend and became a part of our Western folklore.

For this is Webster City, named by its owners when it was first built, way back before the turn of the century. It was not meant to be an outlaw town at all; it was built to be the headquarters of the Webster Cattle Company, an English syndicate, bent on making money out of western land and cattle. As ranches go, it was a nice place considering its time and setting.

Out in what used to be a beautiful, grassy, meadow stood the bunkhouse. It was not the usual type of one, big room dormitory; it was partitioned off into smaller rooms, each with an outside entrance. Along the north side was the kitchen and dining room. It was so elegant, the cowboys called it, "The Webster City Hotel."

Scattered on the hillside to the east, in no particular order, were cabins. These were used by the married cowpokes who brought their families to live with them in town.

The heart of Webster City stood under the western wall of the canyon. It was a combination store, saloon, card room and entertainment center called "The Commissary". It was here that dances were held and holidays were celebrated. One time, it even doubled as a school; the kids, all with cowboy boots on, pegged across the meadow at the twinkle of the bell. But the teacher, to everyone's consternation, forbid the wearing of spurs in the classroom, leaving the boys and some of the girls feeling partly naked. There was too much hooky so the school finally closed down.

Of late years, someone wanted the logs in the old Commissary walls so they jerked them out with lariat ropes letting everything come tumbling down. There is nothing left but a nasty pile of rubble.

The outlaw stories began in the early 1890's. Three strangers rode into Webster City. Their horses were superb, their clothes were new. It took only a glance to tell that these were not the usual run of cowboys. They hitched their horses to the rail and strode into the Commissary. "Can we buy a drink in here?" they asked. "Where is the boss of this outfit?"

A man in charge of the place passed out a bottle and glasses as he replied, "Mr. Fullerton, the boss, has been gone since early this morning. He'll be showing up pretty soon and when he does, he'll stop here for a drink before supper. If you want to see him, take a chair. This is as good a place as any to wait."

The three men sat down and waited. After awhile, Mr. Fullerton came in, angry as a pestered nest of hornets.

"That damned Cassidy Gang is stealing all our cattle. They don't drive them off by ones or twos. They drive them off in bunches," he hollered to no one in particular and everyone in general.

"Mr. Fullerton," one of the strangers replied, "from what I hear, the Cassidy Bunch don't go in for cattle rustling; they like bigger game. What you've got is a mess of two-bit cow thieves. They ought to be easy to get rid of."

"Well, I dunno," Fullerton replied. "Maybe you're right. But my boys are just ordinary, hardworking, cowhands. They're no match for a bunch of gun-slinging outlaws. So we'll have to wait for the sheriff, if we don't go broke in the meantime."

Grinning, the stranger said, "Ah, those rustlers ain't so mean. My partners and I would like a job with your outfit to tide us over for the winter; maybe we can help you with your rustlers. How about it?"

Fullerton looked the speaker and his companions over and seemed to like what he saw because he answered, "all right, you're hired. Feed your horses at the corral and come up to the hotel for supper."

The three strangers worked for the Webster Company all that winter. And although there was no shooting, no killing or even a confrontation with the rustlers, that anyone knew about, the cow stealing ceased immediately.

In the spring, the three men drew their time and rode away. As they were leaving, Fullerton told them, "If you know other men like you, needing work, send them around. I'll give them a job anytime."

One of the men replied, "I'll do that. So if a man says to you, 'Butch sent me', hire him. He'll be a damn good man."

Later that summer Billy Preece, the sheriff of Uintah County and a Pinkerton man showed up at Webster City. After supper that night, as they sat in the Commissary, the Pinkerton man asked, "Have any of you seen any of these men lately?"

The man produced several sketches and photographs. "We'd like to pick up their trail," he added.

"Sure, we all know these three," a more talkative man replied.

"They worked here all last winter but they're gone now. Why? Who are they?" he asked as he picked out three of the pictures.

"Well, this one is Butch Cassidy. This is Elza Lay. And this one is Harry Longabaugh. They are the most wanted men in the U.S.A.," the Pinkerton man answered.

Struck dumb and half unbelieving, the rest of the men around the table sat silent. It was apparent that if any of them knew where their erstwhile comrades were, they were not saying anything about it.

And after that, in spite of the fact that everyone knew that "Butch" was the outlaw Cassidy, whenever a man showed up asking for a job at Webster City and said, "Butch sent me", invariably he was hired. They said it was good rustler insurance.

One by one, you can tick off the better known bandits, who, at one time or another, worked at Webster City: Butch Cassidy, the humorous, smiling leader; Elza Lay, the brainy, educated, right hand bower; Harry Longabaugh, the Sundance Kid, the cool, quiet, left hand bower; Harvey Logan, the hot tempered, Cherokee gunslinger, during his time, probably the fastest gun in the West; Flatnose George Curry, the big, sly fox with the funny nose; Will Carver, the good natured, expert rifleman; and Tom Dilly, the tall, lean Texan. How many lesser lights there were, nobody will ever know because they all used aliases like Brown and Smith and Jones.

Although Webster City was always law abiding, most of its men, being hard working, honest cowboys, still it came to be known as an outlaw haven. This is why most men call it, "The Outlaw Town of the Bookcliffs".

Knowing this much of the story, as you wander in Webster City, do you wonder what was the fate of those notorious men whose spurs once jingled, jangled across the floor of the old Webster City Hotel? Well, it is reported, though some deny it, that Butch Cassidy was shot to death in San Vincente, Bolivia, South America. Harry Longabaugh cashed in his checks with Butch at the same time and place. Harvey Logan shot himself in preference to surrender when a posse had him cornered near Parachute, Colorado. Harvey lies buried near another famous gunman, Doc Holliday, of Tombstone fame, in Glenwood Springs, Colorado. Flatnose George Curry was killed by a sheriff's bullet down on Green River at the mouth of Range Creek. Will Carver ended his career in Texas, trying to beat a lawman who had the drop on him. Tom Dilly, the tall, lean Texan disappeared completely after the shoot-out in which Sheriff Tyler of Moab was killed at the head of Rattlesnake Canyon; what his end was, remains a mystery to this day. Only Elza Lay is known to have died with his boots off down in California, after he had turned respectable and had gone straight for many years.

As it is today, Webster City with all its colorful days behind it is a ghostly place to walk by day and at night, positively haunting. When the sun goes down behind the hill, a thin mist arises from the swampy floor of the canyon, causing the crumbling buildings to appear dim, like wraiths in the pale moon's shimmering glow. From far away, the night birds call and the coyotes howl in the distance. Near at hand, the long grass whispers as the night breeze stirs and there is mourning when the wind blows through the chinks of the cabins.

In an atmosphere like this, one comes to the realization that this village belongs to yesterday and the men of the many legends. To visit it now, although interesting, is a visit with an apparition that lived at a lively pace a long, long time ago and died with the men who made it. It is the ghostliest ghost town in the West.

Note: I know that as Pearl Baker says, Elza Lay's correct given name was "Elzey", but I prefer to use the name he used himself, "Elza" because, not only did he prefer it, it is the name everyone knew him by in his lifetime. Using Elzey is the same as using Robert LeRoy Parker for Butch Cassidy. In either case, the correct name would remove the glitter from the legend.

THE WILD BUNCH

There are few in the United States who haven't heard of that legendary band of outlaws known as 'The Wild Bunch'. But not as many have really known where the name came from. It is generally accepted that one time, when the boys came to town, their rambunctious conduct gave rise to the wild bunch sobriquet. But, undoubtedly, while they probably had a good time at the places they visited, still, from all accounts, the outlaws were not exceedingly riotous. Note the general reputation of the most famous members of the band: Butch Cassidy, the leader, a light drinker and always a gentleman; Elza Lay, educated, refined and cultured; Harry Longabaugh (The Sundance Kid) steady, but quiet and a little retiring; Harvey Logan, taciturn and surly; Matt Warner, merry and gay, but never too far out of the way. Going one by one, through the whole group of the accepted members of the band, it is doubtful if wild actions at a party added up to the name they were given by common usage.

All my life, except while back east to school, I have lived in the Uintah Basin of eastern Utah. My grandfather, my father, my mother, and two of my uncles were among the early settlers of the Basin. They lived here long before 'The Opening', when the Ute Reservation was thrown open to white settlement in 1905-06. My dad was the last foreman of the old St. Louis Gilsonite Mine east of Gusher, Utah, when they closed it in 1904 and moved operations to the Black Dragon Mine in Evacuation Canyon.

In the Uintah Basin almost every member of the bandit outfit was well known, and ever since I was big enough to toddle over next to the fire and listen, I have heard stories told of those wild old days when 'The Wild Bunch' were at the height of their glory. In my time I knew personally some of the real and reputed members of the famous old outlaw band. I knew Matt Warner, Elza Lay, and Henry

(Hen) Lee. I also knew Jim Sprouse, William Donaldson, Joe Toliver, and many others who were on first name terms with Butch Cassidy and his cohorts. I have talked to all of these men at one time or another. In this year of 1969, I am about as much of an Old-timer in this part of Utah as anyone is apt to find still alive. My version of the origin of the name, 'The Wild Bunch', as applied to the storied band of outlaws, does not agree with anything yet written.

I said to my dad one day, "Dad, how did Butch Cassidy's gang get the wild bunch name?" He answered, "They were so much like a band of wild horses the people just started calling them "The Wild Bunch".

At the time, I didn't get the point, but, later on, not long before he died, the famous, old, western character, Hen Lee, dropped into my office to have me do some legal business for him. He put me straight. I didn't know Hen when he first came in, but I wasn't long in getting acquainted with him, because he said, with a grin, "If you are half as good a man as your father was - and I know you ain't - you're a good enough lawyer for me."

I asked, "Who the devil are you?"

He grinned and replied, "I'm Hen Lee, ever heard of me?" Of course I had and I said so. With that grizzled old man sitting across the desk from me, I called all the appointments off and went into a gab-fest about the early days of Uintah Basin. Old Hen held nothing back for as long as we had to talk, and I still have the notes I made after he had gone.

One thing I asked Hen was, "How did Cassidy's men get the name of 'The Wild Bunch'? Do you know?"

"Of course I know," Hen replied. "You see, in the early days there were thousands of wild horses roaming all over the country. It was common for the tame horses to quit civilization and roam the open range with the wild horses. Sometimes a man would ask something like this, "Joe, where's that little bay mare, Dolly, you used to have?" Joe would answer, "Oh, she ran off and is out on the desert running with the wild bunch." Wild horses generally were known as the wild bunch.

"Along about that same time," Hen said, "there was a lot of young fellahs who thought Cassidy and his outfit was tops. These kids liked to copy the outlaws. Once in a while, a young kid, carrying on like that, got the law on his tail. When this happened, the culprit took off to join the wide-loopers and long-riders. The people used to say, 'Billy Jones is running with the wild bunch.' Once all the men riding outside the law were said to be running with the wild bunch. In time, the newspapers and others, applied the name to the Cassidy gang alone."

After Hen told me this, I checked and re-checked the origin of the name with other Old-timers who had the background to know. Invariably, these people agreed with what Hen Lee had said.

Hank Stewart, my uncle, a ferryman on the Green River, below Ouray for many years said, "Yes, that's how Butch's crew got their name. Those outlaws were just like a bunch of wild horses. They ran free, without a rope, a mark or a brand on 'em. They were here today and gone tomorrow. The outlaws resembled a bunch of wild horses so much the wild horse name was hung on 'em and it fit 'em to a tee. Both wild horses and wild men preferred the same way of life, even if they had to run like sixty to keep from getting caught."

The bandits themselves never knew what the people called them until they read it in the papers after some of their escapades. It was a label applied to all outlaws by common usage until the newspapers stuck it onto Butch and his men specifically.

Thus it was, that the parallel between wild horses and their human counterparts, gave rise to an appellation now grown famous in the annals of the west.

THE BAFFLED AMBUSCADE

For years, the outlaw band known as "The Wild Bunch", had ridden rampant over the West. These bandit riders, under Butch Cassidy's leadership, had never failed to make their play, grab the loot and successfully make their getaway. Such exploits as the Castlegate Payroll Robbery, had put Butch and his gang at the head of the outlaw list and their successes raised them to the status of Murieta, the James Boys, and the Daltons, famous names of former days.

But, while their successes were widely known, their one big failure, never reached the public ear. The attempt that failed was surrounded with peculiar circumstances which were almost wholly within the ken of the perpetrators of the attempt. None of them divulged the facts until years had passed.

In the early spring of 1898, Butch Cassidy, Elza Lay[1] and Harry Longabaugh (the Sundance Kid) were riding from Robber's Roost in southern Utah to the Hole-In-The-Wall in Wyoming. They camped one night at an out-of-the-way spring in the Bookcliff mountains of eastern Utah.[2] After supper, when the chores were done, they sat around the campfire talking before they spread their blankets to turn in for the night.

Suddenly, from up the trail, they heard the sound of approaching horses. Instantly, all three men pulled their guns and stepped into the shadows. There was a friendly hail from out of the darkness and three men rode into the light. They were Bill Carver[3], Ben Kilpatrick and a kid about nineteen years old, who called himself Johnny McVey.[4]

Bill and Ben were known to Cassidy; they had been with the Ketchum gang in Arizona and New Mexico and had used the Roost as a hideout while the heat cooled on their back trail. Johnny McVey was a stranger, but his companions gave him entry to the inner circle of the outlaw band.

After they had unsaddled and hobbled their horses, the newcomers came to the fire and a discussion began about the next robbery the outlaws should pull. In the circle of the firelight sat the cream of the bandit riders: Butch Cassidy, himself, a keen judge of character and a mind with the speed of a steel trap; Elza Lay, Butch's chief lieutenant, highly intelligent, cool and calm, the planner for the Wild Bunch; Bill Carver, pleasant, quiet-spoken, experienced and deadly, preferring a rifle to a pistol in almost any circumstance, with speed and accuracy almost beyond belief; Harry Longabaugh, quiet, retiring, sometimes moody and taciturn, but fast and efficient in an emergency, the kind of man to have siding you in any showdown; Ben Kilpatrick, could shoot with the best, never excitable, too ready to draw blood sometimes, but Cassidy could control him; Johnny McVey, young, inexperienced, but he had the makings, and Cassidy seemed to like him. Around the fire that night, Butch Cassidy had the proper men for any difficult job anywhere.

It was early in the year and still winter in the mountains. None of the men were anxious to quit the warmth of the blaze for their scanty bedrolls. With blankets around their shoulders, they sat by the fire and talked far into the night. All were getting low on cash and they covered, one by one, the possibilities of a job that would bring plenty of loot to fill their empty pockets.

Out in Uintah Basin of eastern Utah, was the Ute Indian Reservation. Once a month on "Issue Day", the Indians were given food and cash. They drew a stipulated amount for every man, woman, child and dog in a family. The money was sent in from Price over the army-built "Nine Mile Road".

On the Uintah River, within the borders of the Ute Reservation, was Ft. Duchesne, a U.S. Military post. Once each month the soldiers were paid in gold and silver.

Usually, the Indian annuity and the army payroll came together, both were sent by rail from Salt Lake City to Price, Utah. At Price, the cavalry from Ft. Duchesne met the paymaster and escorted him to the post. It was ninety some odd miles from the rails to the Fort. The road ran most of the way through a wilderness of mountains and desert, devoid of towns or human habitation. The Wild Bunch, for years, had known of the payrolls, but, had never seriously thought of a stickup. The bandits knew that stealing from private outfits was one thing; hijacking government funds, especially army funds, at gun point, was another. So the money had passed without harm or hindrance, to its scheduled destination.[5]

Over the years, the commanders of Ft. Duchesne and the Indian Agency officials, were well aware of the Wild Bunch activity and had been lax in handling the large sums involved in the two paydays. Always the cavalry escort was at the train to meet the paymaster and in addition, various ruses were used from time to time to keep possible robbers guessing. Sometimes the paymaster rode the stage in civilian clothes, posing as a 'drummer'; sometimes he traveled by private rig. In either event, the ambulance and escort were on the road as a decoy. But most of the time the paymaster, the money, and the escort journeyed together. The escort detail usually consisted of eight enlisted men, an ambulance, a driver, the paymaster and one line officer—eleven men in all.

Elza Lay, having lived at the Strip, adjoining the post, before he took the outlaw trail[6], knew all the particulars concerning the transit of the government money. Cassidy and Lay had discussed the situation many times before, but they had never planned to pull a holdup. At the camp in the Bookcliffs that night, however, when somebody brought the subject up, they talked about it again, and the more they talked, the more feasible a successful hijacking appeared.

There were problems to be solved, but these didn't seem to be insurmountable. Every man at the camp knew that the troopers of the escort, had been tempered in the Indian wars of the American Frontier; a surprise would not be sufficient to make an easy mark of the soldiers. This must be an ambush and a massacre. Every man in the escort detail would have to be killed so fast they wouldn't know what was happening to them. It was possible to get more outlaws to help, but, if you cut a pie into too many pieces, there isn't a very big hunk per man. Butch would send for Harvey Logan, but except for him, the six men present would have to do the job.

Harvey Logan (Kid Curry) was the top pistoleer of the Wild Bunch. It is probable that he was the fastest gun in the West during the heyday of his outlaw years. Harvey had blinding speed and pin-point accuracy with a handgun; an addiction, he loved a gunfight. In most instances, Cassidy was reluctant to use Logan, because Harvey had a wicked temper and a speedy trigger finger. But for a job like this, the quarter-breed Cherokee gunman was tailor made for the task. Therefore, Butch wanted Harvey in on the deal.

It seems strange that Butch Cassidy and Elza Lay, neither of whom had killed a man up to this time; who had always argued that bloodshed was not necessary, should all of a sudden, plan a murderous attack from ambush like this army payroll caper. But, the newspapers had begun to print bad stories about Butch and his cohorts, calling them every printable bad name in the dictionary, including "Homicidal maniacs", and "blood-thirsty", and Cassidy was angry. If he was going to have the fame, Butch figured, he might as well have the game.

At dawn the next morning, the camp was astir and over the breakfast fire, the holdup decision was definitely made.

Cassidy sent Longabaugh to the Roost to get Logan, while he and the rest of them, took the Tabbyogg Trail to the Rock Dugout above Nine Mile Canyon on the mesas, the closest outlaw haven to the army road to Ft. Duchesne. On the way, the outlaws rode close to 'The Wells', a stopping place and station for travelers and the stage.

McVey was sent for more grub and ammunition, while the others waited in a place that was well concealed. As evening came, they rode into the hideout that Butch had designated as the rendezvous. Here they would wait until the payload came from Price.

About three quarters of the way down Nine Mile Canyon, the military road from Price turns north up Gate Canyon. Gate Canyon is a narrow, twisting defile; its lower reaches is a causeway ledged in on both sides. In these 'narrows', there are two ways to go for men on horseback, up or down, for horses cannot climb the ledges. There is a place in the narrows, where the canyon, as you ascend it, runs east about three hundred yards, swings around a point and almost doubling back upon itself, runs west about three hundred yards. The point, around which the canyon swings, is the end of a low, ledgy ridge which thrusts out from the mountainside into the canyon. The crest of this elevation can only be reached back where it meets the mountain and its top has many rocks and nooks that make good hiding places for a man. The breadth of the out-thrust is such that a man on top can move from one side to the other in a matter of seconds.

Elza Lay, early one evening, rode the narrows of Gate Canyon. When he came to the long, low ridge, he inspected every detail of it. Then he built a rock monument out of the way, but easily seen on the right hand side of the road. This was the spot Lay picked for the ambush of the paymaster.

That night, when Elza got back to the hideout, he explained the tactics the bandits would use in the ambuscade. Cassidy, Lay, Logan, Carver and Longabaugh, would lie in wait on top of the ridge. When the army cavalcade reached the point, the outlaws would fire simultaneously at their targets. Since troopers, in a body, rode in columns of twos, each man would have his assignment according to the horsemen's position in the line. Carver would shoot the officer in charge and the men riding in the ambulance; Butch would take the first two troopers; Lay the second pair; Longabaugh the third pair;

and Logan the fourth pair. The mules drawing the ambulance must be killed, too, otherwise they might run off with the booty before the brigands could get to them, but this would be after the soldiers were all down. Lay calculated the shooting should all be over in a few seconds.

The troopers, when the firing commenced, could only go up or down the road. Either way, they would have to ride three hundred yards to gain cover. With these marksmen above them, not a soldier would come out alive.

The horses could not be taken on the hill with the attackers. They must be concealed close by. Kilpatrick would be in charge of the horses, and at the sound of the first shot, he would come larruping down with the mounts. He should arrive at the scene at about the same time the ambushers got from on top, down to the road. If all went well, Kilpatrick should have McVey to help him.

McVey, since he wasn't known in Utah, would be the scout. It was up to him to go to the Strip and then to Price to arrange some details Butch and Lay had in mind. And in the end, he would ride to alert his cohorts. McVey was to wait in Price for the cavalry escort. When it came, he must spot the paymaster and how he traveled, then he was to proceed to the mouth of Gate Canyon ahead of the payroll guard. With Lay's field glasses, he was to check the army detail as it left Pete Francis's station. If the paymaster was in place, if everything looked right, he was to ride up Gate Canyon to Lay's monument. At the right moment he was not to shout, wave or make any undue sign or signal; he would merely take his hat off, wipe the sweat band with his bandanna and ride on to Kilpatrick to help him with the horses. But if there was anything wrong, Johnny was to ride to the monument, stop, dismount, and tighten his saddle cinch; then he was to ride to Kilpatrick and warn him. Lay pointed out that the money and the paymaster were inseparable; you would never find one without the other. It would be useless to kill all those men and find the dough was gone. It was up to Johnny to use his eyes.

In Gate Canyon, north of Lay's ridge, there is a place called 'The Shelf Campground'. It was used in 1898 only by men on horseback because a wagon could not get up the trail. It is a small, level meadow. It was above the road, which ran in a deep, natural cut in the solid rock at the base of the Shelf. From the old road in the cut, a traveler could not see onto the campground, nor could it be seen from up or down the canyon. It is a 'dry camp', so few people then or now use it. This is where Kilpatrick was to conceal the horses.

Cassidy, after Lay finished, directed that Lay, who was the best horseman of the Wild Bunch, have charge of the horses and that Kilpatrick go with the ambushers on the hill.

One evening Longabaugh and Logan rode in. They had made good time on their journey, even though they had stopped to get extra horses in case relays were needed. That night, the plans for the hijacking were gone over again. Longabaugh was silent, but Harvey was delighted with the whole scheme.

McVey was sent to the Strip to contact Bob Ricker. Bob was a minor outlaw who had spent time in the Roost with Cassidy. Bob was to keep a sharp eye on Ft. Duchesne and when he saw what he deemed to be the payroll detail leave for Price, he was to wire John Dey at the Cottage Hotel in Price. The message was to be a simple, harmless thing. But McVey, passing as Jim Dey, would know what it meant. Ricker agreed to the arrangement and McVey came back to the dugout.[7]

In a day or two, McVey and Longabaugh left for Price. Johnny was to register at the Cottage Hotel, but Longabaugh was to remain at a cabin a couple of miles out. When Ricker's wire came, McVey was to ride to Longabaugh and Longabaugh would ride to the hideout to alert Butch and his men. This would leave McVey free to keep his eye on the depot so he could spot the paymaster when he came.

It was about this time that Cassidy began to have second

thoughts about the holdup. He wanted to pull some other heists first and as a last gesture make this hijacking on another payday. It was his opinion that an ambush, such as this, would arouse the whole United States and force every member of the band to run for Mexico or South America. In Butch's opinion, when they left the country, they should have as much money as they could get. Harvey Logan, Ben Kilpatrick and Bill Carver insisted that since the plot was laid, and they were on the ground, it should be carried through. If Butch wanted to back out, he should not object if the others pulled the job. If they had to, they could get more help from the rustlers down Nine Mile Canyon. Lay agreed with Cassidy. They were sure Longabaugh would too, but they admitted it was a little late to give up the deal.

The getaway, after the hijack, was planned. They would leave fresh horses in the corral at the dugout. They would leave the holdup site, ride to the hideout, change to fresh horses, ride through the saddle and down to Desolation Canyon on the Green. After they were across the river and in the fastnesses of the Bookcliffs, the money would be counted and divided. At this point, they would split up, everybody to be on his own. They should be far away before any pursuit could get started.

Cassidy and Lay saddled their horses and said they would check out the escape route, since none of them had ever ridden it before. They would be back, they said, in plenty of time to meet the paymaster. In two or three days they were back, and their horses showed the effect of quite a long journey.

McVey, hung around the hotel in Price. He went out now and then to check his horse and once in awhile he rode down to the depot. But, as the days passed, he stuck closer and closer to his room; he wanted to be on hand when Ricker's message came. Finally, the wire arrived. Bob had done his work. Johnny McVey saddled his horse and was off and away to pass the news to Harry Longabaugh. He found Harry at the cabin with Hazel Johnson from

Castlegate. Hazel was a mystery woman who, some years later, ran off with Longabaugh to South America and went by the name of Etta Place.[8]

Ricker was a sharp young man. He had picked up the pay detail leaving Ft. Duchesne. He had sent the message to Jim Dey as directed. He felt satisfied with himself and knew Cassidy would appreciate the favor. But, Ricker, had one bad habit; sometimes he drank too much, and when he did, he talked too much. The evening after the payroll guard had gone to Price, Ricker got soused in Nichols' saloon and bragged a little about what would happen to the Indians' and soldiers' money. No one paid much attention to the drunken cowboy. Apparently, most thought it was another randy boasting about his connections with the Wild Bunch. This happened often at the Strip.

Early next morning, the famous 'Blackhorse Troop' (Blackmen on Black horses) of the 9th U.S. Cavalry, left the post for the rails under forced marching orders. Somehow the news of the planned robbery by the Wild Bunch, had leaked out.[9] The Indian Agent at Whiterocks had heard the news and called the commander at Ft. Duchesne. The Blackhorse Troop was the result.

In the night, Longabaugh, on a spent horse, arrived at the dugout. Lay figured time and distance. He and Logan were on hand to see the ambulance and guard go down Gate Canyon on its outbound journey. As usual, there were eight enlisted men, ambulance and driver and a line officer. It would be three days, maybe four, before the payrolls arrived at the ridge on the inbound trip. Johnny McVey, from here on, was the key man. It was a busy time for the outlaws, none of them saw the Blackhorses go pounding down the road.

Johnny kept his eyes on the depot, he did not see the troop of cavalry ride through Price on its way to Helper. But in the morning early, he saw eight troopers, the ambulance, and the officer pull up, halt and wait. Everything so far, looked good. Shortly, he should be on his way to his friends. The train whistled up the track; in a few minutes it pulled in and stopped. Johnny saw the paymaster and his heavy satchels alight and he saw, too, a whole troop of cavalry get off the cars. The young outlaw knew trouble was on the wing. Johnny got his horse, Blaze, mounted him and went whirling away on the short-cut trail to Soldier Canyon. There was no need now, to watch the paymaster. He had one thing on his mind; warn Cassidy and his men. This was McVey's first job. He was somewhat excited, so he rode his little mount too hard on the tough trail, but he was way out in lead of the cavalry. Blaze was tiring as he crossed Whitmore Park. His rider knew they must go at a much slower pace. At Lee's Station in Nine Mile the horse was limping. Johnny knew he must stop. At a ranch, he turned in at the gate, roused the rancher and tried to buy or borrow a horse. Warren, the stockman[10], wouldn't sell or lend a mount, but he offered oats and hay for Blaze and a bite to eat for his rider. McVey accepted. In the process of feeding, Warren looked at the hoof of the little horse. He found that it had thrown part of a front shoe, and traveling fast the way he had, he had sprained a tendon. With pincers, Warren pulled the broken shoe and the shoe from the other foot. The cattleman knew that night, that the kid was running from somebody or something, but he didn't know until next day about the troop of cavalry. When it came by next morning, he put two and two together.

McVey, after he had eaten, found his horse was cool enough to water. He rubbed Blaze down, fed him some more and decided to rest until daylight.

As the first streaks of dawn lightened the eastern sky, Warren gave the kid breakfast and sent him on his way, telling him not to crown his mount. As Johnny rode, he knew he had not used his head. It would be a shame if he botched the job by not watching as Lay had told him to. Maybe the troop of cavalry was not a guard for the payroll. He would have to find out. He stopped at Pete Francis's Saloon. When he saw a fog of dust back up the road, he mounted Blaze and rode to Gate Canyon. Here he took Lay's field glasses from the case to have a look. The eight man cavalcade came in sight and he saw that it was as usual. He waited. Then a dust cloud shown behind the leaders. With the glasses, he could see the Blackhorses coming.

Ordinarily, people on the road to Ft. Duchesne, stopped at the Francis Station to water their stock one last time before they assailed the long, dry stretch between the Minnie Maud and the Wells. But the soldiers must have watered back up the road somewhere, for they came on at a good clip without stopping. The outlaw knew he had a race now with disaster, and as he whirled to make his run up Gate Canyon, Blaze fell. When they got up, the mustang was limping badly again, the sprained tendon was giving trouble. But Johnny had to go on, he spurred his horse almost every step. But he knew the cavalry was gaining, because he could check their progress by glimpsing their dust. At last he came to Lay's monument. He had won his race, but just barely, for as he came to the piled rocks, the lead troopers were coming around the bend below. He rode opposite the monument, jerked his hat down tighter on his head, dismounted and tightened his saddle cinch. It was too late to ride on, so he just stood by the side of the road.

This military outfit, veterans of many an Indian chase, understood ambushes and they knew this narrow defile was a likely spot for things to happen. At the mouth of the canyon, they had changed tactics. Far out in front, rode two sharp-eyed troopers; after them came the ambulance and six soldiers; behind them came the main body, a whole troop of riders. It was a trap, a counter ambush, the skirmishers out in front, the decoy, and behind, men enough to take care of any situation.

McVey knew if any of the men on the ridge fired, rolled a rock, or showed himself, all would be lost. The lead troopers came to him, paused to look him over. But Blaze moved and limped. This allayed suspicion; the bluecoats rode by.

Soon the ambulance came. This time, Johnny led Blaze down beside the road as if he were taking a lame horse to the grass and water of Nine Mile Canyon. The lieutenant waved and led his command on.

About this time, the troop came into sight down below. McVey led Blaze on toward the mouth of Gate and the Blackhorses passed in a rattle of equipment and a cloud of dust.

They called it 'Cassidy Luck'. But the facts are, Butch had an instinct for avoiding serious trouble. He knew when he first saw McVey, on his badly limping bronco, that something was wrong. He kept every man low and quiet, despite Logan's protests. When the Blackhorse Troop showed up, after that, he had no difficulty with anybody. Soon the buffalo soldiers were gone out of sight, up toward the pass.

When the outlaws were sure the troops were gone, they came down from their perch, thankful for Johnny McVey and for Butch Cassidy. If it hadn't been for them, they would have been killed or captured before the sun went down. Johnny gave the credit to Blaze, the little, tough, mustang pony.

But where was Elza Lay with their horses? In a minute or two, Elza showed up driving their mounts down to them. He had watched the troops go by from the shelf. Two troopers came up to check him out and had seen the empty saddle horses. But Elza had been so dumb as he conversed with them, that they had gone without suspecting anything. Elza had watched the soldiers as far as he could see them up the canyon, then he had come on down to the ridge.

Harvey climbed the iron pole and cut the telegraph line, just for fun. Johnny unsaddled Blaze and turned him loose, he never expected to see him again. This done, he handed his saddle and bridle to

Bill Carver, mounted up behind Lay and they all rode for the hideout. As they looked back they could see Blaze hobbling along following them; he arrived at the dugout sometime during the night.
After that, McVey would never part with him.

The failure of the Wild Bunch to get the government money has
left a mystery. Who tipped the hands of the outlaws to the government officials, so that they were able to foil the ambush?

Harvey Logan,[11] maintained until the day he died, that Butch
Cassidy and Elza Lay, squeamish over the bloodshed that would be
necessary, let the cat out of the bag, but did it in such a way that
none of the bandit crew was killed or captured. Logan could always
see the deep laid plots of Lay in the whole affair.

As for the Agent and the Commander, they were never sure that
an actual attempt to hijack their payrolls had ever been made. There
was a cowboy riding a lame horse to the bitter end; the tall, dark
man on the shelf with saddled, riderless horses; and finally, the cut
telegraph line near where the other oddities occurred. But, this could
only add up to conjecture after the facts were put together a few days
later. The reports cover the use of a troop of cavalry to bring the
money safely to Ft. Duchesne, but no mention is made that an
attempted hijacking had ever been made.

The participating brigands knew that one or more of their number gave the play away. But who or how or where, will always
remain unanswered because those who knew never divulged the
secret while they lived.[12]

Notes:
1. The writer knows the correct first name of Lay is Elzie, but
since the outlaw never used that name in adult life, preferring to use
Elza, the writer uses the name the outlaw was universally known by
and used himself.
2. The Bookcliff Mountains, as used by the writer, is an area in
eastern Utah listed officially on the maps as East Tavaputs Plateau

(Tavaputs means 'Land of the Sun' in Ute). Because the natives of the area always say, "The Bookcliffs", the outlaws would have used the same name, therefore the writer uses it.

3. Lay's description of Carver matches that given by Roy D. Holt, in his article, "The End of Will Carver", True West, June 1970. Only Mr. Holt does not mention Carver's proficiency with the rifle.

4. According to Lay, McVey was the youngest rider who ever rode with the Wild Bunch. He went to South America, met Cassidy and was in on several holdups with Butch, Longabaugh, and Etta Place. He came back to the U.S.A., quit the outlaw trail and went straight. McVey was not his real name and who he really was remains a mystery. It is possible Lay knew his real name, but if he did he never disclosed it. "The Outlaw Trail", by Charles Kelly, pages 289, 290.

5. The safe passage of payrolls to Ft. Duchesne, "Utah Military Frontier", by Thomas G. Alexander and Leonard J. Arrington, Utah Historical Quarterly, Fall 1964, pages 348-352.

6. Elza Lay's residence at the Strip, "The Outlaw Trail", by Charles Kelly, page 85. "The Death of an Outlaw", by George E. Stewart, Old West, Summer 1970, page 17.

7. Bob Ricker at the Strip, "The Wild Bunch at Robbers Roost", by Pearl Baker.

8. "The Mystery Woman, Etta Place", who she really was, Letter to the Editor, by Harry Longabaugh (son of the outlaw), Deseret News, June 9, 1970.

9. The ambush tip-off to the agent and commander, The Salt Lake Tribune, March 1, 1898. Utah Historical Quarterly, Fall 1964, page 352.

10. Personal interview with Doc Warren, Bluebell Utah, June 9, 1966. He is the son of the Warren who cared for McVey's horse and was present the night of McVey's visit.

11. Harvey Logan (Kid Curry) recorded as a pistoleer, The Western Gunman, American History Illustrated, July, 1970, by Mark Sufrin, pages 25, 33.

12. Personal interview with Elza Lay by the writer, early 1920's at Myton, Utah.

Blazing Guns in

The Bookcliffs

The Bookcliff Mountains of eastern Utah are almost as remote today as they were a long time ago when outlaws rode the trails. It is rough country, these mountains, because from where the peaks rise to their tallest, the deep, dark canyons twist and turn down, down in every direction. To the west, the canyons drop into the gorge of Green River, called Desolation Canyon. Northward flows Hill Creek and Willow Creek and all their forks and tributaries. To the south, the great, crooked causeways descend to Cattle Valley and yonder, the desert. To the west, the mountains stretch on and on all the way to the Colorado line and beyond.

Hole in the Wall, Brown's Hole, Powder Springs and Robber's Roost were all used as hideouts by the famous outlaw band known as 'The Wild Bunch', the lore covered well by the pens of both fiction and history writers. But the Bookcliffs have received little attention in books and articles, though they were used by bandits as a retreat as much as any place on earth. Because it was the stomping ground for men on the dodge, the Bookcliff area was the setting for three of the more famous gunfights between law officers and outlaws. Actually, it was these three fights that for one reason or another, blew taps for the lawless activity of the Wild Bunch, in Utah, Colorado and Wyoming.

Civilization has never overrun the Bookcliffs. It is interesting today to view the scenes where guns blazed in those long, gone days. Because the places are so little changed, it is possible to reconstruct the split second picture, in your mind's eye, with all the props and scenery in place. Each will be narrated in the stories that follow.

* * *

Joe Walker, a Texan, probably on the lam from home, showed up in Price, Utah one day in 1891. Joe was a wild young jasper, who seemed hell-bent and trouble-bound. He was in on the fabulous Castlegate Payroll Robbery when Butch Cassidy and Elza Lay took, at gun point, the mining company's gold. Walker had been the one to cut the telegraph line so Butch and Elza could not be headed off by a posse from Price. It was also Joe who met Butch and Elza on the trail, took the loot and went riding away up the Green while Cassidy and Lay decoyed the chase toward Robber's Roost. Even if the pursuit had run down it's quarry, the booty would not have been recovered.

But Walker was no holdup man, his specialty was stealing horses. Joe didn't steal bang-tails; he went out to take the best in the country. Up Green River, in the middle of Desolation Canyon, Joe built a cabin at the mouth of Chandler Creek. He stole horses and drove them there where they were cared for by an old man and his boy. When he had gathered a big enough herd, Walker drove them away to sell on distant markets.

North of Price, the Whitmore brothers, J.M. and George had a large spread. Part of their business was breeding fine horses. Time after time, Walker got away with the best mounts the Whitmores had. Something had to be done. So it was determined by Azariah Tuttle, sheriff of Emery County, Utah, to trail Walker and apprehend him the next time he stole. This was to be a chase to the limit.

Alone, without assistance, Joe drove off some fine geldings and headed for Robber's Roost. This time, the thief was pursued all the way to the San Rafael River, in outlaw country, and overtaken at Mexican Bend. The wide-looper was a crack shot, so the lawmen treated him with care after they had run him into a cul-de-sac. But Joe refused to give up and a gun battle ensued. Sheriff Tuttle was wounded in the hip and was in such pain, the posse withdrew to take the wounded man home for medical aid.

While Tuttle had violated a long standing custom when he penetrated outlaw country beyond a place called Cleveland, still, the shooting of a law officer was not looked upon kindly by the people of Utah. Joe Walker's name joined the governor's list of the twelve most wanted men in the state. From this time on, Joe bore the stamp of a real badman along with Butch Cassidy, Elza Lay, Harry Longabaugh, Harvey Logan and the rest. The usual price of five hundred dollars, dead or alive, was placed on Walker's head.

Despite the bounty to be paid for his apprehension or death, Joe did not cease his thieving activity. He set out, it seems, to make the Whitmores pay for his misfortune. Joe, with two other men from Robber's Roost, led away more Whitmore horses. This time, the thieves headed up Green River for the Bookckiffs. On the way, the outlaws ran into Bud Whitmore, the youngest of the Whitmore boys and Billy McGuire. The desperadoes beat the boys unmercifully, stole the cows they were driving and took their saddle horses, leaving them injured and afoot, far from home. The two kids walked to Price to tell their story. This was the last straw, the manhunt was on in earnest. Sheriff C. W. Allred, of Carbon County, Utah, picked a posse of six men besides himself and started on the trail of the outlaws.

Joe Bush, the celebrated lawman of Salt Lake City, came down by rail to Price. Bush brought two men with him, a tracker and a gunman. He picked up Billy McGuire at Price to set them on the tracks of the hunted men.

Somewhere along the way, Bush and Allred joined forces. Altogether, there were eleven men on the trail of Joe Walker and his lawless companions. The tracks led upriver to the McPherson Ranch, at the mouth of Florence Creek. Here, as a safety measure, they took Jim McPherson into custody to make sure he did not warn the fleeing men. Also, there was one of Walker's confederates at the ranch, probably planted by Walker to keep a lookout on the back trail. This man was forced, at gun point, to accompany the lawmen and guide them. He led them up Florence Creek, almost it's length, then along a narrow, crooked trail up the face of the mountain. As evening came, the party had reached the top and camped in the north fork of Florence Creek. The guide, who has always remained unnamed, through money or fear, was made to tell the whereabouts of Joe Walker and his gang. It was just over the ridge in Post Canyon, a couple of miles away that the outlaws were holed up, the guide said.

In the morning of Friday, May 13, 1898, before daylight and without breakfast, the lawmen got on their way. They went up the trail, over the cow ridge and descended a narrow, wooded defile. As dawn broke, they came to Post Canyon, and there, at a small stream, fed by a clear, cold spring, lay the hunted men, still in bed. Two men lay over against a ledge. Joe Walker and his partner were asleep on the small, grassy bedground with a log at their heads to shelter them from the mountain breeze.

Contrary to popular belief, there was no code duello of the West. Gunlaw was a deadly, ungentlemanly game. A man, especially a lawman, took his gun-slinging opponent the surest way he could— face to face, behind his back, from ambush, any method was permissible and no questions asked afterwards. The officers felt free to get Walker, using the safest, surest way.

After the camp was spotted and each member of the posse told where Walker lay, all dismounted and crept forward in a semi-circle, on foot, with rifles in their hands. There are two accounts of what happened next. One account states that first Allred, then Joe Bush called upon the sleeping man to surrender. The other account says no warning was given; rather, there was a shouted order to fire. Regardless of which account is correct, guns blazed. The two men next to the ledge came out of bed with their hands in the air, these were not shot down. Walker and Herron, bedpartners, turned over and fought back from under the covers. Herron broke away and tried to reach the timber on the hillside close by. He never made it, a bullet caught him on the way and he died on the slope. Joe Walker fought on from his bed and died there with his boots off. It was fast, the whole thing lasted but a few seconds. Afterwards, counting up, it was found fifty rounds had been fired by all concerned, in less than a minute. Surprise had done the trick, two outlaws were dead, two surrendered and not a single lawman had been hit.

There was a sequel to the fire fight in Post Canyon. John Herron was light complexioned and bore some resemblance to Butch Cassidy. When the returning party reached Thompson, Utah, the report went out that not only Joe Walker had been killed, but the famed leader of the Wild Bunch, Butch Cassidy, himself, had been bagged. The bodies of the two dead men were put on display in Price, and it caused the greatest gathering in Carbon County history up to that time. All had come to see the corpse of Cassidy.

When the crowd was at its greatest, the live Butch Cassidy rode down the main street of Price in the back of Jim Sprouse's covered freight wagon. From this vantage point, he gleefully watched the people who had come to celebrate or mourn his fate, as the case might be.

At last, Sheriff John H. Ward, of Evanston, Wyoming, who had known Butch well while Butch was serving time in the Wyoming Pen arrived in Price to make identification positive. Ward took one look at the body of Herron and said, "I don't know who that fella is, but I can tell you one thing, he ain't Butch Cassidy."

The bubble burst, the viewers went home and the remains of Joe and John were buried just outside the Price City Cemetery. They had lived outside the law and were buried outside the limits of the resting places of law-abiding men. Ironically, the cemetery has been enlarged to include the outlaw graves. And in 1969, it was proposed that the places be marked by a monument, a sort of memorial to the dead days of the Old West.

To find the place where the gunfight took place, drive up the

Hill Creek Road from Ouray, Utah. At the summit of the mountains is a sign indicating the way to Post Canyon. The road, the sign indicates, leads down the wooded defile the posse rode that early morning in May, 1898. Hard by Indian Ranger Station is a camp ground. This is the place where the outlaws slept. Near the campground is a log; with a knife, fragments of lead can be dug out of it. It isn't for sure that this lead is from the bullets fired at Walker, but it probably is.

The bedground where the bandits died is there. Campers still sleep on the same old spot, although few know its history. The hillside Herron crawled to is unchanged. He would have been safe had he been able to make it six more feet.

* * *

Flatnose George Curry was Canadian born, but in his early life, the family moved to Nebraska where George finished growing up. As time went by, he moved westward, finally coming to Hole in the Wall in Wyoming, as an outlaw.

George said that in his early years, he had been kicked in the face by a horse, flattening his nose, and marking him for life. This peculiar facial characteristic was the basis for his sobriquet.

Flatnose, though he never attained the eminence of Butch Cassidy as an outlaw, must still have been brainy and sharp because he became the 'Leader of the Hole in the Wall Gang'. He was responsible, too, for several innovations in the art of banditry, which proved his skill and artfulness. He invented the trick of uncoupling the engine and the express car from the rest of the train; steaming down the track a mile or two, then opening the express car to get at its contents. This prevented interference from people on the train and it gave time for a getaway after the job was done.

George was identified as the leader of the bandits who performed the Wilcox Train Robbery. The U.P. Railroad offered a reward of three thousand dollars for the capture of Curry, dead or alive. That much money was a fabulous sum in the '90's. Flatnose knew there were only a few men he could trust. In addition, he could not travel under disguise because of his nasal characteristic. He and some of his trusted men moved out of Wyoming and into Utah.

Since the death of Joe Walker, Utah had been getting tough on Owl Hooters. Honest sheriffs with nerve and determination were taking the trails to run all bandits down. To ease the pressure, most of the Wild Bunch and other desperadoes were moving to New Mexico for awhile.

George Curry, for some reason unknown, stayed in Utah. He worked as a cowboy for the Webster Cattle Company and lived in "Webster City" on Hill Creek. It was here he met Tom Dilly. The two worked together, as cowpunchers in the Bookcliffs. Finally, George quit Websters and was lost to view for a time.

Tom Dilly was a long, lean, black-haired young man from Texas. He had some altercations on his backtrail. He had killed a man in Texas over a girl. He had killed a sheepherder in an argument over a hundred dollars and a horse pasture. He had pistol whipped Sam Jenkins, a cowboy at Webster City. Warrants were out for his arrest so he took to the outlaw trail.

Tom took up where his fellow Texan, Joe Walker, left off. He claimed the cabin at the mouth of Chandler Creek and he began to steal horses and rustle cattle.

Sheriff William Preece, of Uintah County, Utah and sheriff Jesse (Jack) Tyler of Grand County, Utah, had determined to bring Dilly in. Both were searching the Bookcliffs to find their culprit.

On April 17, 1900, Fullerton, the boss of Webster Cattle Company saw a rustler stealing a Webster cow. He thought the thief was Tom Dilly so he rode to find sheriff Tyler. On his way, Fullerton ran into sheriff Preece and told his story to him. Preece and his men rode to the place where the rustler was using his running iron. The wide-looper mounted and made a run for it with Preece on his tail. A running gunfight ensued. The fleeing man headed for Green River and somewhere in the canyon, disappeared from sight. The sheriff followed the canyon trail to the river. As he looked the land over from a bluff, he saw a man on the other side of the stream who obviously had just crossed. The officer assumed this was the man he had been chasing. He took his rifle from the saddle, laid it across a rock, aimed and fired, calling on the man to give up. The man ran for some rocks nearby and returned the fire. In the meantime, Tyler was on the same side of the river as the outlaw and could hear the shots up ahead. He rode toward the sound of the guns. When he got close enough, he recognized Preece across the river. He thought Preece had Dilly cornered, so he dismounted, walked quietly up behind the fighting outlaw. He took careful aim with his rifle, fired once and brought his man down with a shot to the head. At this point, both lawmen thought they had ended the career of Tom Dilly. But, when they got to the man and turned him over, it was found they had killed Flatnose George Curry. They tied Curry on a horse and packed him out to Thompson Springs. At that place, they put a door on two sawhorses, stretched the body on the door, sloshed it down with buckets of water. It seems there was a good deal of joshing, joking and bragging during this process. The disrespect shown the remains of Flatnose was not appreciated by some of the onlookers.

John C. DeVore came down from Wyoming to identify the body. He took his look and confirmed that this was Flatnose George Curry, the leader of the Hole in the Wall Gang. There was a dispute between Preece and Tyler as to which of them had killed Curry. Since the fatal shot had come from behind, Tyler, they said, killed George. And it was to him that the three thousand dollars was paid by the railroad company.

The corpse was packed in ice and George's father came to claim it. He took it home to Chadron, Nebraska for burial. The rock that sheltered Flatnose in his last fight is there close by the river. It still bears the marks made by the bullets from Preece's gun. Where the outlaw fell, there is a dark stain on a rock which could be blood.

Many years after the event, while riding up a canyon, Budge Wilcox, a rancher in the area, found Curry's hideout. It was a dugout in a sheltered place. When Wilcox walked inside, some of George's camp equipment was there. The old fashioned dutch oven was still setting with the lid in place. When Budge raised the lid, there were biscuits left over from George's last breakfast, they still looked fit to eat. But when Budge tried to pick them up, they crumbled into dust.

* * *

Harvey Logan, probably the fastest gun in the West in his day, was the top pistoleer of the Wild Bunch. Typical of gun hawks, almost without exception, Harvey was short and slight of build. In his veins, coursed Indian blood; he was quarter Cherokee and lacked the icy blue eyes of the usual gunfighter of the West. But this did not interfere with his proficiency with a gun. He was quick and accurate, especially with his pearl handled six shooter.

Logan, like others of the Wild Bunch, had gone to New Mexico and while there ran with the infamous Black Jack Ketchum Gang. Somewhere in Arizona there had been a shooting affray and the gang had shot Frank LeSeur and Gus Gibbons to death. The warrants and wanted posters were out. So Harvey, with Black Jack, George Kilpatrick, Ben Kilpatrick and Mack Steen made for Robber's Roost in Utah.

Tom Dilly, after Flatnose George was killed, realized the heat was on. He headed for the safest place he knew, Robber's Roost, knowing there were other men there to help him if lawmen tried to come for him.

Dilly and Logan arrived in the Roost at about the same time. When they came together, Dilly told Logan all the gory details about the killing of George Curry. Harvey was incensed. Curry had been Logan's mentor back in other days of the Owl Hoot Trail. For years, they had been friends and had grown as close as the uncle and nephew they were reported by some to be. Besides, Flatnose had been the leader of the gang from the Hole in the Wall and Harvey had been one of the top members. Harvey didn't like the tale he heard about Flatnose being shot from behind, nor the way in which the body had been treated afterwards. Harvey, in his anger, swore, "I'll go up there and kill that damn Tyler, if it's the last thing I ever get done."

Logan meant to carry out his threat. From that time on, he planned his vengeance. Four men rode for the Bookcliffs; Logan, Dilly, and the two Kilpatricks. On the way, they stopped near Woodside to pick up some top horses Tom had hidden away, then proceeded up the trail. They topped out on the Bookcliffs, contacted some friends they knew and hung around waiting.

The two sheriffs, Tyler and Preece were still in the Bookcliffs trying to run Tom Dilly to earth. But neither lawman knew that Logan and his companions were anywhere within several hundred miles of the area. Otherwise, there is no doubt things would have turned out differently.

From their friends in the mountains, Tom and Harvey found out Sheriff Tyler and Preece were still combing the country looking for Dilly. Furthermore, they were told, Sam Jenkins, Tom's most implacable enemy was riding with Tyler. All the outlaws had to do to get their revenge was to decoy Tyler's posse to their guns.

A trail runs up the west fork of Hill Creek. At the Canyon's head, it crosses over a saddle in the mountains and drops down Rattlesnake. A few yards north of the saddle is a natural clearing completely surrounded by quaking aspen. The outlaws camped at the east edge of this clearing. They had a heavily wooded hillside at their backs.

George Kilpatrick, not well known in Utah, rode down the canyon, a plant to steer Tyler to the waiting gunmen. He hadn't gone far when he saw three men and a boy riding toward him. He saw, as he approached the men, a silver star on two of the men's chests. Somebody already had directed the lawmen up the way the outlaws wanted them to go. But George, this late in the game, couldn't turn back. He rode on to meet the sheriff.

Western custom demands a stop when riders meet in the wilderness. Kilpatrick stopped, curled his leg around the saddle horn and reached for the makings.

Tyler looked George over suspiciously and inquired, "Did you see any horsemen up this way today?"

"Well, there was some fellers driving some horses behind me. I never stopped to talk to them though. They was quite a ways back," the horseman answered.

"Was one of them Tom Dilly?" the sheriff asked.

The stranger replied, "Could be. I don't know Tom Dilly. I'm on my way to Websters looking for a job. This is my first trip up this way."

"Well, maybe we'll see you again," the sheriff said as he checked to his horse and rode off.

Thus, the trap was laid that brought the courageous officer to his fateful encounter.

The rain drift was blowing, intermittently over the mountains. As the posse approached the clearing in the trees, they saw three men huddled around a fire, hats pulled low over their faces and blankets over their shoulders. It was said, the men at the fire were mistaken for Indians by the posse men and this threw Tyler off guard. Maybe so, but this depends on what happened at this point and there are two accounts, each equally reliable.

One account has it that Tyler left Day and Wade mounted on the trail while he and Jenkins rode to the campfire. There was a short conversation, Tyler and Jenkins began to dismount. At this instant, while the swing of dismounting presented the backs of the lawmen to the men at the fire, there was a crash of six-guns. Both officers fell dead, shot in the back. Jenkins had time to exclaim loudly, "Dilly."

This was the way Day told it, claiming to have watched from the trail outside the clearing.

The other account, made by one of the men at the fire, says Tyler had seen and identified some of the horses grazing in the meadow below as stolen horses. He thought he had Dilly cornered at last. The officers saw the men around the fire and knew Tom was there but had no idea Tom had the deadly guns of Logan and Kilpatrick to help him. Tyler took the usual precautions. Day and Wade dismounted, pulled their rifles from their scabbards and stepped into the shelter of the circling trees. These were cover men, to help in a gunfight if necessary, to prevent the escape of Dilly, if he made a run for it.

Jenkins, insisted on going forward with the sheriff because he wanted to be in on the apprehension or death of his greatest enemy. The officers rode into the clearing and part way across it, then dismounted and approached the men at the fire on foot.

As everybody knows, the back of a horse is a very unsteady platform from which to do accurate shooting. Therefore, in a tight place, a man dismounted before he went into action.

The men at the fire, although apparently indifferent to the movements taking place around them, saw every move their opponents made. They knew this was to be a showdown even a shoot-out if need be.

The officers strode straight to the campfire, still unable to recognize the faces under the hats. Tyler spoke, "Come with me, Dilly," able now to identify the long, lean man, squatting in front of him by the fire.

At that instant, the squatting men stood up, discarding their blankets. Harvey Logan, with blinding speed, fired once, twice, hitting sheriff Tyler each time. Dilly's gun blazed, hitting Jenkins. And Jenkins, when he saw Dilly shooting at him, shouted "Dilly! You..." His words trailing off as the second bullet struck him. Dilly almost emptied his pistol into the already dead Sam Jenkins. It is generally conceded, the outlaws had drawn and cocked guns, hidden under their blankets.

There was one shot from the cover men in the trees but it went wild. The outlaw weapons were turned on Day and Wade. Since it was long pistol range, both were able to mount and move out with speed. Wade, the boy, ran for the deepest cover he could find. Day rode down the canyon as fast as his horse could run.

George Kilpatrick, riding back from his decoy job, heard the drum of hooves and took cover in the willows. He saw Day go by, ashen faced and scared. In due time, though, Day found Sheriff Preece and told his story to him. According to Day, there were fifteen to twenty outlaws in the gang on Hill Creek. Preece rode out for reinforcements.

Logan, Dilly and the Kipatricks knew the fat was in the fire and lost no time riding for Hole in the Wall.

When the news of Tyler's death reached the outside, it touched off the greatest man-hunt in Utah's history. The governors of Utah, Wyoming and Colorado sent posses combing the country to pick up the trail of the gunmen. But it was too late, the outlaws were long gone before the chase got off the ground. All outlaws, after that, had to leave for far places.

They say, Harvey Logan was killed on a sidehill in Colorado after a train robbery. He lies in a grave at Glenwood, Colorado. The only thing is, the man supposed to be Harvey Logan, was buried and lay in the grave fifteen days, then dug up for identification. The man who identified him was not sure it was the famous gunman.

Tom Dilly, disappeared from his old haunts forever. He was in South America for awhile, joined friends who were already there. A story persists that he wound up a wealthy man, in England, where he married and lived out his life.

The clearing in the timber has not changed and over against the hill are the charcoals from an old campfire which authenticates the site of the storied gunfight.

The furor caused by the death of Sheriff Tyler was the coup de grace of the Wild Bunch. No more did they ride and rule the outlaw trail. The three shootings in the Bookcliffs taught the law; outlaws could be handled once the public came awake. And there was cooperation between officials and the people.

The land is quiet now, the wild old days are gone. All that is left of those legendary times are the cabins, the rocks and hills at the places where the events occurred. But standing there, among the unchanged things, an aura, a feeling, can be experienced of what it was really like in the Old West of the early days.

MYSTERY OF THE OUTLAW GOLD

I live in Uintah Basin of eastern Utah. From my boyhood days the legend has persisted, that somewhere in the area, near an outlaw hideout, is the cached plunder from a holdup. They say, the treasure is in gold bullion worth thousands, and its hiding place is marked by the grave of a dead man.

The particular yarn I refer to, has several versions, but the warp and woof of the story is as follows:

Five desperadoes got inside information that a big shipment of gold was moving east from a rich mine in the West. Plans were made to hijack the shipment at a certain place along the way. The outlaws laid their plans well. They bought or stole some of the best horses the West afforded, and laid in a good supply of grub, ammunition and possibles, including medicines for gunshot wounds. They waited for the payload.

On schedule, the rich cargo reached the place of ambush and the brigands made their play. There was a brief skirmish, one of the out-laws was shot in the shoulder. But the holdup was successful and the five robbers made off with the booty.

At the first night-camp, one of the five decided to take his share of the spoils and return to his family somewhere in Utah. His part-ners approved, so the man left the party and vanished from the scene. The remaining four rode on heading for St. Louis where they intended to settle down with their stolen wealth.

The bandits knew they would be followed but had no idea a posse was close, until there was a burst of gunfire at a river crossing one day, and a member of the gang was killed. The remaining three out-distanced their pursuers and got away. Along with the posse was a tracker who followed the trail of the escaping bandits with exceeding skill. It was plain the chase would be a long one.

In time, the shoulder of the wounded outlaw became swollen, inflamed and painful. It was apparent that unless he could be doctored, the man would sicken and die. A long stop must be made somewhere.

One of the bandits was an old trapper. He was no stranger to this tracking business. Besides, he knew the mountains of the West like the back of his right hand. The trapper kept saying to the sick man, "Hang on, soon we will come to a place I know. There we will shake those lawmen on our tail and we can stop and get you well."

True to his word, the trapper eluded the posse-men and somewhere in the Nine Mile area they made their camp under a big pinion tree.

The old man went to work on the younger man's bad shoulder, but it was plain, a long time would go by before they could travel on. It was already late in the year; it would be much later before they could leave this place. The three decided it would be best to snug in for the winter. The two uninjured men built a dugout with rock walls and a big fireplace. They moved in to wait out the long, cold months in comfort.

It was in the dugout the wounded outlaw made his fight for life and lost. He died one night and his friends sorrowfully buried him in a grave dug not far from the cabin door.

The two remaining long-riders grazed their horses on the mesa and guarded them as closely as possible. They kept one mount tied at the dugout so the herd could be rounded up at a moment's notice. One day, the younger man saw Indians driving the horse herd from the mesa. He mounted and rode out to prevent the theft. The Indians killed him.

Now, the old man was left alone without a horse. He knew he could never get out of the country with all the gold, so he kept back what he could carry afoot and hid the rest. He found a big flat rock, carved directions to his hidden store on it, placed it carving down, over the smoothed grave of his dead partner near the dugout. He covered the rock with a thin layer of dirt and waited for spring.

When the snow had melted and warmer weather came, the trapper loaded his gold on his back, and depending on his rifle for food, lit out. In due time he arrived in St. Louis, his old home. The gold he carried made him fairly wealthy so he was in no hurry to go west to recover his treasure trove.

He waited too long, for finally, he lay sick of his last illness. Before he died, however, he called two of his nephews to him, told them of his hidden plunder, gave them a map showing the way to the dugout. He said the stone on the grave would unerringly show the way to his concealed hoard and in case the map came into the wrong hands the secret to the stone must still be known, if anyone was to recover the holdup loot.

The nephews were good business men, and on the balance of their uncle's money they did quite well. They had no intentions of leaving home to go into the wilds in search of hidden gold. But, they did make a deal with a friend to retrieve the bullion bars. They gave the map and directions to this friend who started west. He never returned.

When I was a kid the tale held me spellbound each time it was told, but there came a day when I wondered. I researched all the authentic holdups of "The Wild Bunch." I looked up, as best I could, all the famous robberies along the California Trail. In the end, I came to the conclusion that the whole story was a myth.

In the fall of 1967, during deer season, Clark Abegglen, a friend of mine, showed me an old outlaw hideout near the mesas of Nine Mile Canyon. I know there are many old cabins built in out-of-the-way places in Uintah Basin by early stockmen as shelters for range riders.

Each of these is suspected today of having been an outlaw retreat and undoubtedly some of them actually are, but most aren't. This one, however, appeared to be the real thing. It is situated a short way down a canyon and hidden in the junipers and pinions so well you don't notice it until you walk into the old door yard.

The dugout is rock walled. It is old because the timbers of the roof have rotted and fallen in. Parts of the wall have tumbled too, but you can still see where the fireplace was. Apparently the place was selected with a fast get-away in mind. If you go up the canyon, in a couple of hundred yards, you reach a crest, and before you is a canyon turning and twisting down to Nine Mile.

If you go down the canyon from the dugout, there are two trails; one goes down, then up and over a mountain and on across Uintah Basin. The other trail passes through a saddle in the canyon wall, strikes the head of still another canyon which runs a half mile north, makes a right angle turn, and in a few miles empties into Desolation Canyon of the Green River.

Either way you go, the escape route is like a covered causeway with the added deterrent of ambush sites at every turn. Besides this, in the saddle, is a blockhouse about four by five feet square; the door opens on a steep side hill, a porthole looks up the canyon, it was built, including the roof, entirely of massive stone.

Looking farther, I found where a camp had been under a big, spreading pinion tree. I picked up two carbolic bottles which led me to believe someone had been doctored there. In other days, carbolic was used much like iodine is today.

In the fall of 1969, Jack Rasmussen and his wife Nona, John Chasel and his wife Renee, and my wife Elva and I, went to Nine Mile country, looking for the building stones that are plentiful in that area. We wound up not far from the old dugout, and I mentioned it to my companions at one of our stops.

After looking at the structures, the women went on searching for building stones to fit their fancy. My wife, looking for stones not far from the dugout door, called to me, "Oh, look! George, here's a rock with carving on it."

I looked and sure enough, there was carving on the rock she held out to me. It had lain, carving down on the ground. In a minute or two, we had turned up other fragments all with carving on them, all lying face down.

It became evident the pieces had been parts of one large stone. It was apparent too, that the carving had been done by a white man with a metal tool; there were figures and letters and lines, sharply carved. The cutting had been done a long time ago because the freshness had faded to dimness. In addition, the stone and the cuts had become discolored by the minerals in the earth where they had been buried.

With a shock, I remembered the old legend of the trapper's loot. I tried to put the rocky jigsaw puzzle together. Finally, everyone in the party got into the act, but as darkness fell the bits still remained unfitted. I gathered the pieces together carefully, packed them in my truck, and brought them home. Since then, we have worked on the problem and have concluded we do not have all the fragments of the rock.

Five sections fit each other, the rest just don't jibe at all. There are some readable things, like the number 1101 and 1011 depending on which end of the rock goes to the top.

There is a headstone inscribed, also a point which could mean a pointing arrow or trails or canyons intersecting. There are scratches which could be compass points. As for the lines and squares, no rhyme or reason can be made of them without the rest of the stone.

The snow lies deep on the mountains, and while we wait for spring we wonder: Where are the other shards of our rocky jigsaw puzzle? Who, or what, broke the stony tablet in the first place? Above all, is the yarn about the stolen ingots true? If it is true, is the treasure still in its hiding place?

Note to Treasure Seekers:

The treasure, if there is one, was hidden by an old mountain man, who could lay caches that even the sharp, seeing eyes of Indians could not detect. Old trappers hid food and trade goods many times this way, for future use. The gold treasure, will not be in or near an obvious place, so it is senseless to destroy further the dugout, the blockhouse, or other man-made objects in the area. Please leave those things intact when you go out to dig.

THE DEATH OF AN OUTLAW

Saloon at the Babcock Place as it looks today.

The glassless windows stare, like blind eyes, out across a land of desolation. A treasure seeker has ripped up the floor and dug, hunting, I suppose, for gold coins he thought might have dropped years ago by drunks who couldn't keep track of their money. Aside from this, the old buildings, untended for all these years, remain intact. Even the cellar, underground, with entrance behind the bar, the wall built of earth tamped beer barrels, is there, almost as it was in the old days. Most would pass them by, believing them to be the shebangs of some lonely homesteader who starved out long ago, leaving nothing behind worth finding, hence their preservation.

But, in the decades around the turn of the century, this was "The Babcock Place". It was a saloon, a gambling den and a bawdy house. A place of sin, located beside 'The Post Road', an army-built public highway, that ran between Ft. Duchesne and Randlett in the 'Big

Uintah Country' of northeastern Utah. It was built on land, that due to its unique title status, was out of bounds for ordinary law, or for any ordinary law enforcement officers. This place was wild, an outlaw, the legendary "Strip".

On the post of Ft. Duchesne, at the canteens, there was beer, but the enlisted men were forbidden to have anything stronger on the military reserve. As a consequence, the soldiers, a hard bitten lot, during their off duty hours, gathered at the bars on the Strip. Here, they drank, gambled and visited with the painted ladies. There were times, especially after pay-days, when the golden stream of coin, ran fast and free, with all the rambunctious hilarity that implies.

By the Uintah River, near Ft. Duchesne, at either end of the 'Red Bridge', were campgrounds. Freighters and travelers, driving the road between Price and Vernal, camped here for one of their overnight stops. After the long, dusty miles across the deserts of the Indian Reservation, most were ready to wash the dirt from their throats with something a little livelier than clear river water. These men were wont to try the bright lights of the pleasure emporiums on the Strip and add their voices and money to that of The Boys in Blue.

There were always the curious, some from far away places, who stopped to watch the goings on at the wild, boisterous houses, growing more notorious as time went by. Sometimes these men got more than they bargained for. Not that the people at the dens of iniquity were especially quarrelsome, it was only that a man could get what he wanted, be it a drink, a song, or a fight.

The Strip stood athwart the 'Owl Hoot Trail', used often by wide-loopers, long-riders and bandits, heading for the safety of 'Robber's Roost', in southern Utah, Brown's Hole in northern Utah, or the Hole-In-The-Wall in Wyoming. As they moved from one hideout to another, they stopped at the bars on the Strip to dally awhile. They could drink, play poker or visit without fear of a lawman shoving a gun in their ribs. To the outlaw, this was a safe haven.

Butch Cassidy, the Sundance Kid, Elzey Lay, Harvey Logan and others, all members of the noted band of outlaws called 'The Wild Bunch', were seen quite often at the saloons on the out-of-bounds land.

Elzey (Elza) Lay, Butch Cassidy's right-hand man, and Pat Johnson, were partners in a saloon on the Strip, before both chose the outlaw trail. Elzey, after he was pardoned from the New Mexico State Prison, returned there to deal cards for Tom Nichols, at Tom's gaming tables. It was here Lay decided to go straight.

Harry Tracy, the mad-dog killer, the Dillinger of his day, spent a long time at Babcock's while the heat cooled on his back trail. He robbed and beat a well-liked Chinaman near Ft. Duchesne. He had to break and run for the northwest; he died in a wheat field. In his lifetime he killed more than twenty-two men.

Josephine (Josie) Bassett, later Josie Morris of Brown's Hole, subject of many yarns, hung out at the Babcock Place for quite a few years. Josie was a consort of the Wild Bunch and was the greatest woman wide-looper of all time. There was never a man, they say, who dared to cross Josie. She claimed she could outshoot any man who ever came down the pike. No one knows how many times she made good her boast.

There were many mysterious riders, who used the name of Smith, Jones, or Brown, who rode in, stayed on hour, a day or perhaps longer, then rode out again. Nobody ever knew who they really were, where they came from or where they went.

Tinhorn gamblers were there, drawn to this place like flies to honey. They stayed and played. Then like all their breed, moved on, sometimes in a big hurry.

At times, there was music on the desert air, some fiddler came to scrape away till dawn. There was the thrumming banjo. Always there was the harmonics and jews harp. Occasionally, there were sweet voiced strangers, like Tommy Birchell, later the celebrated

"Cowboy Baritone", who sang the tear jerkers: Lorena, Aura Lee, Genevieve, all those sentimental melodies.

Often the coyotes howled from the top of the big, brown hill, either in answer to the music down below or at the lamplight streaming across the barren land from the windows.

Sometimes the roistering went on until the lamps faded in the morning sun.

There were fights, many with fists and some with guns. The records show ten deaths by lead poisoning, but these cover only the demises in which Indians from the Reservation or soldiers from Ft. Duchesne were involved. There were others, and no authority had the right to investigate them. These went unnoted, except by those who were there and saw them. Today they lie in the realm of hearsay. There was no boothill; the dead were buried not far from where they fell. By now, the whispering wind and wandering sand have obliterated the marks of the graves. The number of dead men left after the brawls will never be known.

The name, The Strip, was written in scarlet letters and its ill fame had reached all the way to the offices of the mighty along the banks of the Potomac. It was vowed to the Mormon Elders, that this Sodom and Gomorrah in their midst, would be killed at the first opportunity.

True to their word, the lawgivers in Washington, put the land of the Strip up for sale at a dollar and a quarter an acre. As the land was purchased and went into private ownership, the regular law became effective on the purchased land. Beginning with the year 1901, piece by piece, the old Strip died.

There was townsite formed called Moffat, after the railroad magnate, who was responsible for Moffat Tunnel, through the Rockies. Many of the business houses moved to the new town. The settlement, like many other outlaws, decided to clean up and go straight.

Finally, in 1905-1906, the rest of the no-man's-land was thrown open for homestead entry; the law came to all the outlaw land. The Babcock place was hard hit. It gasped for breath. But it stayed on, paying fines regularly to the proper authorities of Uintah County.

The coup de grace came when Ft. Duchesne ceased to be an active army post. The soldiers marched away in 1910, leaving behind them the empty houses and barracks. The Indian service filled them, but you couldn't sell liquor, not even beer, to Indians, without risking a trip to the federal pen.

The Strip had a short life. It lived, at best, only twenty-two years, then, like some of its human outlaw counterparts, it was shot down in the full vigor of its life. The Babcock Place went down, but it was the last to fall. The only epitaph a man can write for it is, "It died with its boots on."

The wheels have turned many times since 1910. All the marks of the other wild, old establishments have vanished, leaving nothing behind to show where they were. Only this place, by the side of the road still stands.

It was a lascivious sinner, yet it marks one of the most interesting, unusual and colorful spots in the annals of the West. It lived and died, and there will never be anything like it again. The empty shell is there. It gives an authentic likeness; imagination must supply the missing pieces of people, sights and sounds to show how it was in 'The Good Old Days', of the hell-roaring West.

THE OPENING

THE OPENING I

*This is a picture of one of the Settlers of Uintah Basin, in his famous
'buckboard wagon' used for travel long after the automobile.*

Purposely, or inadvertently, one of the most colorful events in
the history of Utah has been overlooked by historians for many
decades. Only lately, has the legendary event gained any notice from
western writers—most of whom keep their eyes forever glued on the
entrance of the Saints into the valley of the Great Salt Lake and its
environs. This, then is a short story dealing with the event known to
most old-timers as 'The Opening.'

From the day of Abraham Lincoln's proclamation of 1861, to

the time of Theodore Roosevelt in 1905, the vast Uintah-Ouray Indian Reservation lay in Eastern Utah restricted for Indian use only. It was a primeval land of mountains, streams, uplands and deserts. Except for Whiterocks, Fort Duchesne, Randlett, and Ouray, all U.S. Government installations, and roads that led to them, it remained unscarred by marks of white civilization.

Then, almost out of the blue, it was done. The great Indian Reservation of the Utes was to be opened to the settlement of white men.

The news traveled like wildfire to the east, to the west, to the north and to the south. People stood waiting.

Now, the government had learned many lessons in the opening of Indian lands in Oklahoma, known now in history as the great land rush of the Cimmaron. This, they opined, would be no duplicate. The Ute Reservation would be settled in a more orderly fashion.

So they worked out a scheme which, in the end, was nothing more or less than a giant lottery. A person could file for a homestead of 160 acres, pay $2.50 an acre and draw a number. That number was his or her right of selection of all fileable land on the reservation. For example, number one had the first choice of all the land on the reservation, number two had the second choice, and so it went until the drawing ended. Of course, there were other rules, regulations and red tape to be complied with, but the above in short, was the general idea.

In this event, people came, not by the tens, not by the hundreds, but literally by the thousands. They were migrating to a new and promising land. My mother and father, who had lived on the reservation since long before the opening said, "During the opening, we stopped on the highest point at the head of Gate Canyon. We could trace the main road all the way to 'The Twist' by the dust and dirt rising up from the hooves and wheels of the steady string of people heading for the government land office in Vernal."

Among these people were some from every occupation known

to man, including outlaws, gamblers, and mustangers. But by far the greatest number were farmers, young and old, rich and poor, coming in for a brand new start.

There were several roads into the Basin from the outside. There was the old Ft. Thornburg Road from Ft. Bridger, Wyoming; the Meeker Road from Colorado; the Strawberry Valley Road from Heber City, Utah; the Colton Road down Indian Canyon. All these roads were used, to some extent, by homesteaders coming in to set- tle. But the big main road that most settlers traveled was the Nine Mile Road, almost forgotten now but once the track of empire. Those hundreds who came in that way drove through Nine Mile Canyon. Here along the creek called the Minnie Maud, the moun- tains towered high above them on either side. The sounds of the clanking wagon echoed and re-echoed from the high ledges, along the bottom of which they drove. To all those who drove that canyon, the memory of it lingers still and has become a legend—like many pioneer roads of the old west. The old road is still there and has the marks of the wagon wheels upon it.

So they came and settled—only they know how or why. And the times were tough. Some starved out and left. Some stayed because they had to. Some prospered; others just lived so-so. All have this to say about those early days, "We'd never have made it if it hadn't been for potatoes and cottontail rabbits. Some day, we'll erect a monument to them little fellers. They wuz mighty good to eat."

It seems to me, looking back at the Opening, that towns, trading centers, churches, schools, and houses sprang up all over. And that without an impact study or a federal grant—impossible!

Were times all bad in the early days of settlement on the reserva- tion? No, oh no! I still close my eyes as we dance or hear the strains of Red Wing, Snow Dear, the Missaire Waltz and Old Dan Tucker; I still smell her hair washed in homemade soap scented lightly with lilac and rain water; her starched, ironed and pretty gingham dress; her sparkling eyes and her sweet smile; and she in my arms. Why my friend, there was a spot of heaven on the old reservation.

THE OPENING II

Somewhere between the Wells and the Bridge, the Nine Mile Road crossed the reservation line. From there on was Indian country until, on the way to Vernal, the 'Sand Ridge' was reached and left behind.

The reservation was established by Abraham Lincoln in 1861. From that time, to the Opening, white man could not settle or use the land of the reservation without permission of the Indian Service. The Ute country extended from the Uintah River to the tops of the mountains in every direction.

The years passed. There was a move to open the reservation to white settlement. The treaty with the Indians said there could be white settlement whenever a majority of the Indians consented. Now the appointed commissioners reported a majority of the Indians were in favor of opening their land to white men. But this has always been disputed. However, the proper authorities in Washington, from the records of the commissioners, determined it was time to allow settlement in the land of the Utes.

A while before the turn of the century, in Oklahoma, the government had experienced the opening of other Indian lands to white men. What happened there is a matter of history.

The Ute Reservation was to be different. It was to be more orderly so that the great rush and abuses of other openings would be avoided. First, the Indians were allotted their lands. Secondly, plans were made to bring irrigation water to Indian lands and the proper arrangements were made to accomplish this. Thirdly, all remaining, unsurveyed land was surveyed. After this was done, the open land would be settled by means of a giant lottery. Every prospective homesteader was to draw a number in one of four places: Grand Junction, Colorado; Provo, Price, and Vernal, Utah. The priority for the pick of the land would be in accordance with the number drawn. Number one had its first choice, number two—the second choice, etc.

The people with numbers were allowed on the reservation to inspect and choose where they would settle. Then they must await their notices.

The notices to the registered number holder went out specifying the day and time they were to report in Vernal to file their claims. If they reported on the day and time specified, they made their filings. If they missed the hour, but were there on the proper day, they went to the first of the daily line with its corresponding priority number. If they missed the day that they were to report, they lost their priority and their number. Fifty were filed in the forenoon and fifty in the afternoon each day.

There were sixty days allowed for all registered claimants with numbers to file their claims. After that, the regular homestead laws were in effect. Any qualifying person could file on land in accordance with regular procedures covered by the prevailing laws on filing on the public domain.

In 1905, the reservation opened and the wagon wheels rolled. They came in an unending line, one, two, three years and more, they kept coming. They came in every kind of vehicle known to man—in wagons, in buggies, on horseback, even a foot. There were wagons loaded with everything the family owned, including the family dog and cat. Little dust covered kids peeked from wagon boxes, especially when Indians were around to be stared at. They were bound for a brand new country to find homes somewhere away out yonder.

They spread out all over the Basin to establish new settlements. Almost overnight, the wilderness sprang alive with tents, cabins, houses and green fields. But the life was hard, some made it, others didn't.

Amanda Felter, one of the early homesteaders said, "When Lee and I came here, we had a wagon, six horses, six cows, six kids and six dollars. We lived and after awhile prospered, but I don't know how. Why, the coyotes came to our door-yard every night looking for scraps of food that they thought we might have overlooked for supper; but it was years before they found anything. Arriving here, Lee drove us to the middle of a brush covered flat and stopped. I said to the boys, 'Get busy, this is home.' That night when we went to bed in our wagon box, I thought to myself, 'Lee, you've got us in a pickle this time and I don't believe you can get us out of it. We'll be too hungry to stay and too broke to go.' The government, you see, bet us 160 acres of land against our $200 (the land cost us $1.25 an acre) that we couldn't settle here and live five years without starving out. I had known Lee Felter was a good man when I married him, but it took life on the reservation to prove just how good he really was. No man will ever come any better."

Another old homesteader said, "Sea gulls rightfully have a great name in Utah history and monuments have been erected to them. But in Uintah Basin, the gull would have to take second place to 'Tawoots,' the cottontail rabbit. Throughout the opening, he was the one unfailing food supply the homesteaders had. He ran by the thousands over the land. He was in every nook and corner of the Basin, so that no matter where you went out here, he was available. Hunger would have stalked many a tent and cabin had it not been for the rabbit. To him, the homesteaders, those who are still around, doff their hats. Today, if he raids our lush green fields in modest numbers, he is welcome. He is no longer required for food, but our gratefulness to him goes back to other days."

Almost all of the homesteaders, together with what was needed from the outside world to sustain them, came over the Nine Mile Road. Strictly speaking, the Nine Mile Road ended at the Bridge or in later days, Myton. Here, at the bridge over the Duchesne, all roads from other Utah points outside the Basin joined. However, since the road from one terminus to the other, in the old days, was a continuous whole over which the main stream flowed, the traffic narrative will continue on to Vernal, the northern end of the old frontier trail.

The way led out of Pleasant Valley, across South Myton Bench, dropped down to the river bottom. In three miles it came to the Bridge, which in later days became the town of Myton.

Myton is rich in history. It is situated on the banks of the Duchesne River near the end of an ancient ford across the river. Father Escalante, the Catholic priest/explorer and the first white man to see the Uintah Basin, camped under the trees at the end of the old ford in 1776. In 1869, a trading post and a station for wayfarers was built where Father Escalante had camped. It was put there for the convenience of the Indians after the reservation had been set apart by President Lincoln. In 1880, a wagon bridge made of wood was constructed across the river by the D. and P. G. Railroad and the U.S. Government. From then until the Opening it was known as 'The Bridge.'

After Ft. Duchesne was built, there was a trading post, a stage station, and a hotel located at the crossing. After the Opening, the Bridge became the town of Myton, named after H. P. Myton, an early Indian Department official and surveyor. It was, in many ways, the most colorful town in the whole Uintah Basin. All the roads from points in Utah joined here, so that all traffic went through the town. It was also the first water and first settlement reached after crossing the long, desert reaches of the Nine Mile Road.

The town sprang into being almost overnight. It became the center for the whole reservation. It was a raw, new, frontier town, filled with the smell of fresh lumber, the sound of the carpenter's hammers, the noise, the hustle of people going places and doing things. All in a moment, it seemed, the open flats were filled with business houses and dwelling places. What yesterday were open flats were turned into streets and yards a foot deep in dust and mud.

Myton was a heterogeneous town. There were people and religions from everywhere, even from foreign lands. As you passed along its streets, you heard the nasal twang of New England, the clipped British accent, the hard R's of the westerners, the soft drawl of Virginia, Kentucky, and the deep south. There were Irishmen, Scotsmen, Germans, Scandinavians, and Mexicans. All these people rubbed shoulders with the Indians, who looked on curiously, and sometimes resentfully, at all this going on in their country.

Up the river, about twelve miles from Myton, was the largest Indian village in the Basin. There were three to four hundred Indians living there the seasons around. It was a village of teepees with some log cabins placed around in a great circle.

Most of the Indians painted their faces in accordance with the old Indian customs. Many still dressed in the same style they had used for centuries. All these Indians, plus those from other places, came to Myton on issue day and to do their trading. They were curious, too, so they came just to watch.

By 1908, there was a bank, three general merchandise stores, a livery stable, two blacksmith shops, a drug store, a hardware store, two saloons, a real estate office, two lumber yards, two lawyers, a doctor, a community hall and amusement center, and a U.S. Post Office. The Indian Irrigation Service headquartered there. It was the center for construction of all Indian irrigation canals and systems.

Stretching a hundred miles and more to the south and east were wide regions of vacant, desert land with the Green River flowing through the middle of it. At this time, on these wide reaches, grazed hundreds of wild horses. They were old natives, descendants of the Spanish horses. The mustangs were small, but they were hardy and their endurance was un-matched. Mustangers made Myton their headquarters. From there they caught the wild horses from the desert country. Their corral was always full where they kept and fed their catches, pending the day they drove them to market over the Nine Mile Road.

The winter of 1909-10 had been a hard one, the snow piled deep over all the Basin and in the mountains. When spring came, it was exceptionally warm and all the streams rose in flood. Myton was built on the river bottom. It was feared the water would leap its banks and flood the town.

E.M. Jones, the hardware merchant, took dynamite to a big bend up the river and set charges, cutting a channel across the bend. He hoped he could divide the water and thus keep the river within bounds. He succeeded far beyond his expectation, for within four hours the river changed its course completely. Mr. Jones saved the town but he left the bridge across which all traffic must pass, high and dry.

The river could not be forded, two men who tried it on horse-back, drowned in the raging torrent. Except for a row boat, used in a quiet place, there was no communication with the other side for two weeks or more. Then the river went down. After that the old ford across the river was used.

The U.S. Government and the State of Utah, joined again and in the summer of 1910, a new steel bridge was built about a mile upstream from the old bridge. When the new, steel bridge was ready for use, there was a big celebration at Myton. Governor Spry came from Salt Lake City. Senator Reed Smoot came from Washington D.C. People came from all over Uintah Basin to be present at this gala event. One of the highlights of the day was when the mail coach arrived from the Wells, driven by Frank Alger. The horses were changed as always. Then at a gallop, Frank drove the mail across the new bridge for the first time and disappeared on the road to Vernal in a cloud of dust. The horses hitched to the coach that day were: Billy, Sally, Maud and Dingo.

Because they feared the river and because they wanted to be on the direct road from the new bridge, the people of Myton moved the old town. In the course of a year, the town moved to a low bench out north of the river. Henceforth, there were two parts to the town—Myton and Old Town.

In the early days the stage left Myton, crossed the wooded bridge, went straight toward Ft. Duchesne for twelve miles through what is now Hartford and Independence. It climbed a low hill, went down Bottle Hollow and was at the army post. In later days a new town, Roosevelt, was settled to the east of Myton. So the road, that is the mail and a part of the traffic, went by way of the new town.

Ed F. Harmston, an enterprising engineer, from a part of four homesteads, laid out the town of Roosevelt in 1906. It was at a location which no sensible person, it was thought, would ever hope to build a town. It was on a dry, hot, dusty bench far away from any stream or supply of water. It was on the banks of Dry Gulch; in those years the gulch was really dry. But Harmston formed the Dry Gulch Irrigation Company, which, at one time, was the largest irrigation system in the United States. Within a year, by means of canals out of the Uintah River, water was flowing to the new townsite.

The town was named after Theodore Roosevelt, who, at the time of the town's beginnings, was President of the United States and had signed the proclamation opening the reservation. It was not because Roosevelt was President, though, that the town was named after him. It was because Mary Harmston, the wife of Ed F. Harmston, had met Teddy when he had been in the Basin some years before. Mary was personally acquainted with Theodore Roosevelt, was an admirer of his, and it was she who gave the town its name.

The town, situated where a town should not be, grew rapidly and in time outdistanced all other towns on the reservation.

After the opening, the old road climbed North Myton Bench, crossed it, and pulled into Roosevelt. It left Roosevelt, climbed Indian Bench, went slantwise southeasterly and dropped down Bottle Hollow to Ft. Duchesne. For years, until hard surfaced roads came, part of the traffic went by way of Roosevelt and some still traveled the route by way of Independence.

MYTON, THE QUEEN OF THE RESERVATION

Above is the old stage and mail station taken at Myton.

Myton, Utah's recorded history began almost two centuries ago when Fathers Dominguez and Escalante, two roving Franciscan friars, made camp and stayed the night of September 17, 1776, near what is now Myton Townsite.

In the 1880's, a wooden bridge was built across the turbulent and dangerous Duchesne River. It was the only bridge along the entire lower reaches of the stream. After the bridge was built, an Indian trading post, a stage station, a sub-agency, and a blacksmith shop sprang into being on the right bank of the river. In those days it was called simply 'The Bridge.'

In 1886, the army built Fort Duchesne. At the same time, the army constructed a wagon road from the post through Nine Mile Canyon to Price, Utah, the nearest railroad town, nearly eighty miles away. The army road, upon its completion, became the main route into and out of Uintah Basin. There were no towns between Price and The Bridge along the way.

Because of the bridge and the new main road, it was literally true to say, all roads on the Reservation led to The Bridge. Here was the gateway to Uintah Basin.

In 1905-06, the Uintah-Ouray Indian Reservation, which up to that time had been forbidden to White settlers, was opened to White homesteaders. One of the three townsites surveyed and laid out by the U.S. Government, in preparation for the opening, was a town which incorporated The Bridge within its limits. This new town was named 'Myton,' after H. P. Myton, the Indian agent for the Reservation from 1899 to 1902.

Then the land rush came at 'The Opening.' Myton, because of its location, quickly became the trading, industrial, and cultural center for the entire Reservation. Within a year, it was booming—lusty, typically frontier, and wild.

If the town was colorful so were its people. It drew all kinds of residents to it: bankers, lawyers, doctors, preachers, barbers, teachers, gamblers, outlaws, gunslingers, Indians, cowboys, soldiers, sheepherders, freighters, farmers, mustangers, engineers, carpenters, writers, miners, 'Mormons,' and 'gentiles' walked its streets. Of course, it had to have tough marshals—some of whom are still remembered.

1909-10 was a year of deep snow and high water. In the spring, E. M. Jones, with a charge of powder, inadvertently caused the river to change its course leaving the old wooden bridge high and dry. In 1910, a new, steel bridge was built and the town moved from 'Oldtown,' on the river bottom up to the low bench it presently occupies.

In its day, Myton had a full complement of businesses like stores, hotels, livery stables, restaurants and many others, including four saloons with gambling dens and one undertaker.

Myton saw the last uprising of the Utes when Billy Muse shot the Indian, Phenno.

In addition, adding tangy flavor, there were shoot-outs on the streets, fights and brawls and other excitements. The little jail was always full. Everything considered, it was a lively place to live.

Despite its notorious reputation, Myton had good, as well as evil. Except for establishments at Indian Agency settlements, it had the first churches, the first schools, the first theaters, the first baseball teams, the first bands and orchestras, the first of almost everything on the Reservation.

Today, Myton is only a shade of its former self. Three fourths of its business buildings have been torn down or burned away and, with a few exceptions, the rest stand empty with glassless windows staring blankly across the old Main Street. But, those that are left are the original. Though dilapidated, they remain unchanged from the heyday of the place, adding charm and atmosphere to its Western lore.

Myton, because of its colorful past, has become a living legend. It was a frontier town, the last of its kind and properly belongs to the Old West of song and story. As the Old West faded so did Myton. Old-timers are right when they say, "She ain't much now; but in her day, she was *The Queen of the Reservation.*"

THE DAY THE BRIDGE WENT DRY

*This is the old wooden bridge that went dry. The boaters are riding on the
lake that was left after the river changed its course.*
—Used by permission, Uintah Regional Library, all rights reserved.

Most of Uintah Basin, in eastern Utah, was restricted Indian
country until the days of 'The Opening' in 1905-1906. So the wild
days of its settling came late. But when those days finally arrived,
they brought with them all the color and unusual happenings that
follow in the wake of the settlement of a new frontier. One of the
true tales old-timers tell deals with the day the bridge at Myton was
left high and dry in the springtime flood.

The snow came early in the fall of 1908. The mountain peaks
and the lowlands, too, were blanketed in white, sometime in
September. Storm followed storm constantly, piling drift on drift. All

roads over the mountains to the outside were snow blocked and the store men rationed their slim supply of staples.

Time after time, the freight outfits banded together for concerted effort, broke through the snow to Price only to find on their return, they must perform the Herculean task all over again. Never before nor since, they say, has there been such a winter in the Big U country.

Then, it was spring. The warm winds blew and their soft caresses melted the snow and ice almost overnight.

Now, a new disaster threatened; the ice went out of the rivers with booming bangs like cannon fire. Every quiet, whispering stream turned into a raging torrent. The angry water came, turgid and roaring, moving everything in its path.

In those days, Myton was the western gateway to the Basin. The famed, army built road, up Smith's Draw, down Gate Canyon, through Nine Mile and on to Price and the railroad was the main highway carrying all the travel. The higher mountain passes of other roads would be snowbound until July.

Myton stood thriving on the banks of the Duchesne River, because, spanning the river at this location was the only bridge along the entire length if this turbulent stream. All traffic, regardless of which route the wayfarer used, must pass this way. In those days, all roads led to Myton.

In the spring of 1909, the safety of the Myton bridge was shaky; the Duchesne River was on the warpath again. Its deep-toned war song sounded incessantly, day and night. Besides, the cataracts of the stream filled the banks to brimming. An inch or two more rise and the streets of the town would flood. Already the crests of the waves were splashing over.

E. M. Jones, the hardware man, had dynamite and an idea. If he could blast a channel across the axis of a wide, curving bend the river made as it flowed to the bridge and Myton, he could draw off part of the water and thus save the crossing and the town. Jones proceeded on his own and never told anyone what he was doing. Ka-boom! Ka-boom! Ka-boom! Three charges went. Then all was quiet.

Suddenly, the roar of the water receded into the distance. Those working to reinforce the banks were astounded. They saw the river fall in its channel until it became little more than a trickle. It was the miraculous hand of God, they thought, not grasping for the moment what had really happened. They threw down their shovels; the town was saved.

But holy mackerel! The river, given an inch by Jones, had taken a mile. It had carved itself a new bed. In a matter of minutes, it had moved rocks, earth, brush, and trees out of its way. Now it flowed straight and true across the bend, leaving Myton off to one side— safe and sound.

The trouble was, the only bridge on the Duchesne River had gone dry; there was no way to cross the raging water. The Duchesne is a swiftly flowing stream. In those days before dams, diversions, and modern irrigation captured most of its water, attempting to ford it in high, springtime flood was suicidal. Already, a mail carrier and a venturesome cowboy had died in the wild torrent. So freighters and other outfitters came and backed up on both sides of the river, waiting. Almost the whole Uintah Basin was isolated from the rest of civilization. How long would this go on, the people wondered. When the solid white on the highest peaks of the Uintah Mountains grew spots, like the spots on a spotted dog, the water would go down, the Indians said.

And so it was, the days went by until the chesty river subsided and the fords could be used to keep the travel moving.

Senator Reed Smoot, Governor William Spry, and the commissioners of Wasatch and Uintah counties got their heads together and came up with a new steel bridge for Myton. In addition, most of the town moved to a new, higher location. In the future, all would be safe from rampaging water.

"Bridge Day" at Myton in 1910 was quite a celebration but that is another tale and merits a story all by itself, perhaps someday someone will write it. For now it is enough to say, the old wooden bridge is gone; it is hard to find its location. The steel bridge is gone too, only the abutments remain, a new, modern bridge replacing it above. "Old Town" and the new town of Myton are there, but both are only ghosts of their former selves. Still, those who were there and remember, know that, in its day, Myton was the "Queen of the Wild Frontier." Around it, many a yarn is woven. All of them smack of the Old Wild West. This tale of the day the bridge went dry is one of these. The name I give the event is the one the old-timers use when they tell of the time, in the 'Early Days,' when the bridge at Myton was left high and dry, off to one side of the river.

THE COTTONTAIL

Each country to its own. Salt Lake Valley has its Seagulls, the plains have the buffalo, and Cripple Creek, Colorado has its jackass.

But out in Uintah Basin, in eastern Utah, there is the small rodent, with the powerful puff tail, that deserves the accolade. His name is the cottontail rabbit.

In the 'Early Days,' at 'The Opening,' in 1905 and 1906, the homesteaders streamed into the Ute Reservation to settle on the last free land on earth. It was a howling wilderness and civilization was far away. There were rivers and streams, of course, but for the most part it was an arid, barren waste. Here the settler must make his home by living on his claim for five years to 'prove up,' or his title to the land went blooey.

They came, they saw, they conquered—some of them—and the rest starved out. But those who made it say it would have been impossible without the cottontail rabbit.

You see, the automobile in those days was practically unknown. There were no refrigerators. The butcher shops in the larger centers had ice, but a trip to town once or twice a month was quite an accomplishment. Fresh meat was seldom, if ever, come by during the long, hot summer. But over the whole country ran the little cottontail. He supplied fresh meat to the settlers.

They say the 30-30 Winchester won the west. This may be true, but in Uintah Basin the gun that did the business was the little 22 rifle of almost any make. With this the homesteader got his rabbits, and if he didn't get them, he got hungry.

As time drew on, the homesteaders' money grew short. As one old-timer said, "When Jim and I settled on our place, we had seven cows, seven kids, and seven dollars, but we made it. Sometimes we had rabbit for breakfast, rabbit for dinner, and rabbit for supper. And

I still think rabbit is mighty tasty when I can get some."

From these stories comes the truth. Not only was fresh meat, like beef, hard to come by, but even if there was plenty, the homesteader couldn't buy it. One of the 'Early Dayers' said, "We spent our money before the canal got built. We were too poor to go and too poor to stay. But as long as we could get bullets, we could get rabbits. And that's the thing that kept us alive. I can't count the times I would have gone to bed hungry, if it hadn't been for rabbits." So it goes, everywhere the Old Boys gather, the story is the same.

In this fast, modern age, the memory of the cottontail recedes farther back, until now, the part he played is almost forgotten. This is why I hasten to write these few words for the record. If it were me, somewhere in a proper place on the reservation, I would erect a monument to the cottontail. I respect the gull, the buffalo, and the jackass, but the rabbit would have my prettiest blue ribbon. Because, you see, I am an Old-timer. I was born, was reared, and have lived all my life on the Reservation. The cottontail is not unknown to me.

THE LAST WAR TRAIL OF

THE WHITERIVERS

Myton as it appeared around 1905 but not in its 'heyday.'

As the days of the Old West were drawing to a close, the fierce Mo-va-tavi-ats (Sun Blanket People, officially known as Whiterivers), one of the northern bands of the Ute Indian Nation, made their final bid for glory. It was war against the intrusion of the 'Americats' (white-men) into the last country on earth the Utes could call their own.

Long before, in 1861, the Great White Father, Abraham Lincoln had set aside a reservation in the eastern part of the territory of Utah. For as long as water runs and grass grows, this big Uintah Country was to be for the exclusive use of the Ute Indian People. Forty-four years the Indians lived without too much interference from the white-men. They were happy.

Then, around the turn of the century, the Awat Towatch (big

men), along the banks of the Potomac, decided to open the Ute Reservation for settlement by homesteaders.

It was unbelievable to the Indians that the words of Father Abraham should be written in the dust, to vanish away in some vagrant springtime wind. So the rank and file of the Indian people treated 'The Opening' as a rumor.

In 1905, came reality. Drawings were held for choice of land. There was the first dribble of settlers into the region the Utes had ruled for centuries. Fences and cabins sprang up on the wide expanses where the Red-man had roamed, unhindered since before the earliest memories of living men. In sullen silence, the Utes watched. Everyone knew the smoldering tinder could burst into flame at the first ill wind that blew.

Feno, a sub-chief, was a trouble-maker and hated the paleface with a passion. At every opportunity, he harassed these men whom he considered to be thieves and trespassers.

One day, at gun point, he forced the stage-driver to drive his coach, with all his passengers, over the edge and down the steep side of South Myton Bench. Only the driver's skill saved injury or death to the wayfarers. Jet Alger, the driver, made the whole, impossible descent right side up and without accident.

Another time, after he had been refused whiskey by a saloon-keeper on The Strip, Feno fired a fusillade through the window. It hit Albert Davis in the hip, a nasty wound from which Davis never fully recovered. Sooner or later, everyone surmised, Davis or Alger or someone else would force Feno to a showdown and trouble would ensue.

Myton, at the time of 'The Opening,' was the largest town on the Reservation. In 1905, it was brand new; smelling of fresh pine boards and tar-paper. The influx of settlers was yet to come, so the town had only a few permanent residents. Those who were there, were building in anticipation of the rush when the general homestead laws would come into effect the following year.

At Myton, formerly known as 'The Bridge,' was an Indian Trading Post operated by Hayden Calvert. In 1905, it was doing a land-office business in general merchandise. One of Calvert's employees was 'The Virginian,' who hailed from somewhere around Richmond. His real name was William (Billy) Muse.

Feno had tried to frighten The Virginian into buying liquor for him. But Muse didn't scare worth a darn; he threw the chief out with the admonition, "Don't you evah come in heah, full of licka again or I will use a buggy whip on you!"

As the Indian left, he threatened, "One day, I kill you, Billy Muse."

Two kids were playing in the yard of their house in Myton. Feno, a little drunk, aimed his rifle and shot close to the youngsters to frighten them. Billy Muse, hearing the screams, came up in time to see the action. He shouted at Feno. Feno turned and pointed his gun at Muse but he was too slow. The Virginian drew his gun and killed him.

A few minutes after the gunplay, the little town didn't have an Indian in it; all had vanished away as if by magic.

That night, the war drums sounded in the big Indian village, on the banks of the Duchesne River at Antelope, a few miles above Myton. The smoldering tinder had burst into flame; the Whiterivers were on the warpath. All night long, the drums beat, accompanied by the wild, chilling war song, rising, ever rising, toward crescendo. The big war fire burned brightly. Around it, the warriors, stripped and painted for war, danced themselves into a frenzy.

The whites, in Myton had been given an ultimatum. "Give us Billy Muse," the Indians said. "We will kill him and bury him side by side with Feno in the same grave. You are in Indian Country. This is the Indian law. If you refuse to do this, we shall kill you all and burn your town to ashes."

"Go on your way. We won't give you Billy Muse. We will try him by our law and if he is guilty, we will punish him," the townsmen answered.

Through the night, couriers rode to warn the scattered white settlers. "Better ride for Myton or Ft. Duchesne," they urged, "lest the gathering war parties of the Utes finds you and lifts your hair."

Night time dust rose on the roads and trails leading toward Myton and Ft. Duchesne. The few settlers were hurrying to add their guns to the embattled settlements.

As day was dawning, many of the women and children from Myton, were on their way to Ft. Duchesne and safety. But the men stayed on, resolved to fight and save their property.

At sunrise, the watchers on the big hill below town, could see the rising dust cloud as the warriors, in a body, rode from Antelope toward Myton. The Indians were determined now to drive all palefaces far beyond the boundary of Ute Territory. They were also determined to capture The Virginian.

The postmaster telegraphed to the commander at Ft. Duchesne, telling him an Indian attack on Myton was in the offering. He got the short reply, "Hold your fire. We are coming."

But the Indians got to the town before the soldiers. They rode up and down main street on the gallop, brandishing their guns and shooting into the buildings. Their high pitched ki-yi (war cry) echoed and re-echoed in the streets.

The white men stood armed behind the doors and windows of their barricaded buildings. "Hold your fire. Don't shoot unless the Indians try to get in or try to set fire to your belongings. Then shoot to kill," were the instructions.

And so they waited, knowing full well the braves were working themselves up to a point of desperate courage, before they tried to force entry into the buildings where many would die.

Colorow, Wero, Redcap, Arapoo and others were there, all veterans of the fight at Meeker and Mill Creek in Colorado, where Major Thornburg and many others had been slain. These leaders were not afraid. Soon, they would lead their men on the final assault.

In the nick of time, the soldiers came. This was the famed old Seventh U.S. Cavalry, some of them veterans and survivors of the campaign against the Sioux when General Custer and his men were killed on the Greasy Grass in Wyoming. They were not afraid, for they were old at Indian fighting.

As the troops approached the town, they could hear the staccato bark of many rifles and the war whoops of the attackers. The order was given; the bugle sounded the charge. Away they galloped in column of twos, the pennon with the big, red seven, leading the way. Across the wooden bridge they rode, sounding like a long, low peal of thunder as their horses hooves pounded on the planking.

The Indians heard the bugle and the thunder of the cavalry horses and retreated out of town and up the river. They retreated, not because they were afraid—after all they had fought the Long Knives before—but Redcap was a good field general. Anticipating the arrival of the troopers, he wished to draw them into a pursuit and smack into a prepared ambush.

The commander of the Seventh was no fool. He entered the town of Myton and halted. There was no pitched battle.

Hard on the heels of the troopers came the Indian Agent from Ouray, bringing Henry Harris with him.

Henry Harris was an educated Pawguan-nuance (Lake Shore People, officially known as Uintahs). Harris, courageously rode alone to meet the chiefs of the warring band. All day long, he sat explaining, talking, and promising. And as the sun went down, his diplomatic skill had made peace between the Americans and the Whiterivers.

The Virginian was escorted out of the country. At his hearing later in Salt Lake City, the findings were, "Not Guilty." The

Virginian had shot in self defense. The Whiteriver chiefs, when they heard all the circumstances surrounding the Feno incident, agreed that the findings of the court were correct.

Though the clouds of war had appeared ominous, though it seemed battle and blood would follow Feno's shooting, incredibly the last war trail of the Whiterivers came to an end without bloodshed.

Looking back, both sides will agree, that had the two opposing veteran contingents of fighting men clashed that fall day in 1905, there would have been much glory, but many would have died. All doff their hats to the memory of Henry Harris, the Indian who talked long ago and saved the peace of Uintah.

THE SHOOT-OUT

"You should have seen it then." Myton-1918.
The crowd at right has been drawn by a shootout; in the group at left
is the author, then a kid reporter (age 12) for the Free Press.
—Used by permission, Utah State Historical Society, all rights reserved.

In 1918, my father and mother operated Hotel Myton in Myton, Utah, then the leading town on the Ute Indian Reservation in eastern Utah. One day, a tall, dark, man, graying over the temples and balding, stopped to stay awhile at our hotel. The stranger had a small black dog he called 'Blackie'. One could see that the two, the man and the dog, were great pals. The dog, like the man, was slightly crippled. The man moved about with a limp. The limp was caused by an old bullet wound, I learned later. One of the dog's front legs had been cut off as a result of an accident some time before.

I had a big, black dog who, in protecting his rich domain of table scraps and beef bones, had become a vicious fighter of great renown around the town.

My father called me to him as the stranger and he stood talking under the shade of the portico which extended over the sidewalk in front of the hotel. "George," he said, "I want you to meet this gentleman. He is a very old friend of mine whom I knew when we worked over on the Strip together. Elza, this is my youngest son, George. George, I want you to meet Elza Lay."

Mr. Lay and I shook hands and then he said, "That little three-legged dog belongs to me. His name is Blackie. He can't fight and he can't run, and I'd hate to see that big dog of yours chew him up. Can you see to that for me, and if you have plenty for a dog to eat, will you see that he don't go hungry?"

Since we ran a dining room as part of the hotel, and since my big dog already showed his friendship for Blackie, compliance with Lay's request was easy. "I will see to him for you, Mr. Lay," I replied.

Elza Lay? I had heard of him, as all teenage boys had in that day and age. But, now, could this be the famous outlaw Elza Lay, the right hand man of the redoubtable Butch Cassidy? Was he one of the real riders of 'The Wild Bunch'?

When I got a chance to ask my father, he told me, "Yes, George, that's the ex-outlaw Elza Lay. He's been out to see his daughter, Mrs. Murdock, in Heber. He hasn't been a bandit for many years now. I'd be pleased if you'd take care of his dog like he asked you to."

I took care of Blackie in sumptuous style and shortly he and I were fast friends. Mr. Lay came around the corner one time and saw me petting his little dog. He saw Blackie lick my hand. From that time on I had a special 'in' with Mr. Lay.

At the time, during off hours from school, I worked on the old Myton Free Press, a small town, weekly newspaper. I did this and that and the other thing, whatever needed to be done. C.B. Cook, the editor, tried to teach me the who, the how, the where, the when and the why of good reporting and as Mr. Lay and I talked, I used the techniques I had learned on him. Only it wasn't the events of the day I tried to find out, but the events of long ago I was after. It was during one of these conversations that he told me about the shoot-out between Johnny McVey and Bill Carver.

The Wild Bunch had planned a hijacking of the army payroll when the money was in transit between Price, Utah and Ft. Duchesne, over the old Nine Mile Road. In the planning process, the men were selected for their ability to shoot with a rifle from the top of a ridge. Johnny McVey, was to act as a scout or spotter or advance man for the Bunch, and he objected a little, saying, "I'll bet I'm the best rifle shot in the crowd, I should be on the ridge."

Bill Carver was a quiet, easy going cowboy, and at McVey's remark, he said nothing. He just winked at Butch Cassidy and let Johnny's boast go by without a challenge.

Butch, seeing a chance for some fun later, said to McVey, "We'll be hanging around here for quite a while, and in the next day or two we'll have a shooting match. Then we'll find out just how good you are. But regardless of that, we want you as a scout because your face isn't known all over these parts. You can find out what we want to know without bringing the law down on our heads too soon."

"Oh, that's it," Johnny replied. "Well, in that case, I'll do the scouting."

Later, when the tedium of waiting became an irking problem, McVey, remembering Butch's promise and wanting to show off his prowess, challenged the Bunch to a shooting match with rifles. Butch, always ready for some horseplay, said, "Now that's a good idea. Bill, since you don't shoot like the rest of us, you go first. If you can't beat him, then we'll each go one by one until somebody comes out the winner."

Carver asked, "What will we use for a target?"

Cassidy picked up six empty cans, he placed them in a row at about two foot intervals, on a log that had been pulled in for firewood. "Now," he said, "whichever one of you can shoot these cans off the log in the shortest time is the winner, and you'll shoot from here." As he was talking, he made a mark on the ground with his boot toe.

The distance was long for fast shooting. By this time the whole crowd gathered around to watch the proceedings.

Johnny McVey was maneuvered into shooting first. He went to the line, raised his rifle to his shoulder, took aim and shot six times in rapid succession, and each time a can rolled. He stepped back with a confident smirk on his face and looked at Carver. It was admitted by all that Johnny was a top hand with a long gun, because his had really been excellent shooting.

"All right, it's your turn," Butch said to Carver.

Bill Carver went to the line, he didn't even put his rifle to his shoulder. He brought it up to the hip, then in a blur of motion, six shoots went off almost in a continuous roar and six cans went spinning, the first can was still rolling when the last can hit the dirt.

Johnny McVey stood dumbfounded, but finally he exclaimed, "Can you teach me to do that?"

There was a roar of laughter from the Bunch, but just the same, the kid was in, mainly because he recognized that he had met his master, and had not been angry over the trick played on him.

Note: Carver used a carbine in the famous Winnemucca Bank holdup. *Outlaw Trail* by Charles Kelly, page 277.

Aeroplane Day in Myton

This is the picture of the airplane as it landed in Myton.

You asked in the Standard of April 10, 1975, about that airplane shown in the photo given to you by Mrs. Marie Benson.

Here is your story:

What you are looking at in that photo is not just a picture. It's a legend because that wasn't probably one of the first airplanes to land in Uintah Basin, it was the first airplane to land here.

It was the summer of 1921. World War I had ended just two short years before, in fact, not all of the AEF had returned from

'Over There.'

Somebody in Myton was in the know. He must have had influence, too, because he found out that a squadron of Army bombers would fly over Uintah Basin on a leg from Salt Lake City, Utah, to Denver, Colorado. Not only that, but he had arranged it so that one of the mighty De Havillands would land at Myton—provided a tarmac (now called a runway) was made in proper length and a windsock was placed on a pole to show the wind direction.

Now, remember, aeroplanes in those days were new and uncommon. Hardly anyone in the whole United States, no matter where he lived, had ever seen one. He had only read about them. And now, here at Myton, away out on an Indian Reservation, one of those giant flying machines was going to come and land—then take off and fly to Denver.

No handbills were passed. No notices were placed in the papers. The word got to every village, town, and farm in Uintah Basin by word of mouth.

The runway was leveled off with teams and levelers. It was on the South Myton Bench high above Begg's orchard about a mile from town.

The ladies sewed a windsock of the right specifications. It was placed on a high pole. Everything was ready, including us kids.

On or before the day set, the crowds of people gathered. Our hotel and restaurant was filled to overflowing, so were all the others.

The campgrounds, all of them, were loaded; they overflowed under the trees and up and down the river. There has never been such a gathering of people, either before or since. This is where the idea came from for the first UBIC at Ft. Duchesne.

Well, the day came for the aeroplanes to arrive. Everyone gathered to the runway up on the bench. They ate hot dogs, hamburgers, chewing gum, and candy. They drank pop by the gallons.

They waited, and they waited, and they waited. But no aeroplanes showed up.

Finally, as the sun was near to setting, Roe Krebs, using a phonograph horn as a megaphone (there were no public address systems in those days) announced that the weather over the mountains was too turbulent. The planes wouldn't come today, but, weather permitting they would tomorrow.

The disgruntled people pulled away. Some said the whole thing was a hoax; the Myton businessmen had pulled it to fill their coffers with money. It was foolish to believe a fairy tale like that—a big bomber coming to a town as small as Myton—scoff, scoff, scoff.

But, they hated to give up their dream. It was like the report of a gold strike down in hell. "There might be something to it," so they stayed or came back like the old prospectors.

The next day, as the people waited, they were skeptical, but still they waited as before.

Then, came Kreb's voice out of the horn, "We have just received a message by telephone. The planes left Salt Lake City. They will be here any minute. Keep your eyes on the skies."

All eyes turned to the west—watching.

An ex-doughboy who had been in France, remarked in my hearing, "You won't miss them. You can hear them before you see them. They make a roar like you've never heard before and you'll never forget it."

The ex-soldier was right. We heard the roar. Then, there they were in sight. There were three bombers flying in V formation. But they flew on past. For a minute or so it looked like they had missed us. Then, one of the trailing planes peeled off, flew down, down, down, and came back circling over the field once or twice. It was terrific!

The DeHavilland was a 'heavy bomber.' It was meant to carry a big load a long way so it had a powerful motor, too heavy for its fuselage and tail. It was inclined, therefore, if lightly loaded, to nose over—breaking its prop and damaging the engine. This danger was greater on a soft track. At Myton that day, it was a soft track. As a

This is a close-up picture of the airplane after it landed in Myton.

consequence, the mechanic climbed out of his seat, and while in the air crawled far back on the tail to keep the nose up in proper balance. After the mechanic was in place, the pilot brought her in to a good landing against the wind. I admired that mechanic for his daring and his courage even more than I admired the pilot.

They landed safely, but the dust and dirt they kicked up was unbelievable.

A youth, like I was then, noticed everything about the plane. The patches on the fabric fuselage and wings must be bullet holes, I surmised. This plane must have been in a fight, but it must have won for here it was still flying. I found out later I was right. It had a set-to with the 'Flying Circus,' commanded by Herman Goering, since by that time The Red Baron was dead. The Spads, fast littler fighters, had arrived in time to even the score and the bomber flew on to complete its mission. Lt. Nwitt had hoped to bomb Berlin, but the War ended before he had a chance to do it.

The pilot, Lieutenant Nwitt and the mechanic, whose name I have forgotten, were met by Myton's VIP's—C.D.Kicher, Dr. R.J.

Enochs and R.E. Waugh—and taken off to town to be entertained. They spent the night at C.D. Kichers, in place of our hotel, where they had reservations. This put me out because I wanted to get better acquainted with those guys.

By this time, my interest in the plane dwindled. I had time to look around me, and what I saw was pandemonium and havoc. About half the people in that day still used horses for transportation. Boy, oh boy! What a mess! Horses had gotten frightened, ran away, and raised hell in general, trying to dodge that big old buzzard. Buggies, two or three were tipped over; riders had been thrown; people had been hurt. Dr. Enochs was busy patching up the injured.

All in all, though, it was fun. There were no serious hurts, just a few bumps and scratches here and there. The people were excited but happy, especially us kids.

Next morning, there was more order. After everything was ready, the plane, in clouds of dirt and dust, took off. We watched it climb and fly away. It flew until it gradually faded out of sight in the blue distance.

Only a short time, a month or so, after their Myton visit, Lt. Nwitt and his mechanic were flying this plane from Denver to Salt Lake. The weather was bad, the plane nose heavy and they crashed in the Uintah mountains near King's Peak. Nwitt and the mechanic died in the crash. They brought the bodies out but abandoned the plane on the mountainside. In 1950, a man from Milwaukee salvaged the plane in pieces, shipped it home, and rebuilt it. It flew again in the 1960's. It flew from coast to coast exhibiting in all the large cities on the way. The Smithsonian wanted it, but I don't know if they got it. So today, it is in perfect order, either in Washington or Milwaukee.

I should like to acknowledge the invaluable assistance of Fred Todd of Myton. Without his information and notes, I could not have completed the information in this article.

ROOSEVELT HISTORY

This is a history of Roosevelt, Utah, a small town in Eastern Utah. It is short, only an outline, gathered from records here and there and from fading memories. The story covers a period when the Old West was still here but was rapidly ending, slipping into the age of technology.

In 1861, Abraham Lincoln, President of the United States, set aside a reservation for the Ute Indian Nation. No survey was made beforehand, it had merely a general description as comprising all the lands from the tops of the mountains to the north, to the tops of the mountains to the south, draining into what later was defined as the Duchesne River.

The area thus set apart was vast. It was larger than some of the states of the Union and larger than some of the nations of the world. There it lay decade after decade, a primeval land, inhabited only by a few hundred Indians, government employees and some Episcopalian Missionaries.

Then came the era of the railroads. Where the rails went, propriety followed. The shortest distance between Great Salt Lake and Denver, and from there east and west, passed through the Big Uintah Country and the Indian Reservation. But those thousands of acres, restricted to the use of Indians only, had to be opened to white settlement.

The Utes, having come to Uintah Basin in the first place to get the 'Americats' out of their braided hair, opposed the fire wagon and its iron trail passing through their country. They knew full well what would happen if it did; their wild, free way of life would be over.

In spite of the Indian opposition, the wheels along the Potomac began to turn. Slowly, surely, but inexorably they turned. Finally, in 1905 and 1906, the Ute Reservation was opened to homesteaders.

The big land rush was on! It was not like the land race along the

Cimarron in Oklahoma, the government had learned its lesson there, so in the Big "U" Country the red tape made the rush much more orderly. But the homesteaders came by the hundreds.

An old Ute said, "When the Americats came, they came by the many manys. They came nose to tail like a string of black ants crossing the sand." Some came from Colorado through Vernal, some through Strawberry Valley, but most came along the stage road from Price through Nine Mile Canyon.

An old-timer, who lived at the Strip before and during 'the opening', said, "It was like the touch of a fairy's wand. Yesterday there was nothing but wilderness and desert. Today there are fences, ditches, plowing, plantings, houses and towns; settlers were everywhere.... It was almost magical."

It has been said that Ed F. Harmston was an enigma. He was an engineer and mathematician on one hand and a dreamer on the other; which he was when he founded Roosevelt City, no one knows.

Way out in the middle of nowhere was a small, flat-topped mesa or bench overshadowed by a higher bench to the west. Nothing grew there but rabbit brush and desert grass. There was a prairie dog town in the center and wild horses grazed across it everyday. The little bench had a dry gulch on one the side flanked by a dry gulch on the other. The nearest stream of running water was miles away!

Ed F. knew the country like the back of his hand. He had surveyed part of it long before the opening. Yet in spite of his knowledge, he chose that dry little desert bench for his homestead claim. One wonders if he was planning or dreaming; it could have been a little bit of both.

Under the law you picked your land, paid $2.25 an acre for one hundred and sixty acres. You must then move on the land, build an abode, improve it, and live there five years. After you 'proved up,' you received title in fee simple by way of a patent from the U.S. Government.

Harmston made his entry and paid his money. But he was too

busy a man to move on and make improvements. He erected a boarded up tent and installed his two sons A.C. (Craig) and Floyd (Nick) Harmston to begin living out his time for him. These sons were the very first residents of Roosevelt, Utah.

A.C. said, "Early one morning, father showed up with all his surveying equipment. We began that day to lay out the streets, alleys and lots of a town. I thought maybe my old man had been sun struck and Nick knew darn well he had, but we kept working day after day until the job was done."

Craig pulled from the old files in his office, a plat of a town drawn on linen paper. It was labeled at the top 'Dry Gulch City.' When asked what it was, he answered, "Well, you see, Dad and I at first called this town Dry Gulch City. That lasted just long enough for my mother, Mary, to hear it. Then she raised the roof."

Mary said, "Not on your life, not if I live here. I'll never be known as a dry-gulcher."

So Mr. Harmston replied, "All right, Mama, you name it."

Mary Harmston, was a personal friend of President Theodore Roosevelt. He was, in her belief, the best president this country ever had, or ever would have for that matter. She corresponded with Teddy, his missives being on White House stationary. So when Ed gave her the opportunity, she spoke up quick as light, "This town will be named Roosevelt City."

The plot was re-drawn; the name was changed and now it bears the name of Roosevelt after Teddy Roosevelt.

Well, now, there was a town platted and named. Its residents were two kids, a dog, a cow, and a small flock of chickens. Its future didn't look bright because there was no water, but nevertheless people started to move in and hauled water for their use from far away.

But Harmston had his plans. He formed the Dry Gulch Irrigation Company, along with others. Soon there were canals, ditches and laterals. Water flowed down many streets and alleys of the town.

When water came, one woman settler exclaimed, "Goodness!

When I woke up this morning, there was water running almost at my doorstep." Beginning there, every kid in town learned to drink his or her water, sand and all, belly-booster from a ditch bank.

Nor was that all, on the drawing board were plans for a reservoir on Pickup's Bench, the higher bench to the west, and pipeline and waterworks for the new city with plenty of pressure. It wasn't long until even this was accomplished.

In 'The Early Days,' Roosevelt was a tent and shanty town. Even some of the businesses began in tents. But of course, these were only temporary, lasting only until something more substantial could be built. When the wind blew hard, as it seemed to do quite often in those days, it raised havoc all over the place, but the people would mend and patch, and with laughter settle down again.

Soon more substantial buildings began to appear including C.C. Larson's rock store, the Rough Rider Saloon, the Consolidated Wagon, a machine company's brick building, the Co-op store, and others.

There it was. It sprang up almost overnight, a town— rocky, dusty, rough, and raw with a purely frontier flavor. And it grew, heaven knows why, but it did.

Even before the tents came down there was a school and some churches of several denominations. The kids from the Reservation were not to grow up 'nincompoops' or irreligious either; that is, not if their parents could help it. The schools were better than you would think. A surprising number of those reservation kids, vernacular and all, who had slept in hollow logs and drank muddy water, made it to the storied "Halls of Ivy", and returned one day with sheepskins from colleges and universities.

A.C. Harmston, when he was asked why Roosevelt grew in its desert setting while other places, which seemed to be much more favorably located, reached a stalemate and some died, replied, "Well, after the opening, Roosevelt was on the main stage road between Price and Vernal. It was also the mail distribution center for the Reservation. Besides, it had telegraph and telephone connections with the outside. It was the 'central'. Aside from that, it was the hub of the whole Uintah Basin." Pointing to a map of the Uintah Basin with a red circle around Roosevelt, he pointed out what he meant. East and west, north and south, do this and you'll see that's what it is, 'The Hub.'

Roosevelt being the hub, along with its other early advantages, quickly became the principal trading center for all the western area of Uintah Basin. In the days of horse drawn transportation, and even today, it is easier to get to, shop and return home in the shortest distance and time.

At first, the settlers hurried in, hoping against hope that they'd beat the railroad in. They might be lucky enough to get a piece of land the right-of-way had to cross, (although the route was always kept secret). If they got the right land, they knew it meant a fortune for them. The question wasn't if the rails would come, the only question was when. The months stretched into years, the years stretched into decades and still the railroad didn't come. It was close a time or two, but failed to arrive. The legend is that David H. Moffat, the railroad magnate, missed getting financed by two hours in Denver. Old Man Gould said he would advance the money, then within two hours changed his mind and pulled his support back.

Then one day, the automobile coughed and spat and purred in. After the automobile came the motor trucks. Soon no railroad was needed. One old-timer said, "We needed them trains once, but not anymore. I'd feel put out if them long drags started to come through here now."

Still, looking back, we know that in the beginning, a railroad would have been a God-send. As it was, everything a homesteader bought had to come on freight wagons winding slowly over mountains and across deserts from Price. They came along the Nine Mile Road from some eighty miles away. Prices were too darn high. Not only that, but everything the farmers had to sell had to go out the same way. It was hardly worth it. The farmers could raise most of what they needed for food; he might have patches on his pants and mamma might have a dress in calico, but they set a mighty hefty table.

What the people of the Reservation needed most was a 'cash crop' to buy the incidentals and pay their taxes. So they went to livestock. Everybody went for either sheep or cattle, and sometimes both. The country, with its wide open spaces and good grazing land, was made for that. They didn't have to haul these products; they could drive them to market on their own four feet. Some went up Avintaquin and over the ridge to Colton; some went up Indian Canyon and over the Hump to Price; some went up Willow and Hill Creek to Thompson Spring; but by far the largest number went out the Nine Mile Road to Price. At certain times of the year, the stagecoach would be late because it had to pass through so many herds of cattle on the way to market along the Nine Mile Road.

Then the creamery companies were founded because the Uintah Basin was a wonderful dairy country. There was a time when every little settlement—Bluebell, Mt. Emmons, Mt. Home, Altonah and Boneta and others—had stations where cream, butter, and eggs were bought. Roosevelt at one time had six cream stations in it. Usually, cream was saved up through the week and taken to the station on Saturday for sale. Needless to say, De Laval cream separators sold like wildfire.

Saturday was the biggest day of the week in Roosevelt, the trading center. Things would really hum as the people came to town to spend their cream, butter, and egg money. The bank stayed open until five o'clock and the stores until nine o'clock. Roosevelt took it in stride, but strangers stood gaping and surprised. This gave rise to the expression only the old-timers understand. When things are busy they will say, "Why this is like cream day in Boneta."

After World War I, a depression struck. Banks went broke; mortgages were being foreclosed right and left. One couldn't sell a thing for a decent price. Cattle, sheep, wool, and hogs weren't worth a dime a dozen. The situation looked black and it actually seemed to be the end after all the years of struggle. Roosevelt was so quiet, even on Saturday, you could hear a pin drop.

Then, out of the blue, without warning, the miracle came rolling in called the "Billion Dollar Crop." It was alfalfa seed. By this time, most of the usable land in Uintah Basin was planted in alfalfa to feed livestock. The experts found the Basin could produce the best alfalfa seed in the world. The new land, the cool nights, the hot days produced seed of premium quality and plenty of it.

The seed industry is faded and gone now. It is hard to explain what happened when the seed industry hit this town, without being accused of lying or greatly exaggerating the facts. But, there are those still around who know. They all agree on the impact to this country of the hayseed.

The seed companies came in, erected seed cleaning plants and bought seed by the tons. Literally, millions of dollars were paid into the Uintah Basin each year. It was better, in a way, than oil because every farmer raised seed, sold it, and walked away with the loot.

At that time, most people still traveled by horse and buggy. But then came cars of every kind and model from the Hudson Super Six, the Rickenbacker, and the Cadillac, down to the 'Tin Lizzy.' Most people held their heads and bought Fords, Chevrolets and Buicks.

Roosevelt rolled. Business had never been so good. Well, the seed business has vanished now. It died from the lack of fertilizers, insecticides, and innovative methods. However, with the new technology in these areas, sooner or later, the seed boom may come back again.

A side product of the alfalfa seed industry was honey; the blossoming alfalfa fields produced honey by the car load. There were both big and little bee outfits. Our honey, because of its quality, became famous from coast to coast. It, too, was a ready source of money that helped Roosevelt grow.

Once in a while a stranger stops a local resident on the street to inquire, "Where is the Indian Reservation and where are the Indians?"

The reply usually surprises them, "You are standing on the Reservation right now!" As for the Indians, just look about you. Sometimes, it may take you a second to recognize them, but they are here. If you want to see them in paint and feathers, hear their chants or see their native dances, you will have to visit during the Pow-wow on the Fourth of July, the Bear Dance in the spring, or the Sundance in the summer. You won't see any of these things on the streets because they are reserved for special occasions.

You see, the Utes are a part of us, some of our business people are Indians. They have given Roosevelt their patronage all these years and have helped us grow. In fact, there have been times when their help made the difference between success and failure, as was the case in the depression of the late twenties and early thirties. Without the Utes, we could never have gotten Union High School when we did; nor could we run our educational system as well as we do without their money.

This might seem like old, old history, but it isn't. Roosevelt is a very young town—one of the newest in the state. You realize this when you know that one of the first two residents of the town, Nick Harmston, is still alive in Orem, Utah. Then, too, here and there as you walk the streets of Roosevelt, you can still see the old settlers, the first who came to live here. They can remember the tent and shanty town, drinking belly-booster out of the ditches, the first school and all the rest.

We are now a thriving, modern community. We have come a long, long way in the time we've had. We have the oil fields and many other resources. They have always been here, but are just now on the verge of development. Roosevelt's tomorrow looks as bright as the stars at night in our clear blue sky.

THE RUMBLE OF THE UINTAHS

Years ago, when white men first came to the Uintah Basin, they noticed a deep-toned rumble that seemed to come from the Uintah Mountains to the north. Most of the time, it happened in the afternoon, sometime between two and four o'clock, give or take a little. Nothing you could set your watch by, you understand. It just happened oftener then than at other times.

It was while that rumble rumbled that everything came to a standstill—a pause in the day's occupations. The horses in the fields stopped grazing and raised their heads to listen; so did the cows. The dogs stopped whatever they were doing and so did human beings. And I suppose if you could see them, so did wild things. It only lasted for a minute, maybe two, then it was over. Then life went on as usual.

What did it sound like? Well, it is very hard to define; many have tried to define it but nobody quite hit the mark. Some said it was like potatoes rolling down a chute into a deep, dark cellar under a house; others likened it to great rocks rolling down a mountainside into a canyon; still others said it was like distant thunder without a cloud in the sky. None of these were quite right, of course, but it will give you some idea of what it was really like.

Strange too, it always seemed to be the same no matter where you were—whether near or far from the mountains, or in the mountains themselves. Needless to say, this rumble was a deep dark mystery, for no one has ever been able to determine what it was... or is.

There have been many explanations for it, or speculations, should I say? As for example, the echoes from the blasting at the open pit copper mine in Bingham, Utah; or the rumbling underground from the shots set off in the deep mines of Park City, Utah. Some newcomers said it was the echoes of those giant German guns that shelled Paris from fifty miles away in World War I. Fine, except that the rumble seems to have pre-dated all of them.

If you asked the Indians what it was, they would come back with that bit of grinning Ute humor: "Indians no savvy. White man savvy; he knows everything." Or "Big Indian making big medicine in the mountains; white men better run." But after the humor the Indians would say, "It was here a long, long time ago before we came. We don't know what or where it is."

I remember listening to my elders discussing the rumble around the table at mealtime. To me, it was eerie. It was weird. It was like meeting something from the unknown face to face. It was as good or maybe better than a good ghost story.

Of course, after awhile, you got used to it and just took it in stride. Except you always listened. When some newcomer, hearing it, asked "What is that?" you replied, "It's the Rumble," as if no further explanation was necessary.

Is the rumble still there? I don't know. It's a noisy world we live in now as compared to what it used to be when I was a kid. There are power saws, lawn mowers, cars whizzing by your door, big eighteen wheelers on the highways, airplanes in the sky, sonic booms. All these things, so who can tell?

I thought I heard it again a couple of years ago way out in the silent desert south of Myton. But I might have gotten it mixed up with something else. Even there, modern machines can fool you.

But honestly, I think it's still there if you can sort it out from all the other noises you hear.

Journey Through a Lost Country

Chandler—The Canyon of Mystery

One of the cliff dwellings found in Chandler Canyon.

At the end of a wilderness road in eastern Utah is the 'Land of the Sun' (Tavaputs). Here the Canyon of Mystery lies. To the white man, it is known as Chandler Canyon; to the Indian, it is the Canyon of the Dead. This great abyss was cut by wind, water, and weather. It runs from the tops of the cool, green mountains, down its twisting length to the Green River in the heart of Desolation Canyon.

East Tavaputs is Indian Country. The great defile belongs to the Utes, but their love for it is overshadowed by their fear; for it is, to them, and to others, a place of uncanny sensations. A deserted wilderness of high ledges, carved monoliths, and brooding silences. On nights of the bright moon, imagination weaves many sights and sounds. It is indeed a haunted place, where one is not surprised if apparitions appear.

Two great spirits prevail in the canyon. When the sun shines brightly and the land smiles, then good is in control and no harm will come. But if the clouds roll over it, the place is dark and sullen. Then evil is master and danger lurks.

An old Ute said, "If the canyon is angry, do not ride the trail into its recesses, for the canyon can kill. It has in the past and it will again. But if the landscape smiles, then it is safe to go. Do not stay in the canyon at night, for then the spirits of the long vanished moquitch (old people) are there. They resent your intrusion into a land they call their own. Ride quietly, friend, do not disturb these precincts with loud noises, for this is the Canyon of the Dead."

Whether it belongs to the dead or not, it certainly belongs to the past, for up in the ledges off the canyon floor are the dwelling places of an ancient race. They were cliff dwellers. They occupied this country a thousand years ago. Their houses occupy the shelves and overhangs high on the rocky walls. Unmolested, the buildings stand now as they have stood through the centuries. So perfect is the state of preservation that it is hard to believe they are so old. Seemingly, they could be inhabited today as they were in those days long in the past. It is one of the great mysteries of all time. Who were these people? Where did they go? Why did they go?

The canyon, where it begins in the grassy meadows, flows north and then turning at right angles, flows west to Awat Paw (Big Water). At the angle where it turns westward is a deep fork running northeast to the mountain top. Up this fork is an old Indian trail. Long ago, an Indian riding this trail, came upon the body of a man. The dead man had built a small fire. As he sat over it, he had fallen forward into the fire, dead. There were no marks, no bullet holes, no

knife slashes upon the body—nothing that showed a death by violence. It was strange, though. The man was an Indian, small in
stature. His costume showed he was not a Ute; he was from some
tribe far away. No one knew from whence he came.

Was he a 'Moquitch' come back to visit the land of his ancient
people?

No one knows. But the trail where the body was found has been
known from that day to this as 'The Dead Indian Trail' and the fork
up which it goes is 'Dead Indian Canyon.'

Do the spirits of the 'Moquitch' still linger in the canyon? On
moonlit nights, they can be heard crying—mourning the loss of this
land and the loved ones left here. A legend of the Utes says this is
true. The white man, if he is honest, can believe the legend if he
abides in the stretches of the canyon in the moonlight.

PASSAGE OF THE RIVER

Once in springtime, we got our boats together and began our
passage of the River—of the turbulent Green River as it flows down
through the canyon in its transit of the mountains; as it flows from

Ouray to Green River, through a land of desolation called now, 'Desolation Canyon.'

Trying to keep my diary of our boating expedition, I found I could not write. For spells were cast upon me by the land and all its glory; by the grandeur of the scenery; by this country which remains as God made it. I took to dreaming only and my pen was stilled and quiet. I knew I could not describe this canyon were I a genius, scribe or poet. All I could do was feel it as we went down—down the River, through great stretches of this timeless land.

How can I describe it for you, this silent land of ages? There are no words to paint the pictures, nor to make you feel the moods forever passing over, as the sunlight, air, and shadows change at each bend and turning in our passage of the River.

It is as if the River were a narrow, winding way. On right and left, in passing, are the structures high—so high above you that they reach to the sky. You gasp in awe and wonder at the size and the grandeur of the many sculptured pieces on the canyon's upper rim. There are the 'Sleeping Monks,' the 'Barking Dog,' the 'Sombreroed Sitter,' the 'Crouching Lion,' the 'Perched Eagle,' all brooding out the days, which run on into ages. There are castles standing high, their battlements unguarded. There are Mosques, there are Cathedrals; but no bells, no voices ringing. There is silence—silence everywhere like a deserted city of the giants. Silence so profound you can feel it deep within you.

Each bend the River makes changes all the scenes around you. New scenes rising skyward take your breath away in wonder. The fleeting shadows passing, and the sunshine on the faces make the landscapes dark and brooding, make them scowl and almost threaten; make them smile and almost beckon, so that you shiver, laugh, and smile in your passage of the River. As the mighty faces change in alternate sun and shadow, or as the mists dispel and gather in morning, noon, and evening, so your mood changes as you watch and dream down the length of the canyon.

In the stillness of the nighttime, in the brightness of the moonlight, the great ledges stand there sleeping and their crests are turned to silver. In the shadows, in the darkness, where the moonlight does not linger, there is mystery and a guessing of what lies within those shadows. But it lies beyond your guessing, so you turn your back upon it. There is mystery everywhere as the moonlight softly pores over all the land about you; and you gaze and dream. For this is an ancient land, grand and forbidding. As you look upon it in the quiet of the night, you wonder, ever wonder of its past.

In your passage of the River, your thoughts go ever backward, to the carving of this chasm; to the years that carved these splendors from the solid rock above you. What sights were then occurring along this mighty river? Were there any men or beings passing by the points and headlands? When did men, with brain and thinking, first explore this gouged out fissure? What sounds occurred by this mighty crouching lion? All are lost now in the antiquity of yesterdays. We shall never know, but we may dream and weave a tale, all untrue of course, of the long ago.

Men were here, there is no doubt, many ages ago. Here and there upon the rocks are pictures, signs, and symbols drawn by the ancients, drawn by men who lived in this deep canyon and made their passage of the River. That race is lost and gone forever from these ledges, from this canyon. All you see now are their drawings, growing dim from the passing time and the wearing of the weather. In the shelter of the ledges, they built their camps for lodging. Where they built their cook-fires the smoke rose upward, blackening the rock above it and the blackness still remains. You may see their campsites in shelter of the ledges as you make your passage of the River.

You will ponder as you view these leavings of the ancients; were they strong and mighty warriors? Were they skillful, crafty hunters?

How did they dress in winter? How did they dress in summer? Did they love this mighty river? Was there laughter, shouts, and singing? Where were born the children of these people? Did they play along these banks, making playthings in the sand? Did these ledges throw back echoes of their happy shouts and cries, as they throw back ours now in our passage of the River? There is no answer, for the crouching lion speaks not, nor do the sleeping monks.

You get one last impression as you look back up the canyon at the end of your passage of the River. As you look back and see the long line of sentries in a row, the monks, the lion, the sitter, and the rest, you think and you almost know, they are waiting. Waiting for what? You do not know. You never will know for the lion speaks not, neither do the monks, nor do any of the rest.

So we come to the end of the boat trip down the River. I was going to describe it as a diarist should, but I never could. As I have said, moods and spells were cast upon me so that I could not write what I saw, day by day. I could only write, inadequately, what I felt.

Someday, if I may, I shall go again down the River, into the deep canyons. Then I shall take pictures of what I see and write day by day what I feel. Maybe, at that time, I shall do more justice to my 'Passage of the River.'

The Watcher

I am the Watcher. And now I shall tell you of a different kind of watching, for on the occasion of which I write, we watched the gorgeous landscapes of the Uintah Basin as they appear from the high places where the pleasant air of 'Indian Summer' wafts across the wide, deserted places of our homeland.

We traveled far over a land of desolation, on the east side of Green River, high into the Bookcliff Mountains, to the land of the Ute Indians. From there, we looked afar over an area of great spaces. We watched the changing world as it lay below us, a world of strange inexplicable charm.

From the green mountain ridges, we looked back over the miles that we had driven and where the desert lay far away from civilization. Its utter desolation is, in itself, a thing of beauty. The many colored headlands, rising high above the mesas, shown in the morning sunlight through the softening mists of autumn, like ghostly, dim paintings. At the bases of the headlands, and flowing all around them, lay the mesas. The sunlight did not reach them and they were turned dark purple in the mists and in the shadows. As the clouds sailed slowly over and the rainstorms moved across them, these headlands and mesas, buttes and valleys, lay in alternate light and shadow which changed them, while we watched, into a land of changing colors, rugged and magnificent. It was a grand panorama of ethereal, haunting beauty. It cast a spell upon us. We were awed and stood silent as if we were in a mighty guilded temple of the Most High.

From one point, which we reached by walking, the land fell away before us in vertical cliffs and ledges, straight down into the gorge of the Green River as it makes its passage through the mountains. It is a chasm cut in solid rock by the wearing of the waters. It was so far down to the river, that it looked like a slender, narrow ribbon, winding there among the colored ledges far below. High up on the gorge sides, where the points of the mountains thrust out into the canyon, the gifted hand of nature has carved many sculptured pieces from the solid rock of ages. There is a crouching lion, a pharaoh seated on his throne, a cowled monk, a castle, a mosque, a minaret and a cathedral. All are gigantic and stupendous. But there were no voices singing; there were no bells ringing. There was only the silence of the wasteland—only a mystic brooding silence. We stood there, never speaking, never moving, struck dumb and still by the colossal splendors there below.

In the deep canyons cutting back from the river, in the bottoms and on the mountain-sides, there were riots of many colors painted by the autumn leaves on the vegetation. The scene was indescribably lovely.

In this country, long ago, dwelt the 'Anasazi' (The Ancient Ones) or the 'Moquitch,' as the Utes called them. Their homes are still there in the ledges. The intangible presence of these people adds a haunting, mystic air to these canyons and ledges. The feeling is so compelling that it is hard to be aware that the Anasazi vanished from these precincts centuries ago. We had a strange, eerie feeling that they were watching us from the shadows and cliff dwellings above, as we explored along the ancient trails of their domain. When we left, we withdrew quietly. We said good-bye in a respectful, silent manner, hoping, after all, that we had not been unwelcome on our visit to the places where the ancients had their homeland long ago.

Our time had come upon us, we had to leave that land of wonders. But we vowed to return again another day. We shall always remember the land to which our wandering took us, for it is a land of enthralling interest; a land of unmatched grandeur; a land of untouched and unsurpassed loveliness; a land of mystic, dreamy enchantment. We have been infected by the subtle virus of what we saw and watched there. We shall never recover. As the years go, by we shall strive to return to it again and again.

We hope the Ute Indians, in their love for such wild places, will hold fast this primitive area. We hope they will preserve this last outpost of the wilderness, in the condition that God made it, so that in the age of broken atoms there will be one place near—a place of peace and quiet, where one can go to rest his troubled soul.

Thus we took a pleasant journey. Thus we watched, and saw in passing, sights like we had never seen before. I have tried to tell you of it, but I know no man can write it—neither genius, scribe or poet—for it is a feeling that you get by watching over an immense land where grandeur, loveliness and dreaminess are co-mingled. It seeps into your being, but there are no words to describe it. I shall tell you only this: that if you watch as we did, you will know what I have meant and have tried to tell you of—this grand old Western Country which we watched on our journey into Indian Country.

I shall see you,
The Watcher